GOOD PRACTICE IN RISK ASSESSMENT AND RISK MANAGEMENT

GOOD PRACTICE SERIES
Edited by Jacki Pritchard

This series explores topics of current concern to professionals working in social work, health care and the probation service. Contributors are drawn from a wide variety of settings, in both the voluntary and statutory sectors.

GOOD PRACTICE IN RISK ASSESSMENT AND RISK MANAGEMENT 2
Protection, Rights and Responsibilities
Edited by Hazel Kemshall and Jacki Pritchard
ISBN 1 85302 441 4
Good Practice Series 5

GOOD PRACTICE IN RISK ASSESSMENT AND RISK MANAGEMENT 1 AND 2
Edited by Hazel Kemshall and Jacki Pritchard
Two volume set
ISBN 1 85302 552 6

GOOD PRACTICE IN CHILD PROTECTION
A Manual for Professionals
Edited by Hilary Owen and Jacki Pritchard
ISBN 1 85302 205 5
Good Practice Series 1

GOOD PRACTICE IN SUPERVISION
Statutory and Voluntary Organisations
Edited by Jacki Pritchard
ISBN 1 85302 279 9
Good Practice Series 2

GOOD PRACTICE IN COUNSELLING PEOPLE WHO HAVE BEEN ABUSED
Edited by Zetta Bear
ISBN 1 85302 424 4
Good Practice Series 4

GOOD PRACTICE IN WORKING WITH VIOLENCE
Edited by Hazel Kemshall and Jacki Pritchard
ISBN 1 85302 641 7
Good Practice Series 6

GOOD PRACTICE IN WORKING WITH VICTIMS OF VIOLENCE
Edited by Hazel Kemshall and Jacki Pritchard
ISBN 1 85302 768 5
Good Practice Series 8

GOOD PRACTICE WITH VULNERABLE ADULTS
Edited by Jacki Pritchard
ISBN 1 85302 982 3
Good Practice Series 9

GOOD PRACTICE IN RISK ASSESSMENT AND RISK MANAGEMENT 1

Edited by
Hazel Kemshall and Jacki Pritchard

Jessica Kingsley Publishers
London and Philadelphia

First published in the United Kingdom in 1996 by
Jessica Kingsley Publishers Ltd,
116 Pentonville Road,
London N1 9JB, England
and
29 West 35th Street, 10th fl.
New York, NY 10001-2299, USA

www.jkp.com

Second impression 1997
Third impression 1998
Fourth impression 2000
Fifth impression 2001
Sixth impression 2002
Seventh impression 2004

Library of Congress Cataloging in Publication Data
Good practice in risk assessment and risk management / edited by Hazel Kemshall and Jacki Pritchard
P. cm.-- (Good practice series : 3)
Includes bibliographical references and index
ISBN 1-85302-338-8 (alk. Paper)
1. Social service. 2. Risk assessment. 3. Risk management.
I. Kemshall, Hazel, 1958- II. Pritchard, Jacki. III. Series.
HV40.G65 1995
361.1--dc220   95-36215
                                      CIP

British Library Cataloguing in Publication Data
A CIP catalogue record for this book is available from the British Library

ISBN 1 85302 338 8

Printed and Bound in Great Britain by
Athenaeum Press, Gateshead, Tyne and Wear

Dedication

For Sue McEwan, who ran all the risks
Born July 22, 1957. Died May 22, 1997

Contents

INTRODUCTION

Risk assessment and risk management are now key issues for all practitioners and managers in the field of social care and criminal justice. Increasingly, responding to the risks of others, preventing risks to vulnerable clients, or running risks to themselves is all in a day's work for the busy practitioner and manager. Risk is often central to the decision to allocate resources or to carry out an intervention. However, with the most notable exception of Brearley (1982), there has been little literature which has addressed the complex issue of risk assessment and risk management. This book attempts to fill that gap by bringing together a number of contributions from both academic research and current practice spanning the spectrum of social care and work with offenders.

The volume begins with an important chapter on the legal context of risk taking. This contribution raises important issues of negligence, duty of care and liability for all those practising with risk. The volume then develops a number of pertinent themes across a variety of work settings and client groups, closing with the penultimate chapter which focuses on risk to workers. Individual contributions are supported, where applicable, with case studies, and additional training material is presented in the final chapter.

A key theme is the relevance of values and attitudes in decision making on risk. For example, many risk decisions are made in a context where philosophies and policies on risk minimization on the one hand, and normalization of service users on the other, are often in conflict. Where this conflict remains understated, agencies and their practitioners are often unclear about the type of risk decisions which need to be made, and the impact of such philosophies upon the types of risk management strategies subsequently chosen is often underarticulated.

These difficulties are frequently expressed as practice issues around client self-determination versus risk to others or to self, lack of clarity about the competing risks of client and carer, and further difficulties in resolving the imbalance between promoting clients' rights and preserving the responsibilities of the worker to others, including the public.

Many agencies are currently producing policy documents to address the issue of risk, but there is little practical guidance and training on how to implement such policies. Workers are left to make decisions in a climate of uncertainty, having to interpret and carry out policies as they see fit. This leaves a number of workers themselves exposed to risk, especially in situations where their decision making has been unsupported.

We made a decision to produce this volume because of the gap in practice based literature on risk work. We felt it was important to include a number of different aspects of risk assessment and management in order to reflect the diversity of risk work in social care. The volume does not attempt to produce a simplistic guide to practice skills in risk work, but rather seeks to locate practice guidance within particular theoretical frameworks and grounded within a knowledge base derived from current research. The intention of the volume is to make the reader think about risk and the likely impact of this issue on her/his current practice. It is hoped that the reader will take issues pertinent to them and use the volume as an individual and team resource to develop good practice.

Risk is a complex practice and policy issue. The knowledge base and awareness of all those working with risk needs to be improved. Training has a crucial role in developing the knowledge base on risk. This has influenced the structuring of this volume, most particularly in the selection of case studies and training material in the final chapter.

We realize that this is a developing area of work and it has not been possible to include every work setting or client group; however, we hope that the reader will find that the knowledge and themes presented in this volume are transferable to other settings.

REFERENCES

Brearley, C.P. (1982) *Risk and Social Work: Hazards and Helping*. London: Routledge and Kegan Paul.

CHAPTER 1

RISKING LEGAL REPERCUSSIONS

David Carson

Should I have risked giving that workshop? It involved applying the ideas to a new topic. I wasn't ready; but they wanted it. I feared embarrassment. I agreed because my risk seemed trivial in comparison with the kind and degree of risks that my audience would be used to taking on an almost daily basis. My risk assessment failed to include getting cross with some members of my audience.

I was leading a one-day, in-house, workshop on risk taking and child protection services. I knew I had 'lost' some of my audience by lunchtime. Nearing the end, working through a suggested outline procedure for taking risk decisions, I was asked, in effect:

> 'If there is no statute or case-law which says we have to do this why should we bother?'

I was told, in effect:

> 'If I have a difficult risk decision to make I discuss it with my senior. The only risk involved is that he or she might not be willing to sign to show that I would be following his or her advice.'

It's not just that I had explained why a proactive and preventative approach to risk was being recommended. Indeed, that was why I had been pressed to provide the workshop. The attitude towards risk taking seemed so entirely wrong. I could have understood a condemnation along the lines of:

> 'Its all right for you academics; you can just generate your ideas, calling in aid "academic freedom" when necessary, without having to accept the consequences.'

That would have been understandable, if a little unfair. But a failure to perceive that risk taking involves the most exciting, the most intellectual and professional parts of the job, although also the most anxiety provoking parts, was irritating and frustrating. It is to be hoped that the law will develop so that such simplistic, defensive, cover-our-backs, attitudes to risk taking may lead to liability. It may not be there yet but it is, this chapter will argue, *en route*.

A kind of justice ensued. A few weeks later that local authority received extensive adverse national publicity for a risk decision that it had taken. Substantially, because the authority and its staff were unable to present the risk decision in a positive manner, within a coherent framework where everyone could quickly appreciate the issues, they suffered badly. In the process a valuable service was lost.

RISK LAW

Litigation, civil and criminal, involves the practice of risk. The parties risk winning and losing. Compensation and other orders (such as custody of a child) can be won or lost. The reputations of witnesses, such as those who took the risk decision, can be made or ruined. But, even though it is so central to the law, 'risk' is not a discrete legal concept. There is no 'law of risk or risk taking.' The key legal concepts are 'negligence' and 'recklessness,' with the latter almost entirely confined to the criminal law. When someone suffers harm because another took a risky decision (or behaved in a risky manner, for that is the same thing) then, provided they know that there might be a legal remedy, and they can find and fund a lawyer, then a negligence action may be considered. It may not succeed for a variety of reasons. In addition, or alternatively, complaints procedures, formal inquiries and disciplinary proceedings may be instituted. Media coverage may be invoked. These will, implicitly if not explicitly, involve consideration of negligence notions. The legal concept has significance outside its own specialist arena.

The key issue, in practice, is whether the person, for example a social worker, acted in a manner comparable to how others would have acted. Hence the member of my audience's (and many others') belief that it all depends upon acting in a way that is similar to reasonable colleagues. But, as we will see, there is much more to it. Relying upon that belief is risky. Can you actually demonstrate that a responsible body of co-professionals would have made the same decision, particularly now that we know harm has resulted? Will your decision-making process stand up to forensic analysis? Should anyone rely upon the data and the implicit value system that you relied upon?

Defensive beliefs and reactive approaches to risk (managing the harm once it has occurred) will increasingly be challenged by developments in risk assessment and risk management. The emphasis is moving to decision-making processes and their management. It might, once, have been appropriate just to rely upon following legal procedures.

> It is clear that the social worker's best protection lies in good practice and in knowing the law and recognizing its potential for use in dangerous situations. The legal framework in which social workers operate has been seen as constraining and even as putting excessive pressures on workers to act in a way that professional discretion would argue against. However, in so far as the law represents a statement of beliefs about necessary action, it is an unavoidable feature of social work. More importantly, knowledge of the law and a correct and careful attention to legal requirements and possibilities offers the social worker important protection. On the one hand, the law provides for client protection;

on the other hand, it provides worker and agency protection. (Brearley 1982, p.149)

It is essential to appreciate that the law, at best, provides checklists, procedures and frameworks. It provides a foundation for professionals to work within and to utilize to justify their risks; it rarely provides direct answers. If practitioners want to avoid the risk of liability then they need to organize the law's concepts and procedures to their own ends, and before the harm occurs.

NEGLIGENCE – DUTY OF CARE

Negligence, the noun, involves at least five separate concepts or tests. Each must be satisfied. Negligent, the adjective or adverb qualifying certain decision-making, or other behaviour, is just one of those five tests. To be liable for negligence (the noun) the person being sued (hereinafter known as 'you'), must owe a duty of care to the person injured (the 'client'). No duty, no liability. Basically, we all owe duties of care to those whom we can, being reasonable about it, foresee we might damage by an act or an omission. Hence you owe a duty of care to your client. It goes with the relationship. Why is the other person a 'client' other than because a particular propensity to harm is foreseen? It extends to people you are assessing for possible clienthood; if you do the assessment badly, well then. And it goes wider. Can you (or should you) reasonably foresee that if you do your job badly, such as by making a poor decision, you will cause harm to a volunteer working with a client? If yes, then you have a duty.

But there are limits. You do not owe duties 'to the world', to everyone who may come in contact with your client. Thus, in those rare cases when a client with a mental disorder attacks a stranger there will be a problem in demonstrating a duty of care (Ritchie 1994). It will depend upon the circumstances. For example, *Partington v. Wandsworth L.B.C.* (*The Guardian*, December 2, 1989) concerned a client with autistic tendencies who was known, very occasionally but suddenly, to attack other people. She was being taken for a walk by residential care staff when she suddenly attacked an elderly lady who had been approaching from the opposite direction. The existence of a duty of care was readily accepted. Mrs Partington, as an individual, may have been a total stranger to the client, the care staff and their potentially vicariously liable employers. But just as drivers owe a duty of care to other road users, so a duty was owed to another pavement user. However, if the client has been discharged from care, and was thus unaccompanied by care staff, it could have been a very different matter. In such a case the question could be whether the decision to discharge was negligent for a duty of care would have existed at that time.

It depends upon whom and what you are. In *M v. Newham L.B.C.* ([1994] 2 WLR 554) the Court of Appeal decided that a consultant child psychiatrist, a social worker and the social services department, could not be sued for their acts and decisions involved in implementing the Children Act 1989. The argument is that although that Act laid down a number of duties it did not specify that they could be enforced in the courts. The presumption is that Parliament intended the duties to be enforced by way of complaints, inquiries and similar. So if those duties cannot be enforced directly then it follows, the Court of Appeal decided, they cannot be enforced indirectly by suing for negligence instead.

But the decision is controversial. It may be changed by the House of Lords, who are deciding an appeal at the time of writing. Some see an inconsistency. Why can a child psychiatrist, for example, be sued for providing negligent medical treatment but not for providing negligent advice concerning a child's protection? There are other, similar, decisions. An education authority cannot be sued for providing its services in a negligent manner, except when acting *in loco parentis*, (*Holtom v. Barnet L.B.C.* (1993) *The Times*, September 30) and possibly when making assessments of need for special education (*E. v. Dorset C.C. et al.* (1994) *The Times*, May 4). Social services departments cannot be sued for negligently making child minder placement decisions, as this is governed by an Act, but they can be sued if an individual worker makes a false statement knowing that it will be acted upon (*T v. Surrey C.C.* (1994) 144 NLJ 319) as this is governed by the common law. The exceptions involve ways of suing that are not based upon claims of breach of statutory duty or negligence.

The *M v. Newham L.B.C.* decision, about the 1989 Act, is under appeal to the House of Lords. Their decision, which will surely involve a review of the other decisions, will be exceptionally important. But, for the moment, social workers and others taking risk decisions that are related to their duties under an Act of Parliament cannot be sued for negligence. They do not owe a duty of care.

Even if those decisions are overturned it does not automatically follow that they may be sued. The courts have always reserved a discretion to decide that it would be unfair to impose a duty of care within the law of negligence. They consider the policy implications. Would it be fair and appropriate? They have decided, for example, that the police do not owe a duty of care when investigating crimes and protecting people at risk (*Hill v. Chief Constable of West Yorkshire*, [1988] 2 WLR 1049; *Alexandrou v. Oxford*, [1993] 4 All ER 328; *Osman and another v. Ferguson and another*, [1993] 4 All ER 344; *Ancell and another v. McDermott and others* [1993] 4 All ER 355). A court may always decide, as others before them have decided, that imposing a duty of care would be a bad policy. It would involve spending resources on litigation rather than providing services, they could argue. Unfortunately this is an untested and likely erroneous argument. Once a practice, for example a procedure for taking risk decisions, is found to be negligent then standards will quickly change in order to prevent further liability. Negligence is a very inefficient quality control scheme. It is slow and dreadfully expensive. But it does tend to keep people 'on their toes' even to the extent of being too anxious about it. Negligence does emphasize accountability for decision-making.

But not being suable in the law of negligence does not solve everything. Your risk decision making can still be the subject of disciplinary proceedings. A complaint may be launched, a formal inquiry established, a prosecution considered. The absence of a duty of care, required by the law of negligence, does not prevent any of these options being taken! They are not dependent upon the existence of a duty of care.

NEGLIGENCE – STANDARD OF CARE

The second requirement of the law of negligence is a breach of the standard of care. (Very similar notions will apply in the case of complaints, inquiries and disciplinary proceedings.) This involves a question of fact rather than of law. Whilst the courts reserve the right to declare a standard of care to be too low this is rarely exercised. It is not for a court to choose its preferred experts or procedure but simply to discover, as a matter of fact, whether a responsible body of co-professionals would have reached a similar conclusion. The standard is not that of the best or even the majority; would a responsible body of co-professionals have made the same risk decision?

That seems simple. 'That member of the audience was right; I only have to do what the majority of my colleagues would have done'. False. First, those colleagues may not be regarded as 'responsible'; consider how many differences of opinion there can be within co-professionals. Second, will a court, will employers, will an inquiry, believe that that is how and why you made your decision; can you prove it? Take the *Partington v. Wandsworth L.B.C.* decision outlined above. Mrs Partington's lawyers thought they would win. If they had not expected to succeed then they would not have risked a court hearing with their client losing and becoming responsible for paying the costs of both parties. They argued that the residential care staff should not have risked taking the young woman, described as 'predictably unpredictable', for a walk or, if they did, that they should have kept a restraining hold on her at all times.

The judge did decide that the staff were not negligent. But he emphasized that it was a close thing! The local authority was almost liable. (Some lawyers know of cases where voluntary organizations have settled, have compromised, *weaker* negligence claims rather than risk losing more money, plus receiving bad publicity, in court.) Notice that the residential care staff had no legal authority to stop the young woman going for a walk; she was not a patient, she was not detained. Notice that it is unprofessional, within the terms of a normalization care philosophy at least, for care staff to be restraining adults that they are taking for a walk. If the judge thought that this was a relatively evenly balanced case then consider how other cases might be perceived.

Perception is critically relevant to risk assessment, which involves evaluating and weighting consequences and their likelihoods. Studies of risk assessment emphasize the subjectivity involved and the opportunities for making mistakes (e.g. and for variety, see British Medical Association 1990; Rachlin 1989; Royal Society 1992; Yates 1992). In particular, consider the effect of hindsight. A risk was taken with a child, patient, prisoner, it matters not. Harm has resulted. In deciding whether a reasonable risk decision was taken the court, inquiry or whatever, will be involved in assessing how likely it was. It will not jump to the conclusion that the child's death was a foregone conclusion; it will be influenced by knowledge of what actually happened. Courts and others are in a very poor position for doing their own likelihood assessments. They only get involved when things go wrong; their experience is based upon the atypical risk taking failure. Risk takers, particularly in areas where the predictive power of the existing data is weak (which is the case where 'unpredictable' human choice is involved), need to predict how their risk decisions will be perceived by assessors and adjudicators. If that had been done in *Partington v. Wandsworth L.B.C.* then the risk decision might have been presented in a much more positive manner. The likelihood of the young woman being violent might have been more explicitly assessed. The negative value, indeed the illegality, of detaining or restraining her might have been more clearly evaluated and stated within a clear statement of a normalization philosophy. Such a presentation would have increased the likelihood that Mrs Partington's lawyers would have advised against suing.

NEGLIGENCE – CAUSATION *ET AL.*

For there to be liability in negligence, the breach of the standard of care must (a) cause (b) harm of a kind which the courts compensate (c) which was reasonably foreseeable. No such harm then no compensation. But such restrictions do not formally apply – although they will in practice – where complaints, inquiries and disciplinary proceedings are concerned. Inquiries are possible, indeed highly desirable, into 'near' accidents. You can be disciplined, dismissed even, for a risk decision which could have, but fortunately did not, cause harm. That inquiries, complaints and proceedings are relatively unlikely into negligent 'near-accidents', in comparison with when harm results, even though they may have been non-negligent, is just one of the many ways in which our monitoring and management of risk decisions is misconceived.

A risk decision is taken badly and harm results. It may be inferred that the harm was due to the negligently taken decision. But there may, in negligence law, be no causal association. The negligent behaviour may justify disciplinary action, and condemnation by an inquiry team, but that may still not be enough for liability in negligence. The law will inquire, in particular, whether the harm would have happened without the negligent act. An elderly patient is discharged prematurely from hospital. She or he falls, at home, and breaks her or his hip. It looks like negligence. But would the fall have happened anyway? Would the same thing have happened in hospital? If the answer is 'yes' then the fact that it occurred at home is not relevant. The negligent risk decision must increase the likelihood of harm resulting and/or the gravity or degree of harm (such as through the consequences of delay in getting a patient back to hospital).

In *Gauntlett v. Northampton A.H.A.* ((1985) *Lexis*, December 12) an acutely mentally ill patient was assessed as being at risk of committing suicide but not to such an extent as to require constant observation. Clinical staff were sued when she seriously injured herself in a suicide attempt. One was found to have acted (actually it was an inaction) in a way which was not supported by any responsible body of co-professional opinion. He could have been (and, one hopes, was) disciplined by his employers and professional body but, despite his negligent act, he could not be sued in negligence. Even if he had done as he should have done the attempt at suicide would still have occurred. There was no causal connection.

A consequence of this causation rule for risk takers, which is insufficiently appreciated, concerns the time dimension. Care providers and planners regularly take decisions, the consequences of which can last for a considerable period of time, for example the discharge of a patient or the release of a prisoner. They are regularly expected to make a prediction about behaviour that will cover a considerable period. That they often have a poor record in such predictions ought not to be too surprising; they have very little control (causal power) over their clients' future behaviour. If a prisoner offends within weeks of being released early then it appears, at least on these few facts, appropriate to examine that release decision for evidence of negligence. But if that prisoner offends some years later then it will become increasingly inappropriate to contemplate a negligence action, formal inquiry or complaint. The offence, even if it would not have taken the exact same form, might have happened anyway. The release decision would not be the appropriate focus for inquiry. More appropriate would be the monitoring of the offender in the community. For example, was the decision not to seek a revocation of a discretionary life sentence prisoner's licence appropriate? That no such decision was formally made, for example the case was not reviewed or 'it went through on the nod', does not prevent it from being analysed as a decision. Preventative action could have taken place; it was not. That the decision, or non-decision, was taken in a cavalier or uninformed manner could demonstrate neglect. Negligence has to do with process as well as product.

RISK DECISIONS

The traditional view of risk, consistent with dictionary definitions, concerns the likelihood of harm or other form of loss. Risks are perceived as inherently evil. This encourages a preoccupation with avoiding them (NHS Executive 1994). But risk taking is often regarded as highly desirable, particularly when associated with choice and recreational activities; betting, exploring caves, sports, bungee-jumping even. Risk taking is also inherent in the work of clinicians and other care providers. The better view, it is submitted, defines risk taking in terms of comparing and balancing likely benefits with likely harms (Health and Safety Executive 1988) and recognizing that risk taking has at least four 'levels' of analysis and responsibility; (1) the assessment and control of specific risk factors, (2) taking account of situational or contextual risk factors, (3) acknowledging and controlling the problems and calling in aid the potential of the decision-making process, and (4) managing the total decision-making process (for a fuller statement of this thesis see Carson 1994).

BALANCE

Releasing a prisoner at the end of his or her determinate sentence can be justified because his or her continued detention cannot be justified. Releasing a prisoner before the end of his or her sentence can be justified if the likely benefits outweigh the likely harms. If a prisoner's motivation for change is not seized upon then that period may pass, making rehabilitation more difficult and continued offending more likely. Of course it is difficult to assess the genuineness of such a motivation and it is controversial to evaluate the values involved, for example public safety, retribution. Indeed the difficulties, where risk decisions affecting human clients are concerned, are so complex, so fraught with uncertainties, so dependent upon subjective factors, that many wish to give up, deny or question the possibility of risk assessment. However, it is always possible to be more explicit and possible to make better or worse decisions. For so long as that continues to be the case lawyers will have a legitimate interest in challenging risk takers' decisions.

If risk takers wish to be happy, if they wish to minimize the chances of a negligence finding against them, if they wish to seize the opportunities that professionalism and responsibility offer them, then they need to take risk decisions, and take them in a manner which can readily be justified. Instead of anxiously asking a senior colleague what he or she would do (creating many problems in the re-telling and summarizing of the facts), hoping for the best and that nobody will notice the decision-making process, they could think the issues through rigorously to discover what decisions they could justify. Instead of waiting on the chance that a court or inquiry would become involved and impose its assessments of the likelihoods involved and the importance of the different outcomes possible, they could declare their own. The professionals involved, such as those involved in *Partington v. Wandsworth L.B.C.*, are better positioned to make assessments of the likelihoods and the values involved, such as the dignity and equal citizenship of people with learning disabilities. They should not risk legal liability through failing to seize their opportunities.

If you have reason to believe that an event is possible, but unlikely, then you should declare and record that likelihood in an explicit form. Unless it can be shown that your estimate was inappropriate it will prove powerful in discouraging any court, or other form of inquiry, from utilizing hindsight in order to conclude that the harm, which has now occurred, was more likely than it then seemed (Wexler and Schopp 1989). The court has to try to avoid hindsight; why not help it?

You decided that the chance of re-establishing relations between the child and his parent was very important, indeed so important that it was worth the low likelihood of the parent harming the child. Unfortunately, harm has occurred; the child has been killed. Can you prove your reasoning process; can you justify your decision? The court hears you saying that you highly valued the chance of re-establishing relations and that that chance was good. But how highly; how good? If you have a risk taking methodology, designed to produce confirming evidence as a side-product, then you have a much greater chance of convincing the court. Explicit valuation systems can be developed. They will always be imperfect and depend upon a considerable measure of subjectivity. They will not be perfectly objective but they present you with the opportunity for demonstrating a considerable degree of consensus. Instead of leaving it to chance (or to a judge who is not versed in care philosophies and practical dilemmas) to decide how important it is, for example, that clients should be allowed to learn from their mistakes, the people involved in regularly making these kinds of decisions could develop some consensus. That consensus can then be used to demonstrate, although it does not automatically follow, responsible co-professional opinion. It may not be possible to attach agreed, mathematically stated (although there are some advantages for clarity of communication in trying to do so) weights to different outcomes but a little work along these lines will quickly demonstrate a degree of consensus on a hierarchy of values or weights.

LEGISLATIVE VALUES

Risk decisions must be made within legal frameworks and tests. But, arguably fortunately, those frameworks are insufficient. Consider section 1 of the much lauded Children Act 1989. It provides a list of matters to be considered when decisions are made about children. But they are not exclusive and the section does not indicate their relative importance. Consider the tests for when it is lawful to detain someone under the Mental Health Act 1983. The Act may provide verbal distinctions but so much more needs to be done before a decision can be taken within their terms. Such legislative tests demonstrate, rather than constrain, the flexibility available.

RISK MANAGEMENT

Does your employer have a safety policy designed to minimize the likelihood of injury to you and your colleagues? Yes, is the answer. The desirability of such policies has long been recognized. Does your employer have a risk taking policy to help you, and your colleagues, take high quality risk decisions that will minimize the likelihood of injury to clients, the public and yourselves? If the answer is negative is that not rather strange? Why not? If the answer is affirmative does the policy help; for example does it promise to support you if you took your decision within the policy's terms and procedures?

Because the traditional approach to risk-assessment and risk taking has concentrated upon individuals' liability (although employers may be vicariously responsible) managers have escaped attention. This, it is submitted, is entirely wrong. Their responsibility takes a different form. It should not be to second guess or to make (and sign for) decisions that are the responsibility of those directly involved with, and having a fuller knowledge of, the specific case. Their responsibility includes, at least, ensuring that decision-makers are: (1) trained in risk assessment and the making of quality, readily justifiable, decisions, (2) provided with quality information, for example predictive data, (3) monitored so that (a) they can learn from their successes as well as any failures and (b) they can intervene to minimize the seriousness of harmful outcomes as soon as this is needed; and (4) provided with a framework for making their decisions which promises to support those who follow their policies, even if harm results (Carson 1994).

The future of risk management involves closer attention to how decisions are made and how decision-makers are managed. The legal framework for the former has existed for some time. It is also, it is submitted, available for the suing of managers who risk legal liability by not appreciating that risk taking is a skill which can be, and deserves to be, developed.

REFERENCES

Brearley, P. (1982) *Risk and Social Work*. London: Routledge Kegan Paul.

British Medical Association (1990) *The BMA Guide to Living with Risk*. London: Penguin.

Carson, D. (1994) 'Dangerous people; through a broader conception of "risk" and "danger" to better decisions.' *Expert Evidence 3*, 2, 51–69.

Health and Safety Executive (1988) *The Tolerability of Risk from Nuclear Power Stations*. London: HMSO.

NHS Executive (1994) *Risk Management in the NHS*. Leeds: Department of Health.

Rachlin, H. (1989) *Judgment, Decision and Choice; A Cognitive/Behavioral Synthesis*. New York: W.H. Freeman.

Ritchie, J.H. (chair), Dick, D. and Lingham, R. (1994) *The Report of the Inquiry into the Care and Treatment of Christopher Clunis*. London: HMSO.

Royal Society (1992) *Risk: Analysis, Perception and Management*. London: The Royal Society.

Wexler, D.B. and Schopp, R.F. (1989) 'How and when to correct for juror hindsight bias in mental health malpractice litigation: Some preliminary observations.' *Behavioral Sciences and the Law 7*, 4, 485–504.

Yates, J.F, (ed) (1992) *Risk Taking Behavior*. Chichester: Wiley.

CHAPTER TWO

RISK ASSESSMENT IN CHILD PROTECTION WORK

Brian Corby

INTRODUCTION

This chapter will focus on risk assessment of intra-familial child abuse including physical and sexual abuse, and physical and emotional neglect. There are many other forms of child abuse currently on the social agenda, for example ritual abuse, organized abuse, institutional abuse, bullying and child prostitution. However, these will not be directly considered. There are two reasons for narrowing the focus. First, although it could be argued that there is a generic aspect to all child abuse (i.e. that children's experience of mistreatment has potential physical and psychological ill-effects whoever the abuser and wherever it takes place), there are particular issues in intra-familial abuse, most notably that the child usually has a close social and psychological tie with his/her abuser and that he/she may continue to live in close proximity to this person. As will be seen, these factors pose particular difficulties for those involved in carrying out child protection risk assessments. The second reason for narrowing down the focus is simply that to deal with the whole range of abuse in a relatively short space would not do justice to the complexity of the subject matter.

CONTEXTUAL PROBLEMS

Before considering the practicalities of doing child protection risk assessment work, it is important to consider contextual issues which help shape and to a large extent determine the parameters of this activity. Consideration will, therefore, be given in this section (1) to the political and social context within which child protection assessments are carried out and (2) to the problematic nature of the concept of child abuse itself.

The Politics of Child Protection

Child protection work does not take place in a vacuum – far from it. Indeed it could be argued that it is the most visible and reported on aspect of modern-day social welfare work. We live in a society which for the most part relies heavily on parents to take responsibility for the socialization of children and young people. The norm, therefore, with regard to state intervention into families is one of non-interference and, as a result, such intervention has to be particularly justified and ultimately sanctioned by the courts. On the other hand, society has a duty to take steps to ensure that children are not exposed to abuse within their families. Achieving the right balance is what is required. The expectation placed on child protection professionals is that they will be able to identify those children who are seriously at risk and ensure that appropriate protective measures are taken, but that as far as possible this should be within the context of the child's family.

This is not an easy task. More than two decades on from the Maria Colwell inquiry report (Colwell 1974), there is still ongoing concern about cases where social workers and other professionals either fail to predict the degree of risk to a child (The Bridge 1995) or take what are ultimately considered to be overreactive steps to protect children (Orkney 1992). One response to this is to lay the blame at the door of these individual practitioners (see Hill 1990). However, this is clearly insufficient. Social workers and other professionals operate in a very difficult environment where there is little agreement about the way forward in a range of areas. For instance, there is still confusion about the link between children's needs/rights and those of parents (Owen 1992); there is no clear agreement about who best should carry out assessments – social workers, psychologists or police, and there is uncertainty about the degree to which professional decisions should be backed by legal authority. The state is highly ambivalent about setting parameters for intervention into families which results in fluctuating approaches and policy reversals. The main thrust of child protection policy from 1972 through to the early 1990s was to ensure that social workers and other professionals recognized the existence of child abuse and responded decisively to it. Current research sponsored by the Department of Health is pointing to the need to provide more general support for families where children are considered to be at less serious risk, rather than to focus exclusively on the matter of child abuse (Gibbons, Conroy and Bell 1994). These and other issues stemming from the nature of the state's relationship with the family powerfully influence child protection assessment practice.

Definitional Problems

Child protection work is made further problematic because of difficulties in agreeing on the levels of seriousness which should properly be the concerns of the state (see Giovannoni and Becerra 1979). At one end of the spectrum, there is general agreement. All children who are persistently physically assaulted or who are sexually violated by their carers are generally seen to be victims of child abuse. However, a good deal of physical abuse and, arguably, some sexual abuse is not viewed as obviously serious. Particularly controversial is the issue of physical punishment. In a society that endorses 'smacking' of young children, there can be no hard and fast rules about when punishment becomes abuse (see Freeman 1988). Physical and emotional neglect cases raise even more issues of value about what constitutes good enough parenting, and pose awkward questions about the role of poverty, stress and illness as causative or contributory factors (Wolock and Horowitz 1984). While from the child's point of view all the aforementioned acts are likely to be experienced as abusive, the issue for child protection workers is far more complex because of the social context within which they are operating.

THE BACKGROUND TO RISK ASSESSMENT IN CHILD PROTECTION WORK

Current child protection assessment methods have been shaped and built up over the past 30 years. Although this development has by no means been a smooth one, knowledge of how it has happened is important to aid under-standing of the present situation. In particular it is important to note how different professions have been involved in shaping child protection assess-ments. This interdisciplinary aspect is both a strength (in that it ensures that a wide range of perspectives are brought to bear on the problem of child abuse) and a weakness because of the difficulties of coordinating these perspectives and of avoiding professional rivalries.

Physical Abuse

In the field of physical abuse, the medical profession played a key role early on (see Kempe *et al.* 1962; Pfohl 1977). It made important contributions to the detection of child abuse through the use of X-rays and blood-clotting tests. Another key contribution was the development of a theory of causation of child abuse (Steele and Pollock 1974) which dominated child protection work from the early 1960s through to the mid-1980s, and is still influential. This approach emphasized the emotional deficits of parents (usually mothers) as key causative factors in child abuse. Parents who themselves had had emo-tionally depriving experiences as children were considered to be unable to provide satisfactory emotional care and support for their own children. This 'inadequacy' resulted in aggressive or neglectful behaviour towards them. Children of such parents were perceived to be at risk of further abuse without intervention which focused on the psychological needs of these parents.

Another contribution of the medical profession in this field has been the attempt (largely unsuccessful) to predict, and therefore prevent, physical child abuse from happening. This will be discussed in more detail in the assessment practice section.

The 1980s saw a broadening of the approach to understanding physical child abuse with more emphasis on social, social psychological and cultural factors. Concerns raised by public inquiries (DoH 1991a) have led to greater concentration on risk assessment with the social work profession taking a lead role.

Neglect

In the field of neglect, again the medical profession has been influential in theorizing why some children fail to thrive (Iwaniec, Herbert and McNeish 1985) and has devised techniques such as the use of percentile charts which can be used in clinics and by health visitors to detect and monitor this phenomenon. Social work researchers, particularly in the USA (Polansky,

Ammons and Weathersby 1983), have tried to devise checklists for assessing neglect. However, a major problem in this field is the issue of what constitutes good enough parenting. There are problems in agreeing upon acceptable standards and norms given the considerable differences in culture and class between assessors and assessed in the vast majority of cases.

Sexual Abuse

Sexual abuse assessment has raised considerable controversy in the past decade in Britain. The focus of concern has been more on determining whether abuse has happened or not, rather than on future risk of it, although there are obviously links between the two. Because of the lack of physical evidence available for the discovery of all but the most extreme forms of sexual abuse (see below), much emphasis has been placed on the child's testimony and behavioural indicators. However, with regard to the former, there are major problems because children are often under threat not to reveal (Furniss 1991) and, in the case of younger children, they often do not have the language and understanding to communicate their problems (Macfarlane and Waterman 1986). Psychiatrists and psychologists have devised various techniques (play therapy, use of anatomically correct dolls, child-centred interviewing techniques) to improve their assessments (Bentovim *et al.* 1988), and these have been taken up by social workers as well. However, these methods have been subject to much public criticism (Cleveland 1988; Orkney 1992). At present, assessment of the kind that is acceptable as evidence in court is bound by strict rules of procedure (see the Memorandum of Good Practice (Home Office 1992)) and the police have increasingly taken a prominent role in this work. One consequence is that many other professionals feel blocked in developing assessment procedures.

With regard to behavioural indicators, checklists have been devised (see Porter 1984), but they are of limited usefulness because the behaviours identified are also indicators of general disturbance. According to Beitchman *et al.* (1991), only those related to sexually precocious behaviour have any specific value.

There has been little progress in identifying sexual abuse by means of physical examination. The work of Hobbs and Wynne on child buggery (1986), using reflex anal dilatation tests, has largely been discredited as a result of the way in which they were applied in Cleveland. Currently, there is much confusion about how to assess sexual abuse of children within their families in a way that is acceptable to society, and this in turn has obvious implications for assessing future risk.

THE PRACTICE OF RISK ASSESSMENT

When considering practice issues, it is important to be clear about what is meant by the term 'risk assessment'. Wald and Woolverton (1990) use the following definition: 'A process for assessing the likelihood that a given person (usually a parent) will harm a child in the future' (p.486). There are three main stages in child protection at which risk assessment work is carried out: at the preventive stage, at the initial investigation stage and later on in the child protection process when major decisions are being taken which could affect the long-term future of a child already considered to be at high risk.

In the strict sense of the meaning of risk assessment, preventive assessment fits the definition best, in that a set of criteria are used to predict from a whole population those most likely to harm their children, and the results of these predictions can be tested.

The focus in initial investigations is a dual one – first, on whether abuse has taken place and who was responsible, and second, on the likelihood of a recurrence of the abuse without the input of services or resources. While there may be a close connection between these two concerns, it is important that practitioners remember that they may also be distinct. Children could have been seriously abused, but because of changes in family circumstances, be at very little future risk. On the other hand, children who have been ill-treated with only minor consequences could be at serious risk in the future.

With regard to what will be called long-term risk assessments, it is not always easy to distinguish between assessment and intervention. Some of the methods used to assess risk involve working with parents over a long period to test their potential for becoming safe parents. Monitoring the progress of families where children have been rehabilitated after removal can be seen as a form of ongoing assessment. Thus, it can be seen that risk assessment at the different stages of child protection work involves a wide variety of activities. These stages will now be considered in more detail.

Preventive Risk Assessment

As stated above, the aim of risk assessment at this stage is to predict and thereby prevent physical abuse happening by screening whole populations of parents of new-born children to select out those most likely to abuse and target services on to them. Examples of approaches to this form of assessment are to be found in Kempe and Kempe (1978), Lealman et al. (1983) and Browne and Saqi (1988). The main criteria used for this type of assessment are the quality of the interaction of the parent (usually mother) and child as observed by nurses, midwives and health visitors, and a list of factors derived from research into child abuse. For instance, Browne and Saqi's (1988) list includes the following factors:

(1) History of family violence.

(2) Socio-economic problems such as unemployment.

(3) Infant premature, low birth weight.

(4) Parent abused or neglected as a child.

(5) Step-parent or cohabitee present.

(6) Mother less than 21 years old at the time of birth.

(7) History of mental illness, drug or alcohol addiction.

(8) Infant separated from mother for greater than 24 hours post-delivery.

(9) Infant mentally or physically handicapped.

(10) Less than 18 months between birth of children. (p.68)

There are considerable practical and ethical problems attached to this type of assessment. Although it is possible to predict many parents who turn out to abuse their children physically (between two-thirds and four-fifths), in the process a large number of non-abusing parents are included in the prediction. Browne and Saqi (1988) found that only six per cent of those they identified as potential abusers had abused their children within two years of the assessment. Lealman *et al.* (1983) also reported a very high false positive rate. These rates are largely unacceptable, given the socio-political background to intervening in families to protect children outlined in the previous section. Parton (1985) and Dingwall (1989) have subjected this form of preventive assessment to close scrutiny. Dingwall is of the view that these approaches merely single out lower class parents who are seen as difficult or troublesome by professionals. Another factor to be considered is the emphasis on mothers' parenting potential. This does not seem justifiable considering that males may be responsible for half of all physical abuse (Corby 1993, pp.65–66). Finally, there are ethical concerns surrounding the apparently covert nature of these types of assessment.

Initial Risk Assessments

It should be pointed out that preventive assessments of the kind outlined above are not part of mainstream child protection practice in Britain. Social workers and other professionals are largely engaged in dealing with individual referrals about child abuse. They are faced with allegations of abuse having happened or concerns that they might be about to happen and they have to decide whether or not to intervene and, if so, how. Assessments of this kind often have to be made quickly with a view to deciding whether a child needs immediate protection.

The Procedures Governing Initial Risk Assessments

Procedural guidelines for initial child protection assessments are set out in Area Child Protection Committees' handbooks. These handbooks are based on national guidelines deriving from two main sources – the 1991 Working Together guidelines (DoH 1991b) and the Memorandum of Good Pactice referred to above (Home Office 1992). The general procedure for this type of assessment is as follows:

(1) Abuse referrals should be made, first, to social workers in social services departments who are expected in all but immediately unsubstantiated allegations or cases of minor abuse to consult with the police and decide whether to conduct a joint video interview of the child. The purpose of the joint interview is largely to determine whether there is sufficient evidence to prosecute an alleged abuser. Another purpose is to ensure that a child does not have to recount his/her story over and over again to different professionals, a concern resulting from the outcome of the Cleveland inquiry).

(2) Children may also be medically examined subject to their consent (depending on their age and understanding) and that of their parents. If parents refuse consent, their wishes can only be overruled by a court decision. The wishes of children considered of sufficient age and understanding cannot be overruled by courts.

(3) Under the 1989 Children Act, police and social services departments have powers to apply for protection orders if they feel children are at immediate risk (sections 44 to 46); social services departments may pay for alternative accommodation for an alleged abuser who is willing to leave the family home (schedule 2.5.); they also have the power to seek authority from the courts to carry out assessments of children at risk if parents are preventing them from doing this and the courts are satisfied that the child is suffering, or likely to suffer significant harm (section 43).

(4) In cases where abuse is thought to have happened or is likely to happen, a child protection conference is held involving all professionals in contact with the family concerned, the parents and the children (if they are of sufficient age and understanding). The national guidelines recommend that this conference take place within ten days of the allegation.

The Process of Initial Assessment

There are few guidelines in procedure handbooks about the content of assessment. Some handbooks include information about types of injury that should be cause for concern (in the case of physical abuse), suspicious child behaviours (more particularly in cases of sexual abuse) and social/psychological factors that have been correlated with child abuse. However, these provide only the bare bones on which to build assessments. The reality of assessment is quite complex. First, child protection assessment involves different professionals with different backgrounds, concerns and responsibilities. Second, as stressed in earlier sections, except at the serious end of the abuse spectrum, there may be a wide variation in judgement about what is abusive enough to warrant intervention. Third, professionals are operating from a limited knowledge base about why child abuse happens and in what circumstances. Fourth, they are faced with a good deal of denial, disagreement and indignation from parents. Fifth, they are required, as far as possible, to provide protection for children in the context of the family and to use compulsory measures only where there are no alternatives.

Given these difficulties, it is particularly important for practitioners to use some form of plan/scheme within which logically to itemize and evaluate concerns.

First, it is necessary to be clear about the nature of the issues presented in a referral, in particular to distinguish between general concerns about a child's welfare, suspicions that a child may be being abused and allegations that a child is being abused or is likely to be abused. Concerns about a child's welfare may develop into a child protection issue, but this should not be assumed to be the case at the start. Suspicions about abuse need substantiating and the general view held since Cleveland is that this should be done by gathering further information and close monitoring of the situation before initiating action. (This raises interesting questions about parents' rights and working more closely with parents in the spirit of the 1989 Children Act – see section on the consumer's perspective. It could be argued on these grounds that concerns of these sort should be shared with parents as soon as possible.) There is less dispute about responding to allegations of abuse or likely abuse. The expectation is that such referrals will be responded to by social workers and the police as quickly as can be arranged, and this will entail informing parents of concerns.

Second, (and the following comments refer to cases of alleged abuse or likely abuse) it is important to establish facts surrounding the abuse. What is the nature of the alleged or likely abuse? When was it alleged to have happened? What were the circumstances? Who is alleged to have abused or be likely to abuse the child? Does the alleged abuser deny the abuse? If there is a non-abusing parent, what is his/her view of what happened or is happening? Securing this information is not as easy as it seems. The facts are frequently disputed. There may be denial by parents/carers that the abuse happened at all or, if it did, that they were responsible. They may feel that the alleged abuse was not serious enough to warrant investigation and that there is no likelihood of their children being at risk in the future. Farmer (1993) in a study of families with children on child protection registers found that such disagreements over what she termed commission, culpability and risk were a prominent feature of social worker–parent interactions. There is now much more uncertainty about the weight to be a given to a child's account of abuse as a result of research (Mantell 1988) which throws into question the previously held view among many health and welfare professionals that children must be believed when they make such allegations (particularly in respect of sexual abuse). There may, or may not, be medical evidence of abuse which will verify that it has happened even though it is unlikely to help identify the abuser. In the field of sexual abuse, such evidence is rare.

Third, having disentangled the available facts, there is a need to make decisions about the future risk to the child. This will usually entail gathering information from other professionals, considering previous referrals and any prior involvement with the family over child care and child protection issues, and evaluating the seriousness of the abuse currently being investigated. The coordination of this task is usually the responsibility of the investigating social worker. The initial assessment is usually finalized at the child protection conference. How is this risk assessment carried out? What guidance do social workers and other professionals have in trying to predict future risk to children?.

Initial Risk Assessment Checklists

What knowledge we have suggests that social workers in Britain have not up to recently explicitly used rational methods of assessing risks (Corby and Mills 1986; Campbell 1991; Higginson 1991). In physical abuse and neglect cases, for instance, Corby and Mills found the following factors to be implicitly influencing conference decisions:

(1) Assessment of parental character.

(2) Cooperativeness of parents.

(3) Previous history of child abuse.

(4) Availability of police and medical evidence.

(5) Seriousness of injury.

(6) Age/potential vulnerability of the child.

(7) Suspicion surrounding the cause of the injury.

Waterhouse and Carnie (1992) found a slightly different set of factors operating in sexual abuse cases:

(1) Attitude of the non-abusing parent to the alleged perpatrator.

(2) Access between referred child and alleged perpetrators.

(3) Type of alleged abuse.

(4) Age of child or young people.

(5) Attitude of alleged perpetrator to allegations.

(6) Parental attitude to social work investigation.

Corby and Mills (1986) have argued that there is need to make the use of criteria such as these explicit, and that professionals need to check through these factors in a systematic way as an aid to deciding on the level of risk at the initial assessment stage.

Over the last ten years, there has been considerable attention paid to developing sophisticated risk assessment instruments in the USA (see Wald and Woolverton 1990; English and Pecora 1994; Milner 1995). These instruments are used at all stages in child protection intervention; that is, at a broad screening level and with individual cases both at initial investigation and later when decisions are being made about rehabilitation. The best of the instruments take into account a very wide range of variables including demographic/social factors (e.g. whether parents are biological parents or not, their ages) biological factors (e.g. neurological and physical health problems), cognitive/affective factors (e.g. low levels of child development knowledge) and behavioural characteristics (e.g. use of alcohol, drugs). They include information about individuals, their families and the communities in which they live. They take the form of either check-lists, structured interview schedules or personality measures, or a combination of any of these. The most comprehensive and widely used approach is that of the Child Abuse Potential Inventory (Milner 1986) which claims a very high success rate.

These developments have aroused considerable interest in Britain. However, there is need for caution about their use. First, it should be stressed that many of the risk factors have questionable scientific validity as predictors. Research into child abuse cases, though extensive, still has far to go before it can provide the type of certainty in prediction that would be acceptable to society (see Corby 1993, Chapter 4). Second, there is the issue of how to weight risk factors. For instance, should they be added up and scored, and this score be used to determine the level of risk? Wald and Woolverton (1990) question the validity of such an approach. They consider that the interaction of factors is probably more important than a cumulative total, but then warn that 'nobody is able to point out which interaction of factors makes a difference' (p.495). They also question the idea of linking levels of risk to scores because there are no clear indicators about where the cut-off points should be drawn.

This may all seem disheartening to those seeking to sharpen up initial risk assessments. However, check-lists can be usefully applied to assessment work as long as their limitations are realized. Wald and Woolverton again have important things to say about this. Drawing from the American experience, they argue that the use of check-lists can sharpen professionals' thinking about the issues involved in child abuse risk assessment. At the very least, such activity ensures that consideration has been given to a wide range of factors in a relatively consistent way. However, they stress that risk assessment instruments should not be used in a mechanistic way and that, given the current state of knowledge they are an aid to, not a substitute for, clinical judgement. In particular, they express concern that agencies may be attracted to such instruments because of their perceived potential for reducing the need for expensive resources, such as experienced and well qualified practitioners.

LONG-TERM ASSESSMENT

The previous section has dealt with assessments at the investigation and early decision-making stage of child protection work. This section deals with assessment of children and families who have already been assessed as being high risk and about whose longer term future decisions have to be reached. While the knowledge base for making these assessments is in many ways the same as for initial assessments, there are some contextual differences.

First, as just referred to, the children and families who are the subject of long-term assessments have already been selected from a wider population. The children have been identified as being at a relatively high degree of risk, and the focus is on how to reduce the risk in situations where their parents/carers wish them to remain in their care or return to it, if they have already been removed. In the field of physical abuse and neglect, this issue has been seen as the most pressing one of all. Most of those children whose deaths from child abuse were the subject of public inquiries were in one or other of these situations. Some continued to live with their parents after being assessed as at high risk (e.g. Tyra Henry, Charlene Salt, Doreen Aston); others were returned to them after periods in protective care (Maria Colwell, Jasmine Beckford, Gemma Hartwell). There has been much activity and debate about how best to manage risk in these situations.

Before considering these developments in more detail, however, it should be stressed that the focus of concern at this stage should be risk reduction, not risk elimination. The risk of children being reabused by their parents/carers can only be eliminated by permanent exclusion from any ongoing contact with them (see Hensey, Williams and Rosenbloom 1983). In many cases this is not possible because the evidence for taking such courses of action is often not available. Also, it is generally considered unacceptable to deny parents further opportunities to demonstrate that they can be good parents. Finally, the fact of a child's being in care can create further risks in terms of his/her psychological well-being and future development. Therefore, the calculation of risk is not carried out in a scientific vacuum; rather, it takes place in a socio-legal environment which defines preferred courses of action. In this environment, much long-term assessment work involves weighing up the costs and benefits of different courses of action and opting for the least detrimental alternative.

On the credit side, it should be pointed out that in cases where children are in care, risk assessments can often be carried out in better conditions than those in which initial assessments are done. Access to the child is not problematic. Usually, there will be more time within which to carry out the assessment, and parents/carers may be more cooperative. Overall, professionals should have more control in these conditions. The opposite, of course, is true after children have been rehabilitated, or where they were not removed in the first place. In such circumstances, parents can be very resistant to intervention and attempts to carry out assessments.

The Lessons of Public Inquiries

Many of these difficulties have been highlighted in public inquiry cases. Although focusing on reports into these cases could be seen as a rather negative way to develop thinking about risk assessment, they do contain a wealth of useful information which should be drawn upon. There are two summaries of findings published (DHSS 1982; DoH 1991a) and also a very useful analysis by Reder, Duncan and Gray (1993). It is only possible to select out a few of the many important messages that the inquiries contain. However, these issues stand out:

(1) The importance of keeping an accurate account of events with particular focus on the need to maintain a record of injuries. A record of this kind can be a considerable aid in assessing the seriousness of risk to a child (see The Bridge 1991; Fox 1990).

(2) The need to ensure ongoing contact and communication with parents and children (Cleveland 1988) and to assert authority in this respect should it prove necessary (Aston 1989; Carlile 1987).

(3) The need to ensure that front-line practitioners are experienced, have expertise in and commitment to child protection work, and are well supervised (Beckford 1985; Aston 1989).

(4) The need for those carrying out assessments to avoid sexist, culturalist and ageist assumptions. The Beckford inquiry showed the effect of failing to involve fathers in assessments (Beckford 1985); the Henry inquiry showed the danger of making assumptions about individuals based on ill-informed cultural stereotypes (Henry 1987), and the Sukina case highlighted the importance of listening to what children say (The Bridge 1991).

(5) The need to involve other professionals and to ensure good communication between them in the assessment process (all

inquiries emphasize this, but see the recommendations of
Cleveland (1988) in particular).

The Use of Checklists

In the field of physical abuse, the checklist approach referred to in the previous
section has also been applied to long-term assessments. Greenland (1987), in
the wake of the Beckford inquiry, drew up the following checklist of factors
associated with 100 child death cases investigated in Canada and Great
Britain.

For parents

(1) Previously abused/neglected as a child.

(2) Age 20 years or less at the birth of first child.

(3) Single-parent/separated; partner not biological parent.

(4) History of abuse/neglect or deprivation.

(5) Socially isolated – frequent moves-poor housing.

(6) Poverty-unemployed/unskilled worker; inadequate education

(7) Abuses alcohol and/or drugs.

(8) History of criminally assaultive behaviour and/or suicide attempts.

(9) Pregnant – post-partum – or chronic illness.

For children

(1) Was previously abused/neglected.

(2) Under five years of age at the time of abuse or neglect.

(3) Premature or low-birth weight.

(4) Now underweight.

(5) Birth defect – chronic illness – developmental lag.

(6) Prolonged separation from mother.

(7) Cries frequently – difficult to comfort.

(8) Difficulties in feeding/elimination.

(9) Adopted, foster- or step-child.

(Greenland 1987 – see pp.185–187)

The criticisms raised in relation to the use of check-lists and other instruments
in short-term assessments apply here as well. The predictive value of many
of the factors is limited. For instance, the link between alcohol and child abuse
is a tenuous one (Orme and Rimmer 1981), and the rate of intergenerational
transmission of abuse is 30 per cent (Egeland 1988). Greenland argues that in
the case of children who have already been seriously abused, the existence of
five factors for parents and five for children is sufficient to consider the child
at serious risk. This notion of adding up factors and determining risk by a

total score, as we have seen, is not without problems. Greenland is not unaware of some of the limitations. He considers that his high-risk checklist should form 'part of the assessment process and (it) can play a useful part in the identification and management of high-risk families' (Greenland 1987, p.170).

The Department of Health Guidelines

In 1988 in response to criticism from the Social Services Inspectorate that systematic assessment of families where children were at risk was not taking place, the Department of Health produced a guide for carrying out long-term assessments (DoH 1988). One of the major influences on this was the work of Dale, Davies, Morrison and Waters (1986) who used family therapy techniques to 'assess' parents who had seriously ill-treated their children. The focus was on getting them to accept the seriousness of what they had done and to develop awareness of their own (often deprived) childhood experiences. Parents who did not respond to this form of assessment were considered to be dangerous and not suitable to be entrusted with the continuing care of their children.

The DoH guide comprises 167 questions which examine a wide range of issues about the life-history of the child and the parents, the quality of the parents' relationship, their interaction with the child, their support networks and material circumstances. In many ways, it is a comprehensive document and can be seen as a worthy attempt to fill the assessment gap identified by the Social Services Inspectorate. However, it has considerable flaws. Many of the questions do not seem particularly relevant to the issue of risk to children. For instance, question 78 suggests that parents are asked if in their teenage years they were involved with drugs or alcohol and if they were in trouble with the police. Question 97 asks if parents have ever been in trouble with the police and if they have any convictions. Question 112 asks parents to describe their sex life and to say whether they use contraception. Not only is it hard to see the relevance of this type of questioning, but one can also envisage parents resenting what they might well perceive as over-intrusiveness.

In many ways, this guide is pointing in the right direction. It is important that risk assessments incorporate a wide range of theoretical perspectives and go beyond the immediate aspects of abuse incidents in order to develop a causal understanding. However, it is hard to see how the current document could be usefully applied in most practice contexts.

Risk Assessment in Sexual Abuse Cases

Family therapy techniques of the type used by Dale *et al.* are also used in long-term assessments of children who have been sexually abused. These have been pioneered at the Great Ormond Street Hospital for Children (Bentovim *et al.* 1988). The strength of this approach is its emphasis on the interactionist perspective as opposed to use of linear causation ideas and the checklist. The focus is on getting abusers to admit what they have done and to assess their potential for more openness and emotional honesty in the future. Progress in these aspects is considered to be linked with less risk to the child.

Other Developments

In general terms, there have been many developments in long-term child protection assessments in the last few years. A notable change has been greater emphasis on interaction between parents and parents and parents and children as a source of evidence of risk (Asen, George, Piper and Stevens 1989 and Reder *et al.* 1993). Much of this kind of work is being carried out in clinical settings and family centres. This development, allied to careful use of the check-list approach, seems at present to be providing the basis of a sensible way forward.

ASSESSMENT – THE CONSUMER'S PERSPECTIVE

There has been a considerable shift since the publication of the Cleveland Report in thinking about the role of parents and children at the receiving end of child protection work. Prior to that, there was little obvious concern for the rights of either. Those of parents were seen as forfeited by virtue of the fact that they were suspected of ill-treating their children and those of children were thought to be merely in relation to the right to protection. The change in thinking brought about by Cleveland, and reflected in the Children Act 1989 has resulted in an expectation that parents and children will be more actively involved in assessment of concerns about them. This is not an easy thing to achieve given the conflicts that seem intrinsic to the notion of state intervention into family life. Nevertheless, there are some important lessons that this more participative approach has for child protection assessment.

First, parents and children (where appropriate) need to be fully informed of the purposes of assessment, the process and how the findings of the assessment will be used.

Second, there is a constant need to check out the views of parents and children (where appropriate) with regard to the assessment. Do they share the concerns of the professionals and if not, why not? Do they share some concerns and not others? What are their views about future risks to their children? What forms of intervention, help or monitoring do they think would assist in reducing any risks?

Third, it is important that the assessment be time-limited and that the assessment outcomes and the reasons for reaching them be shared openly with parents (and children where appropriate).

Fourth, it needs to be recognized that parents and children do have rights in these situations – they have a right to make representations under section 26 of the 1989 Children Act and, in some areas, to sub-committees of Area Child Protection Committees.

It has to be remembered that, except in the relatively small number of cases where children are under statutory orders, or where parents are being charged with criminal offences, parents and children are under no obligation to work with child protection professionals. Hence there is need for considerable skill and expertise in engaging them along with an understanding of and respect for their rights.

CONCLUDING COMMENTS

Risk assessment in child protection work is still at an early stage of development. There is an understandable desire to achieve a firmer, 'more objective' base on which to determine child abuse risks, and this should not be discouraged. More effort should be made to develop explicit approaches to risk assessment which can be tested for validity and, therefore, be used with more certainty in practice. In the meantime, however, the current limitations of risk assessment work should not be overlooked.

In this chapter, considerable attention has been paid to the context in which child protection assessments are carried out – at both macro- and micro-levels. It has been emphasized that at the macro-level there is still great uncertainty about the extent to which the state should intervene in families to protect children. This is a value issue that will not be resolved by the development of more scientific approaches to risk assessment. At the micro-level, perhaps because of societal ambivalence, there are many barriers to conducting assessments as rationally and comprehensively as many professionals would like.

Given these limitations, the quality of those carrying out risk assessments seems to be a key factor. It is important that child protection practitioners, from whatever discipline, have both a general child care and a more specific child protection knowledge base; that they specialize in child protection work; that their experience is retained in front-line practice, and that they accrue with their experience greater influence on the decision-making process (along with the responsibility that that entails). Finally, it should be stressed that risk assessment is pointless if the resources needed to achieve risk reduction are not available.

REFERENCES

Asen K., George E., Piper R. and Stevens A. (1989) 'A systems approach to child abuse: management and treatment issues.' *Child Abuse and Neglect 13*, 45–57.

Aston, D. (1989) The Doreen Aston Report. Area Review Committee of the London Boroughs of Lambeth, Lewisham and Southwark.

Beckford, J. (1985) *A Child in Trust*. The report of the panel of inquiry into the circumstances surrounding the death of Jasmine Beckford. London Borough of Brent.

Beitchman J., Zucker K., Hood J., Da Costa G., and Akman D. (1991) 'A review of the short-term effects of child sexual abuse.' *Child Abuse and Neglect 15*, 537–56.

Bentovim A., Elton A., Hildebrand J., Tranter M. and Vizard E. (eds) (1988) *Child Sexual Abuse within the Family: Assessment and Treatment: The Work of the Great Ormond Street Team*. London: Wright.

Browne K. and Saqi S. (1988) 'Approaches to screening for child abuse and neglect' In K. Browne, C. Davies and P. Stratton (eds) *Early Prediction and Prevention of Child Abuse*. Chichester: Wiley.

Bridge, The (1991) *Sukina: An Evaluation of the Circumstances Surrounding her Death*. London: The Bridge Child Care Consultancy Service.

Bridge, The (1995) *Paul – Death Through Neglect*. London: The Bridge Child Care Consultancy Service.

Campbell, M. (1991) 'Children at risk: How different are children on Child Abuse Registers?' *British Journal of Social Work 21*, 259–75.

Carlile, K. (1987) *A Child in Mind: Protection of Children in a Responsible Society.* The report of the commission of inquiry into the circumstances surrounding the death of Kimberley Carlile. London Borough of Greenwich.

Cleveland (1988) *Report of the Inquiry into Child Abuse in Cleveland 1987.* London: HMSO.

Colwell, M. (1974) *Report of the Committee of Inquiry into the Care and Supervision Provided in Relation to Maria Colwell.* London: HMSO.

Corby, B. (1993) *Child Abuse: Towards a Knowledge Base.* Buckingham: Open University Press.

Corby, B. and Mills, C. (1986) 'Child abuse: risks and resources.' *British Journal of Social Work 16*, 531–42.

Dale P., Davies M., Morrison T. and Waters J. (1986) *Dangerous Families: Assessment and Treatment of Child Abuse.* London: Tavistock.

Department of Health (1988) *Protecting Children: A Guide for Social Workers Undertaking a Comprehensive Assessment.* London: HMSO.

Department of Health (1991a) *Child Abuse: A Study of Inquiry Reports 1980–1989.* London: HMSO.

Department of Health (1991b) *Working Together under the Children Act 1989: A Guide to Arrangements for Inter-Agency Cooperation for the Protection of Children from Abuse.* London: HMSO.

Department of Health and Social Security (1982) *Child Abuse: A Study of Inquiry Reports 1973–1981.* London: HMSO.

Dingwall, R. (1989) 'Some problems about predicting child abuse and neglect.' In O. Stevenson (ed) *Child Abuse: Public Policy and Professional Practice.* Hemel Hempstead: Harvester Wheatsheaf.

Egeland, B. (1988) 'Breaking the cycle of abuse: implications for prediction and intervention.' In K. Browne, C. Davies and P. Stratton (eds) *Early Prediction and Prevention of Child Abuse.* Chichester: Wiley.

English, D. and Pecora, P. (1994) 'Risk assessment as a practice in child protection services.' *Child Welfare 53,51–473*.

Farmer, E. (1993) 'The impact of child protection interventions.' In L. Waterhouse (ed) *Child Abuse and Child Abusers: Protection and Prevention.* London: Jessica Kingsley Publishers.

Fox, S. (1990) *The Report of the Inquiry into the Death of Stephanie Fox.* London Borough of Wandsworth.

Freeman, M. (1988) 'Time to stop hitting our children.' *Childright 51*, 5–8.

Furniss, T. (1991) *The Multi-Professional Handbook of Child Sexual Abuse: Management, Therapy and Legal Intervention.* London: Routledge.

Gibbons, J., Conroy, S. and Bell, C. (1994) *Operation of Child Protection Registers.* London: HMSO.

Giovannoni, J. and Becerra, R. (1979) *Defining Child Abuse.* New York: Free Press.

Greenland, C. (1987) *Preventing CAN Deaths: An International Study of Deaths due to Child Abuse and Neglect.* London: Tavistock.

Hartwell, G. (1985) *Report to the Social Services Committee*. Metropolitan Borough of Birmingham.

Henry, T. (1987) *Whose Child? The Report of the Public Inquiry into the Death of Tyra Henry*. London Borough of Lambeth.

Hensey, O., Williams, J. and Rosenbloom, L. (1983) 'Intervention in child abuse: experience in Liverpool.' *Developmental Medicine and Child Neurology 25*, 606–11.

Higginson, S. (1991) 'Forty case conferences-distorted evidence.' *Community Care.* 17th. May, 23–5.

Hill, M. (1990) 'The manifest and latent lessons of child abuse inquiries.' *British Journal of Social work 20*, 197–213.

Hobbs, C. and Wynne, J. (1986) 'Buggery in childhood – a common syndrome of child abuse.' *The Lancet ii*, 792–6.

Home Office (1992) *Memorandum of good practice on video recorded interviews with child witnesses for criminal proceedings*. London: HMSO.

Iwaniec D., Herbert M. and McNeish A. (1985) 'Social work with failure to thrive children and their families: part II. Behavioural social work intervention.' *British Journal of Social Work 15*, 375–89.

Kempe C., Silverman F., Steele B., Droegemueller W. and Silver H. (1962) 'The battered child syndrome.' *Journal of the American Medical Association 181*, 17–24.

Kempe, R. and Kempe, C. (1978) *Child Abuse*. London: Fontana.

Lealman, G., Haigh, D., Philips, J., Stone, J. and Ord-Smith, C. (1983) 'Prediction and prevention of child abuse – an empty hope?' *Lancet i*, 1423–4.

Macfarlane, K. and Waterman, J. (1986) *The Sexual Abuse of Young Children*. New York: Holt, Rinehart and Winston.

Mantell, D. (1988) 'Clarifying erroneous child sexual abuse allegations.' *American Journal of Orthopsychiatry 58*, 118–21.

Milner, J. (1995) 'Physical child abuse assessment: perpetrator evaluation.' In J. Campbell (ed) *Assessing Dangerousness: Violence by Sexual Offenders, Batterers and Child Abusers*. London: Sage.

Milner, J. (1986) *The Child Abuse Potential Inventory: Manual* (2nd. ed) Webster NC: Psytec.

Orkney (1992) *Report of the inquiry into the removal of children from Orkney in February 1991*. London: HMSO.

Orme, T. and Rimmer, J. (1981) 'Alcoholism and child abuse: a review.' *Journal of Studies on Alcohol 42*, 273–87.

Owen, M. (1992) *Social Justice and Children in Care*. Aldershot: Avebury.

Parton (1985) *The Politics of Child Abuse*. Basingstoke: Macmillan.

Pfohl, S. (1977) 'The "discovery" of child abuse.' *Social Problems 24*, 310–23.

Polansky N., Ammons P. and Weathersby B. (19830 'Is there an American standard of child care?' *Social Work 28*, 341–6.

Porter, R. (ed) (1984) *Child Sexual Abuse within the Family*. London: Tavistock.

Reder P., Duncan S. and Gray M. (1993) *Beyond Blame: Child Abuse Tragedies Revisited*. London: Routledge.

Salt, C. (1986) *Oldham District Review Committee: review of child abuse procedures*. Metropolitan Borough of Oldham.

Steele, B. and Pollock, C. (1974) 'A psychiatric study of parents who abuse infants and small children.' In R. Helfer and C. Kempe (eds) *The Battered Child*. 2nd. edition. Chicago: Univ. of Chicago Press.

Wald, M. and Woolverton, M. (1990) 'Risk assessment: the emperor's new clothes?' *Child Welfare 69*, 483–511.

Waterhouse, L. and Carnie, J. (1992) 'Assessing child protection risk.' *British Journal of Social Work 22*, 47–60.

Wolock, L. and Horowitz, B. (1984) 'Child maltreatment as a social problem: the neglect of neglect.' *American Journal of Orthopsychiatry 54*, 530–43.

CHAPTER 3

CHILDREN WITH DISABILITIES

Philippa Russell

CHILDREN WITH DISABILITIES: THE CONTEXT FOR RISK MANAGEMENT

The past decade has seen major changes in policy and practice for children with disabilities. There has been increasing inclusion of disabled children within mainstream education and other services. Government policy has determined that long-term NHS care is inappropriate for even the most severely disabled children and the *Disability and Discrimination Bill* is a reminder that disability – historically the 'cinderella' of equal opportunities policies – will now be a major issue in looking at how statutory services respond to the wishes and aspirations of disabled people within their local communities.

It has been estimated (Office of Public and Census Surveys 1989a) that there are approximately 360,000 children with disabilities or major medical conditions in the United Kingdom (around 3% of the child population). Of these children, 159,000 are very severely disabled, usually with multiple disabilities and health problems. The epidemiology of childhood disability is changing, with more children surviving neonatal problems; very premature births; childhood accidental and non-accidental injury and simply living longer with degenerative conditions because of improved medical care. Of these 360,000 children, OPCS found that all but 5,500 live in family homes – whether natural or substitute. But of those children living away from a family home, thirty-three per cent were regarded by natural and substitute families as 'too difficult' because of health or behaviour problems to care for at home. Thirty-three per cent were regarded as having 'family problems' which meant that the family was an unsafe place for them to remain and 15 per cent (almost certainly a substantial under-estimate) were known to have been abused.

But for those children who remained at home, there were potential risk factors present. Forty-five per cent of parents felt that *their* health had been adversely affected by the additional care of their child. Fifty per cent felt that the care of their *other* children suffered because of lack of adequate support. Families with a disabled child were substantially worse off financially than a comparable group of parents without a disabled child, with family incomes lower; expenditure increased and with *single* parents much more likely than comparable group of parents without a disabled child, with family incomes lower; expenditure increased and with *single* parents much more likely than their peers without a child with special needs to be living wholly on state benefits. Hence OPCS, together with a survey of research into the lives of children with disabilities and their families (Baldwin and Carlisle 1994) concluded that families with disabled children were inherently more vulnerable than families with non-disabled children; that multiple factors affected their ability to cope, but that constant pressures of care and low income were particularly significant. The Audit Commission (1994) in *Seen but not Heard: Coordinating Services for Children in Need*, similarly concluded that complexity of services and multiple access routes were confusing for families and that only 25 per cent of families in their survey felt that support was 'well coordinated'. All three studies concluded that quality of support was variable; that many parents were isolated and vulnerable and that changing factors in family life (i.e. greater mobility; more single parents; a volatile employment market and changes in the social security system) meant that families with disabled children could be doubly disadvantaged in making sense of the 'system' without additional support.

CHILD PROTECTION ISSUES AND CHILDREN WITH DISABILITIES

The past decade has seen greater public (and professional) awareness of disability, with increasingly positive images about the capacity as well as incapacity of disabled people to make decisions about their own lives and to contribute directly to the planning and development of support services. Positive images are insufficient, however, without a corresponding awareness of the increased vulnerability of disabled children and their families to abuse within a variety of settings. Kennedy (1990), Westcott (1992) and Russell (1994) all note this increased vulnerability, due to multiple factors including poor communication skills; lack of opportunities to develop appropriate social skills and 'street-wise behaviour'; greater dependency on others for intimate personal care and – in many cases – a disbelief that anyone would wish to abuse a disabled person. Russell observes the greater likelihood for young disabled people of use of services outside their local community and the problems faced by parents who may be dubious about the quality of a service, but have no choice but to use it. The Allan Roehr Institute (1988) looking at the abuse of disabled children and adults in Canada also notes the dangers of 'institutional life which creates an ideal backdrop for abuse; isolation and emotional deprivation are major risk factors'. Although it is against government policy that disabled children should live in long-stay NHS institutions, many disabled children still attend residential schools; use a range of respite or short term care services and may use day services which are outside their local community and involve long travelling times. Hence active communication with and review of services for disabled children will be critical in ensuring that they are 'safe'. Equally important, greater empowerment (with the involvement of children and families in decision-making at every level) will contribute to clarity of decision-making and minimize risk because assessment and care management can become partnership activities with shared understanding and goal setting.

However, notwithstanding ongoing concerns about the quality and coherence of care for disabled children and families in the community, there have been some positive developments which theoretically at least make good practice in risk management in social care a real possibility. The Children Act's focus upon the paramount welfare of the child (and the inclusion of children with disabilities within mainstream children's legislation for the first time) has begun to have a significant impact upon policy and practice. The 1993 Education Act and its associated Code of Practice on the Identification and Assessment of Special Educational Needs (together with the 'Pupils with Problems guidance) has emphasized the need for joint working between social services, child health and education within assessment and care as well as education management.

The revision of the assessment and action materials for children 'looked aft er by the local authority' (Ward 1995) has firmly included disability related issues within the new materials – and noted that in education as well as social services led assessment, the aspirations and wishes of the child or pupil are now an integral part of the process. We have had a decade of rhetoric (with some reality) on 'partnership with parents'. The next challenge – and critical to good practice in risk management – is partnership with parents (usually the principle care-givers) and their children. There has been little work in a disability context on conciliation issues when parents and children disagree – although social services departments have extensive experience of such work with children who are regarded as being 'in need' or 'at risk' within the wider care system.

'Risk taking' and 'risk management' will always be complex for children with disabilities. Not only do parents often have a major (and often laborious) range of care tasks to perform, without which the child could not remain in the community, but definitions of 'risk' may be more complex. Parents, schools and others may wish to try alternative treatments and therapies, some very demanding and segregating to the child. There may be additional issues about the length of time for which a particular intervention or treatment is carried out and about possible 'risk' elements within it. Decisions about elective surgery or medical treatment may be particularly challenging, particularly when consequences may be unclear and when there may be concerns that the child does not fully understand the possible consequences. Within the social care and educational sectors, there has been particular concern about the risks of potential litigation if treatment or control approaches are used which could be deemed to be illegal. Some restrictive treatments as shown in the Pindown regime (Levy 1993) can indeed be abusive. But if there is no agreement on acceptable controls for a child with autism and very challenging and aggressive behaviour, then the child concerned may experience another form of abuse; in other words, a very restricted environment, lack of stimulation and possibly referral for a residential placement.

Another issue explored below relates to the complex relationships which most disabled children experience in their everyday lives. Many parents comment on the multiple professional advisers, the wide range of providers and the difficulty of coordinating and understanding information and advice without a clear 'care management' approach. An example of the challenges of multiple support is show by Jenny's case set out below:

'Jenny' is eight years old. She has cerebral palsy and learning difficulties. She can walk short distances; has limited speech (though good understanding) and communicates through her lap-top computer and Makaton. She attends a special school, with a part-time integrated placement in a local primary school; she goes to a range of after-school activities and (because her single parent mother works) has two child-minders. Twice a year she goes on a residential integrated holiday scheme and occasionally spends a week-end on a local authority family placement scheme. She needs some help with personal care, though she is rapidly becoming more independent. A major issue for most of her activities is transport – she uses taxis, a community transport mini-bus, a school bus and (sometimes) a variety of lifts from volunteers and family or friends. Jenny is in contact with up to 100 different people in any one week! In terms of personal safety there are major issues about the checks necessary; about Jenny's own understanding of 'keeping safe' and about the sensible balance between intrusion and protection in supervising her various contacts.

Jenny is very typical of the 'new generation' of disabled children. In many respects her life is rich and varied. She has the opportunity to sample a wide range of educational and social activities. Her mother works, but the child care arrangements appear reliable and friendly. But challenges remain. Jenny's social care, by its very diversity, is carried out by multiple carers who frequently have to help Jenny with a degree of intimate care. Jenny's parents (and social services) do not 'know' many of these people well. Jenny can communicate but her skills are limited for *rapid* communication. She is also very anxious to appear what she calls 'ordinary' and 'not to tell' about things that may worry her at school. Jenny does not have a learning disability. But if she did, with very limited expressive language, there would be even greater concerns.

Aspirations towards 'ordinary life' experiences for disabled children pose potential tensions when using ordinary community services. They also necessitate vigilance and clear criteria for raising concerns amongst *everyone* supporting a particular child. As noted below, they also presuppose much more open and honest discussion with disabled children and young people about how to develop assertiveness skills; about how to be 'street-wise' and about whom to tell when things seem to be going wrong. Many disabled children will have great difficulty in making private telephone calls; writing (or posting) letters or indeed in 'dropping in' to places where other children might feel they would be heard. Even staying behind at school to talk to a teacher will be problematic if the child has to leave promptly on expensive school transport.

FAMILY SUPPORT: PROVIDING SAFE ENVIRONMENTS AND AVOIDING THE NEED FOR 'RISK MANAGEMENT' AS A SPECIALIST ACTIVITY

Parents have had a mixed press in terms of 'risk management'. They may be perceived as partners with professionals (particularly when children are young) but they may also be seen as 'over-protective'; 'unrealistic' or 'negative' when greater independence or any life changes are proposed. In practice families *must* be seen as the corner-stone of good quality risk-management strategies. As noted above, the vast majority of children and young people with disabilities will live in family homes. But family support is nationally variable and many parents hesitate to ask for support, often seeing themselves as 'coping families' or even imposing self-rationing because they see themselves as 'not needing as much help as the family down the road'. As one parent (personal communication; Russell 1995) commented at a parent workshop:

> 'I don't feel *guilty* because I have a disabled child. Professionals are always talking about guilt, but John isn't anything to be ashamed of! He's my son and he has some very special needs. My problem is that I *do* feel guilty about asking for help. We live in a nice house, we both have jobs, we have a good school and some nice neighbours. But in my local MENCAP, I see parents who have nothing. Yes, some of their children are much easier than John. Yes, I think they have more ordinary lives – but what lives! Miserable homes, miserable environment, often last in the queue for everything. I *can't* ask for respite care, I can't ask for anything when I see them. But really John's disability has had a huge impact on our family life. But I can't be the one to ask for help, I really can't. We're all told about these 'levels of need', criteria for services, and I think my local authority 'zones' us all. Five bedrooms and a nice garden, and no-one ever *asks* you if you're all right. Sometimes I think someone should ask us, they should come and see how we manage John. Nobody would know if we did abuse him when he behaves so badly, would they? What do they mean by *family support?*'

'John's' parent queries some of the basic assumptions that are made about determining 'need' when families are caring for some quite challenging children – and she asks whether social services departments are really satisfied that they know what quality of care is available within apparently affluent families who are also carers. The Audit Commission (1994) in *Seen but not Heard*, reflected on definitions of family support for children in need and offered the following definition:

> Family support is an activity or facility aimed at providing advice and support to parents to help them in bringing up their children. This could mean as little, to one group of politicians and managers, as continuing the provision of a health visiting service whilst to another it may mean a complex interweaving of local and regional services provided by a range of public agencies. (p.39)

Barbara Hearn (1995) in *Child and Family Support and Protection: A Practical Approach* expands the Audit Commission definition, proposing that:

> Family Support is about the creation and enhancement, with and for families in need, of locally based (or accessible) activities, facilities and networks, the use of which will have outcomes such as alleviated stress, increased self esteem, promoted parental/carer/family competence and behaviour and increased parental/carer capacity to nurture and protect children. (p.19)

She goes on to hypothesize that in looking at family support and risk management, definitions of family support should at least require that families are enabled to use resources as and when they need them and to use their own skills to assist others. She sees 'developing networks of care within communities to enhance child rearing as another element necessary to compensate for the social isolation which, alongside poverty, often underpins the deterioration into physical abuse and neglect'. Although her report is focusing upon child protection issues, the core principles are equally relevant to families with disabled children – not least because they are frequently isolated from 'networks of care' within their local community and professional advice may be limited because of lack of expertise in a particular disability or special need or because of lack of awareness of all options in increasingly generic child care services.

RISK PREDICTION AND ASSESSMENT

As children with disabilities increasingly use inclusive services within their local community (and as the numbers of children with very complex needs increases within most communities), assessment and planning arrangements to permit reasonable levels of risk become more important. The following 'case studies' illustrate the dangers (and the opportunities) in assessment arrangements of children with disabilities and special needs.

'Mrs Shah' has two daughters with learning and physical disabilities. She lives in a run-down block of flats in an inner-city area. She arrived in Europe two years ago with her daughters; her husband had worked in the UK for twelve years, with periodic visits home. She speaks little English and the health visitor has been unable to get access to the flat when she has visited – though she is sure Mrs Shah was inside at the time. The GP has raised concerns about the girls' health and care and various notes have been put through the door asking Mrs Shah to visit the local child development centre. She has never attended. The health visitor notifies social services, after talking to a neighbour who says Mrs Shah is very depressed; she can hear her crying and, no, the girls do not go to school nor do they ever go out. The social worker, who finally gains admittance, finds Mrs Shah very depressed; the girls are both in bed in their bedrooms in the middle of the day and the envelopes are all on a side table. There is little food in the kitchen and she leaves considerably concerned.

(1) Mrs Shah feared that her daughters would be taken away from her (she did not understand the literature provided on local services in the family home).

(2) She was seriously depressed; she missed her own community and family. Her husband was working long hours away from home and she could not easily leave the home.

(3) She needed practical advice on the most effective care of her children – a parent adviser from a local community scheme subsequently introduced her to the local school where she found friendship, advice and is now learning English through a community project.

(4) Mrs Shah is now visiting 'new' parents in her own community and encouraging them to join a parents' group. She feels she has a 'new life' but is desperately worried that *she* was regarded as a potentially abusive mother and that there are very limited services available to families in ethnic minority communities to help them 'access the system'.

Mrs Shah is continuing to provide a high level of care to two severely disabled daughters. To enable her to continue to provide a reasonable standard of care, she will need continuing advice and support. The Housing Department is about to rehouse the family on the ground floor so that she can take a wheelchair out without help.

'Rodney' is a good looking boy of eleven years old; he is an only child and his parents are prosperous professionals. Rodney has learning disabilities and is thought to have autism; his behaviour is often bizarre but he has a wide vocabulary (not always used appropriately) and is physically advanced for his age. Rodney's parents are unhappy with his diagnosis and are trying a range of alternative therapies and treatments. Rodney is on a rigid exclusion diet and an equally rigid behavioural programme (both through private clinics). His parents have asked the school to implement the programmes, but neither Rodney's teacher nor the educational psychologist are happy. They feel Rodney's life is being unnecessarily restricted and that he is unhappy and would benefit from a more child-centred approach. Rodney's parents announce that they will remove Rodney from school and educate him at home. Rodney is increasingly unhappy, is self-mutilating and will 'steal' any food he can access at school. The school is aware that Rodney spent three years earlier in his life in an independent school which provided a range of 'therapies' *in situ*. His parents removed him after a major argument with the staff, but some of the current treatments go back to that period. In addition to his self-mutilation, a swimming teacher notices that Rodney's back shows signs of beating. The parents strongly deny ill-treatment and threaten to sue the school. Social services are asked for advice.

Rodney's family pose a different challenge. They are desperately anxious to help their son and their anxieties are increased by the fact that Rodney is very much their 'miracle' child, born after *in vitro* fertilizsation and a long and expensive fight against infertility. Neither parent had ever contemplated the possibility of Rodney having any difficulty or disability, although he was very premature and his twin siblings died in the first two weeks. Both parents believe they must try everything and see the school as obstructive. They view social services negatively but are positive about a local paediatrician who has given them a good deal of emotional support. Both parents are tired and stressed by Rodney's hyperactivity. Both are firmly of the view that the school is taking risks in permitting children to use a local swimming club and argue that the care assistant is probably responsible for Rodney's bruising because of his irritating behaviour. They claim that no one understands Rodney's real potential and they won't send their son to school to be abused.

Investigations into Rodney's situation raise an interesting range of issues around family support when the parent is at least in part the *purchaser* of services; when the family is affluent – but where the child's difficulties may pose major challenges in a mobile and successful family life-style – and where the child's behaviour is difficult for everybody to interpret. Fundamental to the situation are the unresolved emotions around Rodney's birth – the fought-for survivor of multiple births and the anxiety of parents who expected to be able to succeed in bringing up their child without outside 'interference'. Concern was being expressed about Rodney's very difficult behaviour in part being due to some of the alternative treatments he was receiving; to his parents' high levels of stress and to the inherent conflicts between school, home and alternative therapists.

However, Rodney is also typical of many of the challenges which affect a local authority concerned about a child's welfare when the child has as a disability and challenging behaviour. Attempts to find a respite care family placement for Rodney had failed after three break-downs because of his destructive and aggressive behaviour. The local residential respite care house had similarly refused to accept him except on a one-to-one basis. Rodney had already been excluded from his *special* school twice and was under threat of permanent exclusion after he had (accidentally) injured a younger child and the parents had threatened legal action against the LEA. If Rodney were to be removed from the family home, there would literally be nowhere for him to go – except to a residential school or independent residential home, probably several hundred miles from his family home.

In practice a full reassessment of Rodney's needs revealed a number of answers. The school suggested that the paediatrician who had been very supportive to the parents (and who had known them for nearly ten years) should coordinate the assessment and that he should be asked to facilitate the initial discussions with the family. It was recognized that the assessment outcomes would be critical to determining whether Rodney should remain with his family and if not, what would happen to him. Rodney's teacher, who was closely involved in the assessment, argued strongly that the parents were tired but trying hard. She suggested that notwithstanding the exclusions, Rodney was making progress. He now had an 'individual education plan' (as required in the Code of Practice and 1993 Education Act) and this included for the first time specific activities for the parents to carry out at home. She felt Rodney was making progress and supported the paediatrician, who felt that Rodney might have a 'glue ear', which was causing a minor hearing loss. The minor hearing loss would be more significant for a child with limited language and might have accounted for his poor relationships with his fellow pupils. An audiology examination showed that Rodney did have a hearing deficit (not due to glue ear) and that his so-called 'attention deficit' was in part due a simple inability to hear instructions. He now wears a hearing aid and there has been an improvement in his response to verbal instructions and comments.

Concern remained about Rodney's back and the possibility that he was subject to physical abuse. Both the staff at the swimming club and Rodney's parents had strongly denied any abuse and it was agreed that the weals could not easily have been incurred at the swimming pool because of the lack of privacy on club nights. As Rodney usually insisted on swimming in a tee-shirt, there was no certainty about the date of their appearance. However, a non-teaching assistant in the school commented that she thought that Rodney's behaviour had irritated some older (non-disabled) children and she thought there might have been some bullying and pushing in the playground. Rodney and other children from the special unit were supervised but Rodney's physical agility and energy meant that he often ran off on his own. Investigation revealed considerable bullying and teasing in the school. Nabuzokov (1993) has clearly shown the *increased* risk of bullying for pupils with special educational needs. The school now has an anti-bullying and behaviour policy, and it is not thought that a similar incident could occur again.

Rodney has continued at his school; his parents, after discussion with the paediatrician, a paediatric neurologist and a child psychiatrist have weighed up the evidence and discontinued the alternative therapies, with the exception of vitamin supplements. Rodney's hearing has improved with the hearing aid and he is more manageable. The school's programme has made it easier for family and teachers to work together and Rodney's father in particular feels he has now 'got something I can do'. Both the parents admitted that they needed help and are seeing a counsellor. The family is still very stressed; Rodney's behaviour is still often aggressive and difficult but the 'risk' elements have been reduced. Most important, Rodney's and his parents' real difficulties have been acknowledged and expressed in a way which enables services to respond appropriately.

'Kelly' has Down's Syndrome and is three years old. She is a bright sociable child but her mother (a young single parent) is increasingly dissatisfied with life. Her parents are in the North of England; her boyfriend deserted her when Kelly's disability was diagnosed. 'Sue' is living in a short-life flat in an inner city area. Kelly attends part-time a local nursery school and Sue and Kelly in theory attend a Family Centre. In practice Kelly is frequently neither at school nor the centre. Sue has just discovered that she can express a preference for a school in Kelly's statement and is demanding full-time special school 'so that I can get my life together again and get some space'. The LEA rejects the preference. The health visitor is concerned that Kelly is spending time in the flat alone and Sue is increasingly truculent about what she sees as 'interference' in her life. She walks out of a local parent support group saying she has nothing in common with all those middle aged women!

Kelly's care poses some different challenges in terms of risk assessment. Her mother is young, poor and isolated. She wants to 'get on with her own life' and there are real concerns about the quality of care (and personal safety) offered to Kelly. Kelly would be regarded as a child 'in need' even without her additional disability. But what additional factors should be taken into account in assessing the 'risk' of Kelly remaining in her family home because of her Down's syndrome? First, Kelly's special educational needs mean that she has had an educational assessment; her LEA and her nursery school have identified a range of strategies to encourage her development and early learning. Statutory *educational* assessment includes reports from child health and social services and it is a useful framework for looking holistically at a child.

Second, Kelly may be more at risk than other children of a similar age because of her limited speech. She is a lively child and doing well but, without much expressive language, any discussion with her will need to take account of *how* she can communicate and (in Kelly's case) of an 'interpreter' to share her use of Makaton signing for communication. Kelly will also need plenty of stimulation; developmental play activities and opportunities to improve and extend her verbal skills before she starts school. A Family Centre might be a good place to start, but Kelly's mother rarely takes her.

Third, there are real risks in Kelly being left on her own when her mother goes out. The short-life accommodation may be unsafe; there is a frequent risk of break-ins and Kelly's sense of safety may be limited.

Fourth, Sue is young herself, wanting to 'get on with her life' and desperate to get day care and 'have a break'. Without support, she may decide that she cannot cope and Kelly may slip into local authority care.

For Sue and Kelly, there were solutions. The LEA insisted that Kelly did not need a special school placement, because there was not a full-day nursery school placement available, Kelly was offered half-time nursery school and a specialist child-minder with a particular interest in children with learning disabilities. Sue was encouraged to go back to college two days a week, and was given very strong messages that Kelly must *never* be left on her own either during the day or at night. Recognizing that Sue wished to have a social life and that neighbourhood baby-sitting was unlikely in the area she was living in, the social services department introduced her to a carer in a local family-based short term care scheme and arranged that Kelly would spend one night a week with her family. The carer was specially selected because of her age and maturity, because it was acknowledged that Sue had herself experienced very little real 'mothering' and needed some role models in order to change her expectations of Kelly and herself. The health visitor agreed to visit regularly and to encourage Sue to attend regularly for Kelly's health checks and immunization – and also agreed to keep a general eye on Kelly's welfare and development. Sue was given a clear 'care plan', setting out the different support available; the expectations for her cooperation and regular review dates. Sue has remained adamant that she does not want to join a parent organization, but she is now attending occasional meetings of a parent support group which provides a wide range of social activities for its members. It is generally agreed that there are some risks in Sue's care of Kelly, but that these risks relate more to her youth; social isolation and disadvantaged living situation than to Kelly's Down Syndrome. Kelly is now developing well and Sue will shortly move to a new housing association flat.

Kelly, Rodney – and Mrs Shah – all present challenges in terms of family support; assessment of the quality of care provided and awkward decisions about what should or could be done. In practice the assessment of risk (and the action taken) was relatively simple in each case. Mrs Shah could not read English; her spoken English was poor and she had not surprisingly neither read the contents of the brown envelopes that kept falling through her letter box nor had she answered the door to 'strangers'. The only visitor, the social worker, was unable to communicate properly because the interpreter had failed to materialize and Mrs Shah's own key concerns had to await a community worker speaking her language.

RISK TAKING – SOME KEY FACTORS IN ASSESSMENT

'Risk Taking' can be variably interpreted in the context of children with disabilities. Russell and Wertheimer (in press) in a self-advocacy project for young women with learning disabilities found that the young women all expressed the desire to be more independent, 'to learn to go around London on my own', 'to go out without my brother looking after me', 'to go to college on my own'. They were conscious of a loss of freedom which was also a loss of self-esteem when they compared themselves to their non-disabled peers. One group of young women described their feelings through two imaginary young women, 'Miss Can' and 'Miss Can't'. Miss Can was independent; mobile; earning; sociable and smart. Miss Can't – the epitome of the young women's fears – was immobile, 'held back', unemployed. The parents, when invited to comment, put the young women's wishes in their own perspectives. One mother (personal communication) observed that:

> 'It's easy for professionals to talk about "letting go", letting '"Annie" travel on the bus on her own, letting her have a boyfriend. But she really

doesn't know how to take care of herself. And she certainly doesn't know about men – yes, I over-protect her. But just suppose something happened! It would ruin her life, she hasn't got any survival skills.'

Annie's mother may have been unrealistic. But no one had helped her develop an independence training programme for her daughter. Diana Lamplugh (1995), looking at safety and disability, has stressed the need for *all* young women (and particularly young disabled women) to know how to be 'street wise' and look after themselves. Equally, there can be no naive assumptions that young people with disabilities 'don't know about men'. Personal relationships should precede sexuality but without practice, many disabled children will be unprepared and very vulnerable.

'Jackie', a young woman with spina bifida (Russell, in press 1996), gives another perspective on risk-taking:

'I was desperate to become more independent. I was at a residential school because my mother had ME and she really couldn't cope. Actually I liked my school; they made me feel really "normal"'. Most of us had medical problems as well as disabilities and I think our school was unusual in helping us to take responsibility for our medication and treatment from quite an early age. They didn't just give us the pills and the inhalers. My friend had epilepsy and they went to great lengths to explain why regular medication mattered and what symptoms she should look out for. She took part in the reviews and she was very responsible. Plenty of my friends at other schools got very rebellious when they were teenagers. They wouldn't take medication; they'd mess up their diets and do all sorts of silly things. I guess some people need to break out now and again! But this wasn't breaking out – it was much more not understanding and not doing something important. It's the same with independence training. We've got to get more independent, so someone has to take the risk of letting us do some risk taking for ourselves.'

Risk-taking does not only apply to disabled children, it may apply to disabled adults whether or not their children have a disability or special need. 'Marcia' has brittle bones and has one daughter 'Melanie', who also has brittle bones. Marcia is a committed, competent and confident mother. In her adapted house, she and her daughter have few difficulties. But Marcia's parenting has been under constant scrutiny. There have been arguments about whether it is 'safe' for her to carry Melanie in her lap in the wheelchair, about her ability to care for an active child (Melanie is more mobile than her mother) and about her capacity to care for her daughter if she is ill. Marcia is irritated with what she sees as unnecessary criticism and mistrust. She knows her own capacity; she is clear about when and where additional help is required. She is confident that Melanie is developing well.

Marcia's local authority have responded to her concerns by utilizing the USA concept of a 'Family Services Plan', which involves all the relevant statutory services and gives a clear specification for support and review arrangements. The plan enables the local authority to ensure that Melanie's care is secure and appropriate and Marcia to be specific about her need for support. The plan has enabled Marcia to re-schedule the times of the home helps to cover the difficult beginnings and ends of days, and to negotiate some further (minor) housing adaptations to enable Melanie to become more independent as she gets older. Her social services department have also been able to satisfy themselves that she can provide care and help with daily living tasks and that Melanie is thriving.

Marcia, acknowledging that many local authorities meet very few families with disabled parents, has set up a local disabled parents' group to set some targets for the local community care planning arrangements. The parents' group in turn is working with the local authority to draw up some assessment criteria to ensure not only that children are 'safe' but also *how* best to support disabled parents and also to address the emotive issue of 'young carers' and how they can be supported when caring roles are reversed. Marcia acknowledges the importance of appropriate standards of child-care for *all* children, but rejects simplistic notions about disabled parents being 'at risk' simply because of their disability. She also stresses a problem which is commonly acknowledged by parents of disabled *children*, namely the emotional and personal difficulties of asking for help if that help is clearly only available on a 'rationed' basis and where there has been no preceding assessment to identify strengths and difficulties and plan for the future.

CARE AND CONTROL – SOME CHALLENGES (AND OPPORTUNITIES)

There has been wide-spread debate across the child care system about *acceptable* means of care and control. The debate has extended into schools (where children may actually be excluded simply because no one can determine what levels of controls or sanctions would be acceptable) and into family homes.

'Judith' has a son 'Paul', who is seven years old. Paul suffered a serious head injury in a car accident and now has severe learning difficulties; epilepsy and very challenging behaviour. Paul is mobile, interested in (and able to manipulate) locks and bolts and frequently runs away. He has been involved in two further minor car accidents when he ran into the road. Paul's respite carer and his child-minder have both said they can no longer take responsibility for him and Judith is desperate. She has three other children. Recently she has discovered that Paul's behaviour tantrums can be modified if he is given 'time out' for up to 20 minutes in a locked room on his own. Her social worker tells her she is breaking the law and the use of locked time-out is illegal. Paul's school retaliates by saying that they had the same advice, but they believed that the systematic and monitored use of 'time-out' might make Paul's general behaviour more acceptable and enable him to re-integrate back into a range of community activities. Paul's father meanwhile says he has had enough and proposes to move out, taking the other children with him. Judith says she has no alternative but to ask the local authority to 'look after' Paul or *she* will feel at risk of hitting him.

Paul's story is not uncommon. In effect, his quality of life is directly affected by uncertainty about how to control his behaviour and about how to assess 'levels of risk' in any of the options available. Christina Lyon (1994), in re-examining the legal basis for interventions with children with challenging behaviour and learning disabilities, has stressed that on certain occasions intervention may be *right* in order to protect the child. But any intervention or sanction should be based on a clear rationale for that intervention; with precise record keeping about *when* and *where* particular approaches or controls are used. Risk-taking in Paul's situation will not be appropriately managed if simplistic and 'crisis intervention' approaches are used. Everybody concerned (including Paul himself and his parents) need to share their knowledge about when and why difficult behaviour occurs; what seems to work and that the various services (in particular the school and parents) would welcome in terms of improved support.

In Paul's case, the school, child-minder, respite carer, parents and social services all shared in a re-assessment which in this instance included a clinical psychologist with extensive experience of working with children with challenging behaviour. Everybody concerned was asked to keep a detailed diary for two weeks about how they did (or could not) manage Paul's behaviour. In consequence, a detailed management plan was developed which included the limited and carefully controlled use of 'time out' (with a staff member or parent always outside the room). The psychologist identified one or two 'rewards' for Paul for modifying his behaviour and over a period of time these greatly reduced the time spent in a separate room. The LEA agreed to fund additional non-teaching assistant time over a time-limited period to help implement the programme over a three months period and Paul's parents visited the school weekly to discuss progress. Paul is still a challenging child. But his respite carer is now caring for him for one night each fortnight. Paul's siblings have been involved and are more confident because they understand their brother's problems. Because disagreements about 'risk taking' may relate as much to the physical environment of the child as to the steps taken to reduce the risk itself, an assessment by an occupational therapist has led to Paul's home having some additional adaptations (in particular shatter-proof glass on all windows and safety catches) and improved garden fencing so that the risk of Paul 'escaping' and having a further injury has been greatly reduced.

Policy and practice for children with learning disabilities and associated behaviour problems has always been challenging for social services. Issues raised in the 'Pindown' Inquiry (Levy 1993) and in Lyon (1994) about the frequent gap between the rhetoric and the reality of the use of so-called behavioural approaches and disagreement about the assessment of relative risks or benefits for the child in question have demonstrated the uncertainties in managing problem behaviours. However, non-intervention (because of its severely limiting consequences of withdrawal of education etc.) may also be abusive and there are clear messages for *all* statutory services to work together to:

- Develop an interdisciplinary 'code of practice' on evaluating the use of sanctions and controls and controversial treatments on a local basis.
- Observe, record and act on behaviour problems *before* they escalate into major problems.
- Involve children and young people in such decision making and in understanding their own behaviour.
- Recognize the impact on professional and family carers of the day-to-day management of very challenging children and the need to give practical and emotional support and advice right from the start.
- Ensure that Area Child Protection Committees are aware of the potential tensions within the assessment of control and treatment issues for children with learning disabilities and challenging behaviour and that they are able to give appropriate advice and support. To achieve such an objective, they may in turn need training in disability related issues in order to make informed judgements. SSI (1994) has noted the lack of disability specific competence in many Committees and conversely the lack of awareness about child protection issues in many disability services.

LISTENING TO THE CHILDREN

Children with disabilities are seldom active partners in their own care management – although the new assessment and action materials published as part of the *Looking after children; positive parenting, positive outcomes* (1995) offer an important opportunity to ensure that their views are always given a significant place in any decision-making. 'Risk taking' in the context of disabled children, as noted above, will include:

- Judgements about the *ability* of a disabled child to travel independently; choose friends; make decisions about day-to-day life.
- Decisions about treatment: what do disabled children think about behavioural or other therapy; about treatment regimes which may be painful, uncertain and where the outcomes are variable?
- Issues relating to 'care and control' – children do not always know best, but the principle of enabling them to *contribute* to decision-making about difficult decisions is widely accepted for children without special needs.
- Prevention of abuse – the welcome thrust towards greater inclusion of disabled children within community facilities and services needs to be balanced by appropriate and clear criteria for assessing the competence of those supporting them – and their greater vulnerability to abuse because of their disability and communication difficulties.
- Avoidance of simplistic notions of 'inability' about disabled people (in particular the potential parenting skills of disabled parents) and

the corresponding reluctance to listen seriously to disabled children and adults.

SSI (1994), in their report of the first national inspection of services for disabled children, highlight a number of key factors in *effective* consultation with children and young people, namely:

- The importance of recognizing that different parts of a service will be at different stages in working directly with children. Some staff (in all categories of service provision) may feel deskilled and hesitant in raising sensitive and sometimes potentially negative information with children.

- Consultation with children must take into account any linguistic; cultural, social or communication needs. Many children will need 'interpreters'. They will also need sufficient accessible information on which to base a decision. Staff will need training and support if they are to take children's views seriously.

- Children can become partners in their own treatment or behavioural programmes. Some schools are moving towards much greater involvement of pupils following the introduction of individual education plans under the Code of Practice. But such partnerships need to focus on recording 'achievement' and ensuring there is a common understanding about the purpose of any intervention.

- Access to independent advocacy, representation or befriending schemes may be crucial for some children (particularly for those 'looked after' by the local authority). There has been little systematic information about the use of 'independent visitors' for children living away from home.

- Participation skills can be learned and children who are *routinely* involved in day-to-day decisions when things go well will have fewer difficulties when major decisions have to be made.

- Access to complaints procedures are important for children with disabilities like all other children – but children with disabilities may have greater difficulty than others in making complaints if they do not have independent access to telephones; cannot write or need communication aids.

The same report concluded the involvement of children with disabilities in decision-making should be carefully monitored; that it should proceed at a pace and in a place which was supportive to children and took account of age, disability and level of understanding. They also strongly recommended that there should be clear policies and guidance within all services for staff on the ascertainment of wishes and feelings of children, with *written* procedures for everyone (including parents) to ensure that children's feelings were taken seriously. Acknowledging the real problem of communication in some instances, SSI also suggested that when children's views were recorded, they should be confirmed as accurate with the child in question and shared with the parents.

RISK-TAKING: PARENTS' WISHES AND CONCERNS

'Being the parent of a child with a disability is being a parent 24 hours a day, 52 weeks a year. In theory the community gives you support – but only of course if your child is small, easy to manage and looks cuddly! What irritates me is that parents are always being castigated as 'over-protective'; 'old-fashioned'; 'holding their children back'. But if you do let your child come home from school alone and he falls and you end up at casualty, they are all looking at you like a child abuser and saying why didn't you watch him? It's all very well talking about 'dignity of risk' when you are not the parent. But we parents are there, picking up the pieces after disasters. I wouldn't mind so much if the professionals didn't keep going away. Six months of wonderful ideas and they're off, never seeing the consequences! Having said that, we are over-protective. We need help in letting go…but that means being really honest and supportive about mutual worries and concerns. No wonder they call us 'informal' carers – no one really knows what we do, but to me there is not much informal about it.' (Parent at parent workshop, personal communication Russell 1995)

Parents (natural or substitute) are the primary care-givers for all disabled children. Kiernan, (1995), in *A Different Life*, followed the life experiences of a number of young people with learning disabilities from their family homes. In many respects the moves were challenging because in some instances the young adults would be doing activities and 'taking risks' which had not happened when they lived at home. Kiernan concluded that any plan for children or adults with learning disabilities should take account of the health, well-being and existing coping strategies of the parents. He noted that many parents had emotional, physical and practical problems associated with caring and that these stress-related difficulties could have significant effects on decision-making. Parents at a time of transition described themselves as having to face substantial re-adjustments, in some cases akin to the process of grieving. Many found using support services (even when requested) difficult because they worried about the quality of care. Kiernan concluded that in decision-making with parents, careful thought should be given to *appropriate support*, including:

- **Support in the home:** parents need help which they feel is appropriate to their needs and should be offered in ways which are acceptable to parents and their children. Some parents described how they refused help because they felt it was intrusive or not good enough. Parents often found it difficult to be critical of scarce services and could conceal difficulties in consequence, which would subsequently cause crises and unplanned placements.
- **Support outside the home:** risk taking and effective assessment and care management will often require a range of perspectives; good quality day and respite care can contribute to learning about children and planning appropriate steps to independence;
- **Pro-active interventions:** parents strongly preferred 'proactive' regular contact from a social worker or a community nurse rather

than occasional contacts for special purposes. Telephone contact was valued when the family was particularly stressed, but the emphasis was overwhelmingly on *knowing* the family, their wishes and needs and planning accordingly.

- **Offers of help followed by action:** disagreements about levels of risk taking often reflect disbelief that support will be available and mistrust that changes in provision are proposed without ongoing action and review.

- **Consistency:** the Audit Commission (1994) and SSI (1994) both noted the multiple interventions in children's lives and the lack of effective coordination. Disagreements about quality of care are most probable when there is no single consistent key-worker or care manager for families (and parents' satisfaction with provision is be considerably reduced without a 'single door' contact).

- **Professional support should reflect genuine interest and concern:** Mutual respect and trust make for good decision-making. Parents in the Kiernan study felt it was crucial to have good relationships with social workers and community nurses. One parent commented that known and trusted professionals became like friends who could say *anything* (supportive or critical) and there could be genuine and open debates about appropriate care.

IN CONCLUSION

Professor Nicholl (1986), describing working with parents whose care of their children posed challenges in terms of quality of care, hypothesized that there is a *Murfit's Law*, which should guide all work with 'risky' or 'challenging' families. The 'Murfit' family (not their real names) are a large family with complex family relationships and a number of children with special needs. Over the past decade they have formed a long, complex and sometimes thought-provoking relationships with their professional advisers! Dr Nicholl notes that professionals increase in direct proportion to the number of problems. But the more professionals are involved, the more difficult decision-making becomes. Professionals talk more to each other than to the parents. Assessments become quasi-team meetings and, worst of all, professionals lose track of the fact that *sometimes* parents do better on their own!

Professor Nicoll's comments are salutary reminders that 'risk taking' is a partnership which calls upon the resources of families as well as of their professional advisers. In the case of children with disabilities it needs to take account of the special and additional needs of children and families because of disability – but any policies on risk taking need to be put firmly in the context of good child care practice. But as *The Children Act 1989 Guidance and Regulations, Volume 6, Children with Disabilities* comments:

> In many cases children with disabilities will need continuing services throughout their lives. It will therefore be particularly important that for these children, the assessment process takes a longer perspective than is usual or necessary for children without disabilities, who will

usually cease to have a need for services after reaching adulthood...the Children Act's emphasis upon partnership and prevention is designed to enable family resources to be strengthened and for children to be brought up and protected within their own homes if at all possible... Child protection is always complex and potentially contentious. In the case of children with disabilities, who may have communication or behaviour disorders, assessment of degrees of risk will be even more complex. (Section 5.2, p.9)

The same guidance saw the safeguards for children with disabilities as being good quality assessment which builds up:

a holistic and realistic picture of the individual and family being as- sessed, which takes into account their strengths and capacities as well as any difficulties. (Section 5.3, p.9)

In effect 'risk taking' is part of a wider assessment and review process which ensures that families with disabled children are actively involved in their own assessment and care management, where there are no global assumptions about 'ability' or 'inability' and where both disability and child protection services acknowledge the need for greater cooperation and collaboration.

REFERENCES

Allan Roehr Institute (1988) *Vulnerable: Sexual Abuse and Children with Disabilities*. Ontario: Allan Roehr Institute.

Audit Commission (1994) *Seen but not Heard: Collaboration between Social Services Departments and Health Authorities in services for children 'in need'*. London: HMSO.

Baldwin, S. and Carlisle, J. (1994) *Social Support for Disabled Children and their Families: A Review of Research*, HMSO/Social Services Inspectorate (Scotland).

Department for Education (1994) *The Code of Practice on the Identification and Assessment of Special Educational Needs*. London: HMSO.

Department of Health (1993) *The Children Act 1989: Guidance and Regulations, Volume 6, Children with Disabilities*. London: HMSO.

Hearn, B. (1995) *Child and Family Support and Protection: A Practical Approach*. London: National Children's Bureau.

Kennedy, M. (1990) 'The deaf child who is sexually abused: is there a need for a dual specialism?' *Child Abuse Review 4*, 2, pp.3–6.

Kiernan, C. (1995) *A Different Life*. London: Mental Health Foundation.

Lamplugh, D. (1995) *Keep Going Safe*. London: Suzy Lamplugh Trust.

Levy, A. (1993) *The Pindown Inquiry*. London: HMSO.

Lyon, C. (1994) *The Legal Basis for the Control and Treatment of Children with Learning Disabilities with Challenging Behaviour*. London: Mental Health Foundation.

Looking after Children: Management and Implementation Guide (1995) London: HMSO.

Nabuzokov, D. (1993) 'Bullying and children with special needs in school.' In D. Tattum (ed) *Understanding and Managing Bullying*. London: Heineman.

Nichol, A. (1986) 'The laws of Murfit.' *Archives of Disease in Childhood 61*, 188–189.

Office of Public and Census Surveys (1989a) *Report 3: Prevalence of Disability among Children.*

Office of Public and Census Surveys (1989b) *Report 5: Financial Circumstances of Families.*

Office of Public and Census Surveys (1989c) *Report 6: Disabled Children: Services, Transport and Education.*

Russell, P. and Wertheimer, A. (in press), *Something to Say: Group-work with Young Women with Learning Disabilities.* National Children's Bureau.

Russell, P. (1994) 'Children with disabilities and special needs: Current issues in child protection.' In A. Levy (ed) *Re-Focus on Child Abuse.* London: Hawksmere Press.

Russell, P. (1996) *Working with Parents of Children with Disabilities and Special Educational Needs.* National Childrens Bureau.

SSI (1994) *Report of First National Inspection of Services for Children with Disabilities.* London: HMSO.

Ward, H. (1995) *Looking after Children: Research into Practice: The Second Report to the Department of Health on Assessing Outcomes in Child Care.* London: HMSO.

Westcott, H. (1992) 'The abuse of disabled children: A review of the literature.' *Child: Care, Health and Development 17*, 4, 243–258.

CHAPTER 4

A FRAMEWORK OF RISK ASSESSMENT AND MANAGEMENT FOR OLDER PEOPLE

Jane Lawson

Risk assessment and management is an area where workers feel stressed and under pressure. Decisions made in such a climate are often of a poor quality. Although risk taking can never be an area of precise prediction, a structured framework within which risk is assessed and managed is important. Definition and articulation of all the elements that will contribute in the risk assessment is of primary importance. This definition will assist in:

- formulating a logical informed opinion
- constructive discussion with other key individuals involved
- managing conflicting opinions and interests
- lines of accountability
- justifying actions.

Hampshire County Council Social Services Department is in the process of producing a policy and framework to assist staff in achieving such structure and definition in risk taking. The policy relates specifically to practice in the assessment and management of risk in relation to older people. Such a framework cannot take away the need for individuals to make difficult decisions. It cannot prescribe what to decide but is a way of deciding and tools to assist in the decision making process.

This chapter examines: the need for such a policy document; the important components of a policy and framework for practice in the area of risk taking.

WHY IS A RISK POLICY IMPORTANT?

A range of guidance locally and nationally encourages staff to support users/carers in the taking of risks. There is a clear need to support this with policy and with a detailed framework for practice if users/carers as well as staff are to:

- make sound risk decisions
- feel good about the decisions they have made
- fully understand and articulate why they have made specific decisions.

A policy and framework for practice will assist:

- in providing a consistent service
- in assisting clear and accurate decision making
- in more clearly justifying decisions made
- by promoting openness and clarity about the values and principles which underlie risk taking decisions
- by facilitating the learning of general lessons from specific decisions made
- in underpinning training in risk taking
- in giving support to those making risk decisions
- by giving greater definition and structure to an area of work where the high degree of volatility and lack of 'normal expectations' in the lives of older people sometimes conspire to cloud important factors.

PUTTING PRINCIPLES INTO PRACTICE

Principles and values are central in all areas of work with older people if a quality service with the consumer at the centre is to be provided. When working with vulnerable people fear of harmful consequences can lead staff to lose sight of those principles in favour of 'safe options'.

It is essential that individuals define for themselves the values and principles playing a key part in the decision making process. How far are they prepared to go in upholding those principles? In articulating this clear definition the decision making process can be much more open and honest.

The following are some of the key principles and values underpinning the assessment and management of risk. Issues relating to putting those principles into practice are also identified.

EQUAL OPPORTUNITIES

All work must take into account and respond to a person's race, religion, culture, gender, sexual orientation, disability and communication needs.

Why is the principle of equal opportunities particularly important in this area of work?

Such principles as those of user focus and self-determination cannot meaningfully be put into practice if this principle is not adhered to.

How might a policy promote equal opportunities?

It is hoped that the need within the following framework for individuals to articulate elements of the decision making process will assist in promoting equal opportunities. It might do so by exposing anxieties based largely on prejudice or assumption.

User Focus

The person who is deemed to be at risk is the main focus of attention and concern. Their needs must not be clouded by issues relating to others.

PROCESS OF PUTTING THE PRINCIPLE INTO PRACTICE

The following questions need to be addressed openly and the responses articulated separately for users, for carers and for other key individuals:

- What do they want (outcomes)?
- Why do they want this outcome?
- What do they value most?
- What anxieties do they have?

Carer assessment forms will assist in separate assessments and will highlight areas of conflict.

Reasons for a decision in favour of addressing the wishes of one individual rather than another in situations of conflicting interests will be made explicit. They will often focus around issues of rights, independence, self-determination.

Encouraging Independence

Users have the right not to have their independence unnecessarily restricted due to the anxieties of others. Restrictions often have a negative effect on quality of life. Wherever possible enhancement of quality of life is the primary aim.

HOW MIGHT A POLICY PROMOTE THIS PRINCIPLE?

The framework outlined here will demand clear articulation of all steps in the decision making process. These will have to be recorded and clearly communicated to users and others involved. This will demand that any anxieties and decisions based on these are explicitly justified. Users or their advocates will have a much clearer basis on which to question decisions.

Self-Determination

All users will be presumed capable of exercising informed choice unless multi-agency assessment (involving user/carer/advocate) determines otherwise. When working to this principle the issue of equal opportunities is central in the process of enabling individuals to make their own choices in the context of their own culture and values.

IMPORTANT FACTORS IN CONSIDERING THE APPROPRIATENESS OF THE USER DETERMINING THEIR OWN OUTCOME

Circumstances where an individual is considered incapable of making their own choice might include those:

- Where the individual does not know they have a decision to make.

- Where the individual does not understand the choices available or the consequences of those choices.
- Where the individual cannot communicate their decision. However, in these and other circumstances they can only be deemed incapable of making the decision where every reasonable effort has been made to assist their understanding of the situation and the communication of their wishes. This will include arranging the support of an advocate and/or interpreter where necessary and possible. It is important to start from the assumption that the individual is trying to find some way of communicating their wishes rather than that they cannot do so.

There may be situations where individuals seem to be able in terms of knowledge and understanding to make their own decisions. However, they may be subject to undue pressure to support a particular course of action, perhaps pressure from a professional or a relative. Workers will need to determine whether the older person is making the decision of their own free will as well as assessing their ability to make the decision.

The above begins to look at the question of which of us has the authority to make decisions about their own life.

The framework here promotes the view that:

- Everyone has the right to be heard and their views recorded.
- Conflicts will be made explicit and recorded.
- The decision making process will be open and articulate and involve key individuals fully.
- The reasons for the decision made will be clear and recorded fully.
- This clarity will assist accountability
- In some instances legislation may assist in decision making.

Confidentiality

Maintaining confidentiality is an important principle in all work.

ISSUES RELATING TO PUTTING THE PRINCIPLE INTO PRACTICE

There are, however, situations within which absolute confidentiality will compromise other aspects of good practice. In such situations an open discussion of the issue will be demanded.

In the area of risk taking where complex decisions often need to be made it will be necessary to share information with line managers and with other professionals involved. It should be explained to users and others that if intervention is to be effective this sharing of information will need to take place.

Where difficult decisions regarding confidentiality arise in situations of serious risk, then the reasons for decisions/actions should be recorded.

Staff Support

Workers and managers will need the support of their employing agency. That agency will need to make a statement about the existence of such support where a specific policy and framework have been followed through. Such a policy and framework will support staff in demanding shared responsibility and accountability:

- By requiring all workers involved in a situation to make explicit their assessments and recommendations.

- By ensuring that through the supervisory process managers will know how and when risk decisions are being made and thereby share responsibility for them.

Risk taking is a complex and far reaching area and it will be necessary for staff to work not only within a policy and framework but within their legal responsibilities and other relevant policies and procedures.

A FRAMEWORK FOR RISK ASSESSMENT

David Carson (1988b) points to a definition of risk taking in stating: 'Risks should be taken to achieve specific goals in the light of possible harms occurring' and 'Taking risks involves deciding that the potential benefits of a proposed act outweigh the potential drawbacks' (p.248). So risk taking is choosing whether or not to act to achieve beneficial results in an awareness of potential harms.

This definition forms the basis of a framework for risk assessment. It identifies the importance of defining outcomes (nature and degree). It also introduces the notion of likelihood with its image of weighing the achievement of beneficial results against the awareness that harms might result.

Definition of Possible Outcomes

Definition of possible outcomes is important. In achieving this definition individuals will be looking at:

- Why are they considering taking the risk at all?
- What are their hopes?
- What are their anxieties?
- In what way and to what degree are various individuals likely to be affected by the decision?

Choices may then have to be made about which/whose aspirations/outcomes are more important.

Individuals will then need to ask:

- **How important/and of what value is each possible outcome to individuals involved?**

For example:

- How much does the individual value their independence? Enough to risk a fall and having to wait until someone comes to help them up from the floor?

- For another individual in the same situation with a different perspective: How profound an effect on that individual's life results from the fear of their relative falling?
- Which perspective is to take precedence in the decision making process?

Such decisions involve making judgements about whose aspirations are most important and about whether the potential harmful consequences which might result from attempting to realize those aspirations are too great/likely for the risk to be taken.

Consideration of the principles outlined earlier may assist individuals in articulating how they are making decisions. Openness about the basis on which decisions are made is central in this work as without this, decisions can neither be justified nor challenged.

In defining possible outcomes and the likelihood of those outcomes occurring those involved will:

- have clearly articulated what they are concerned about
- have sufficient data to attempt to quantify the level of concern (i.e. the combination of severity of outcome coupled with how likely that outcome is to occur)
- have a well articulated understanding of the benefits/value to the user/carer or others of taking the risk.

Likelihood

The risk assessment process must go on to look at how likely the identified outcomes are to occur and to record relevant factors clearly. Those relevant factors might include:

- data about e.g. weight gain/loss, levels of medication, medical condition and likely consequences
- past experience – either relating to the specific issue at stake in the specific situation or relating to other similar situations
- motivation to succeed or change
- experience to date in the risk taking process towards achieving a goal. How many steps of the process have so far been successful?

Again, the assessment of likelihood will be a subjective one but the factors taken into consideration need to be clearly set out.

Tables 4.1 and 4.2 show headings/formats for arranging information in a clear articulate way.

Table 4.1 One section of Hampshire County Council Social Services Department's Care Management assessment form

Hampshire
COUNTY COUNCIL

Social Services
DEPARTMENT

CLIENT REFERENCE NO.

Name: ....

Risk Factors

PROMPT: Positive risk taking (eg personal development, daily living, leisure/work and associated risk); risk to self (eg alcohol/substance abuse, self-neglect, memory loss, suicidal ideas); risk of exploitation (eg financial, sexual); risk of offending; risk to others (eg aggression, irresponsibility, other challenges); risk to property; person's values.

Please make sure that you structure the assessment in the following way:

1. **Specific areas of strength/need** that have been identified.
2. The person's **level of ability** in the areas identified.
3. Whether the person **wishes to take any action** regarding those strengths and needs identified.
4. How the person **prioritises** their strengths and needs.
5. Whether the person's **views are shared** by other people involved in the assessment, if not specifying any different views expressed.
6. Any **statutory/protective** responsibility identified or action required to discharge this duty.

NOTES:

People involved in this assessment:

"I confirm that I have been involved in this assessment and agree with what is documented".

	Name:	Signature:	Date:
User ⟶			
Assessor ⟶			
⟶			
⟶			

Table 4.2 A questionnaire type format for organizing information regarding the risk decision.

Based on the work of David Carson (see bibliography)

RISK TAKING

Name of User:...

Date:...................................

What benefits do you hope to achieve with the user? (i.e. why is it worth taking a risk?)

How will the benefits enhance the user's life, experience and/or dignity? How important do you (and the user) rate the benefits?

What types of harm may occur, while trying to achieve the above benefits, to the user, to members of the public, and\or to property? Estimate how likely each type of harm is to occur. (Harm may mean e.g. physical harm, distress or embarrassment).

**Table 4.2 A questionnaire type format for organizing
information regarding the risk decision. (continued)**

Based on the work of David Carson (see bibliography)

What steps do you propose taking to minimize each type of harm? List
each step, relating to reducing the likelihood and the degree of harm.

Who has been consulted about the risk decision? Have any major problems or disagreements been raised that have not been resolved?

Describe the decisions made and action to be taken. Comment on how
you propose to monitor the situation. What records will be kept and
when you will review progress?

HOW FORMAL IS THE PROCESS?

An element of risk is part of everyone's life but it is important that risk is defined and management of risk planned in formal caring relationships. Risk issues must be carefully considered in all cases.

The level of consideration of the aspects of risk taking will vary in relation to the complexity of the decision to be made. The following are examples of situations in which the framework will be required to the fullest extent:

- Where there is concern about particularly serious outcomes to either the user or others (e.g. family, carers, neighbours, staff).
  - **major life changes**

    > **for example**
    > an older person is concerned at the prospect of giving up their own home to go into a residential care home.

  - **illness**

    > **for example**
    > An older person might be at risk of hyperthermia if they remain in their own home.
    > **or**
    > a carer may suffer exhaustion if they continue to offer the level of care required by an older relative.

  - **injury**

    > **for example**
    > a resident in a care home wishes to go out to the local pub. She is physically and mentally frail and may be at risk of injury on the roads.

  - **death**
  - **exploitation/abuse**

    > **for example**
    > where a relative might be considering their inheritance before the need of an older relative for nursing home care.

- When individuals within a situation dissent from a carefully considered and explained action plan despite the clear indication of significant hazards. These are situations requiring careful consideration of the principles of user focus and self-determination.

  > **for example**
  > where a woman aged 80 years lives with an adult son who physically abuses her particularly when he has been drinking. The woman refuses to have anything said against her son. She wishes to continue living with him and to take no action against him for his abusive behaviour. She has been informed of the possible severe consequences of the abuse which appears to be increasing in severity.

- Where there is the potential to apply legislative measures to restrict liberty/freedom of choice.

> **for example**
> the use of guardianship under the 1983 Mental Health Act or powers under Section 47 of the National Assistance Act 1948, the latter might come into force where a relative is neglecting the needs of an older person to such an extent that they are not receiving adequate care and attention and are forced to live in insanitary conditions.

- Where previous experience clearly indicates the probability of high risk.

> **for example**
> A hospital inpatient was admitted with a fractured femur following a fall at home. The admission followed close on the heels of previous inpatient treatment for similar injuries, also caused by falling at home. The patient wishes to return home without any assistance as soon as the necessary hospital treatment is completed.

- Where the level of uncertainty with regard to harm or loss being incurred is high.

> **for example**
> - not enough is known about the knowledge, skills and qualities of key persons
> - the course of action proposed is setting a precedent
> - the situation is unknown and could rapidly change.

ASSISTING THE DECISION MAKING PROCESS

It is important to note that risk taking should not be about taking once and for all decisions but it can be:

- A process comprising a series of decisions or small steps towards a goal.
- A process constantly being modified by the people involved in it and the circumstances surrounding them.

Each step of the decision making process, must be shared with others, monitored and reviewed (as appropriate) leading to the next step in the process.

Information about the way in which risk decisions have been made should be available to assist relatives/carers understanding. It should also be shared appropriately by staff working in different settings, for example fieldwork and residential settings.

Within the decision making process the following will assist:

(1) Staff Supervision

The opportunity for the worker involved in an 'at risk' situation to share thoughts with a senior member of staff in supervision must be made available in the assessment, decision making process, and the management of risk. Risk assessment and management is an area of work where workers feel stressed and under pressure to make decisions quickly. The supervisory process must seek to minimize the consequences of pressured decision making.

> Supervision can achieve this by:
> - being supportive
> - checking out that workers have looked at all aspects of the situation
> - questioning the values underlying decisions
> - providing some emotional distance from the situation
> - bringing the experience of other situations to bear on specific decisions.

More detail relating to the role of the supervisory process is to be found in *Good Practice in Supervision* (Pritchard 1994).

(2) The Multi Agency Staff Group and Planning Meetings

The multi-agency staff group is important in terms of:
- gathering relevant information from all perspectives
- pooling relevant expertise
- the group might challenge the basis upon which a worker is evaluating a situation

> **for example**
> one professional might argue that a woman's accommodation is unsuitable due to large numbers of cats posing a hygiene threat. Another professional might balance this view by putting forward the idea that the cats provide emotional well being.

- resource decisions
- joint accountability, i.e. a corporate decision in the light of all available facts with the discussion of differing views/values/ principles. A particular course of action to be carried out by named individuals will be a consensus decision.

A more formal approach will be needed in the form of a planning meeting/care planning meeting/Care Programme Approach in some instances. Examples of when planning meetings will be necessary are:
- Where there is concern about particularly serious outcomes.
- When individuals within a situation dissent from a carefully considered and explained action plan despite the clear indication of significant hazards.
- Where there is the potential to apply legislative measures to restrict liberty/freedom of choice (e.g. Guardianship orders).

- Where previous experience clearly indicates the probability of high risk, (perhaps the same risk has been taken in the past and harm resulted).
- Where several workers from a variety of agencies are involved, (indicating a high level of complexity in the situation and a need to bring all relevant knowledge/expertise to bear on the situation).
- Where there is conflict between key individuals.

PROCESS ISSUES AND CONTENT OF THE PLANNING MEETING:

- The planning meeting should not be chaired by a worker directly involved in the situation but by their line manager
- All of those agencies/individuals must be invited:
    - who can contribute to an understanding of the circumstances
    - whose agreement and co-operation will be needed to effect a care plan
    - who are likely to be involved in monitoring the risk (even if they have not been involved to date). This will include individuals from Social Services Department, statutory agencies, private agencies and voluntary agencies
- Users and Carers will be invited to the meeting. Where users and/or carers are to attend it is essential that issues/information which could potentially be distressing to them are discussed with them prior to the meeting. On this basis they can then make an informed decision as to whether to attend the whole of the meeting, or part of the meeting, or not to attend at all.
- Consideration must be given where appropriate to the possibility of appointing an advocate to speak on behalf of the user.
- The meeting must record key individuals' knowledge of/involvement in the situation in question.
- It must ask for opinions and assessments to be shared.
- It will identify the key stakeholders in the situation – what people have to gain or lose. This will clarify whose needs are being met.
- The meeting will then appraise the above information and offer recommendations on:
    - an agreed plan of action
    - specification of roles and responsibilities of agencies/individuals
    - a suitable key worker to co-ordinate risk management within the care plan
    - monitoring and review arrangements
- The meeting will formally record key information, opinions, assessments and recommendations. This will include any dissent from the majority view. It will also insist on written reports from key individuals who are unable to attend.

- The recommendations and information recorded at the meeting will be circulated to all participants promptly following the meeting.
- A separate planning meeting will not be necessary where risk assessment and management is explicitly planned in another forum.

Positive contributions of planning meetings can be:

- organizing and articulating the available information
- exposing hidden agendas
- facilitating a more objective approach
- controlling anxieties
- managing uncertainty
- sharing accountability
- gaining the commitment of all involved to a strategy for proceeding.

Whilst the planning meeting can make some decisions about definite actions to be taken (e.g. those underpinned by legislation) in many circumstances it can only make recommendations. The high degree of volatility in many situations of risk will demand that workers make decisions outside the meeting. It will, however, have provided a framework/an approach within which the worker (in consultation with their supervisor) will be assisted in making day-to-day decisions.

Caution must be exercised since the meeting can lead to individuals no longer feeling responsible for their own decisions/actions. They may come to rely on 'the meeting said so'. This can result in a shift to a more dangerous (sometimes too dangerous) course of action. Recording of individual opinions in the meeting can help to overcome this to an extent.

RISK MANAGEMENT

The decision as to how to proceed will not usually eliminate risk. Risk will almost always continue and a process will be developed for the management of risk.

Part of the process of managing the risk will lie in the definition of time limits in terms of:

- the frequency of reviews
- the frequency and intensity of monitoring arrangements
- the extent to which agencies will continue to be involved in a situation where risk taking has been an issue.

The above must be carefully considered decisions against the background of risk factors identified in the assessment process.

There must be a clear plan identifying the input from individuals who are being relied upon to make the management of risk possible. It will be particularly important to identify individual responsibilities surrounding any critical events or steps to be taken in the life of the individual deemed to be 'at risk'. It will be more usual to take a series of small steps in risk taking towards the achievement of a goal. This approach will assist in that the outcome of previous risk decisions can inform future decisions.

Using the assessment process, risk management will take steps to increase benefits and to reduce the likelihood of harms occurring. This might be achieved by:

- re-allocation of resources
- additional resources
- changes to the user's environment
- influencing attitudes/motivation/feelings.

Managing risk in the lives of older people will require an acknowledgement that their lives often present a high degree of volatility. Timing of reviews and monitoring arrangements will need to take account of this. Goal planning will have to be open to sometimes significant shifts due to changing needs. Risk management issues should be included in care plans and care programmes. This should be done with sensitivity to the degree to which an individual can understand and accept the reality of their situation.

- In this way users and carers (both formal and informal) will wherever possible have signed up to and be fully aware of the risk assessment and decisions. They will therefore, have more realistic expectations of each other.
- In the management of risk it is essential that everyone who has ongoing contact in the situation shares information and maintains awareness.

HEALTH AND SAFETY

In managing risks to users it is essential that the safety of staff is given equally serious consideration. Where there is a perceived risk to staff this can be assessed in a similar way to that outlined above.

Providers will be in a position to clarify the assessment of the degree of risk to staff involved. This will then be looked at alongside the assessment of risk to the user.

The process involved in ensuring the health and safety of staff is looked at in more detail in Chapter 12.

In summary the process outlined above looks like that outlined in Table 4.3.

Table 4.3 Key steps in risk assessment/risk management

Risk Assessment	Risk Management
Define what is to be achieved (i.e. what is the point of taking the risk)	Clarity in the definition of decisions to be made will lead to sounder decision making
Decide on the degree of formality with which the decision will be made	Where possible take small steps in a process of risk taking to achieve a particular goal
Define possible outcomes benefits and harms	Work to increase benefits and minimise harms
Assess relative importance/value of various outcomes to key individuals	Use the supervisory process in assessment and management of risk
Assess how likely each potential outcome is to occur	Consult with other professionals and key individuals
Consider who will be affected by the decision and how	Manage conflicting opinions openly and clearly
Be in a position to justify decisions/actions	Agree a plan of action
	Specify roles of key individuals
	Define reviewing and monitoring arrangements
	Include risk management issues in care plans/care programmes
	Consider health and safety of staff. Assess risk to staff in same way as to service users

Refer back at every stage to the Principles underlying this work

ACKNOWLEDGEMENTS

This chapter results from work with the Hampshire County Council Social Services Department in producing a policy document relating to risk and older people. Advice and guidance have been provided by:

Rosemary Archer, Assistant Director, Hampshire County Council Social Services Department. Glyn Jones, Principal Adviser (Services for Older People). Members of a core group within the Social Services Department participated in the consultation process. They include: Maureen Condon, Sandra Grime, Chris Martin, Anne Meader, Rodney Nash, Geoff Richardson, Mark Surtees, Sue Stickley, Leon Tourle, Sue Wall and Graham Willis. My thanks too to Joan Hudson for her administrative support.

REFERENCES

Bedford, A. (1987) *Child Abuse and Risk*. London: NSPCC.

Brearley, C.P (1982) *Risk and Ageing*. London: Routledge and Kegan Paul.

Carson, D. (1988a) 'Risk taking policies.' *Journal of Social Welfare Law 5*, 328–332.

Carson, D. (1988b) 'Taking risks with patients: Your assessment strategy.' *Professional Nurse*, April, 247–250.

Carson, D. (1990) 'Risk taking in mental disorder: Analyses, policies and practical strategies.' Conference proceedings (Southampton University) 23.3.90.

Carson, D. (1994) 'Risk taking with special reference to mental disorder services.' Conference proceedings – London 29.11.94.

Davies, B., Bebbington, A. and Charnley, H. (1990) *Resources, Needs and Outcomes in Community based Care*. Aldershot: Avebury.

Faugier, J. and Greenwood, M. (1993) 'Outside risk.' *Nursing Times 89*, 40, 56–58.

Pritchard, J. (ed) (1994) *Good Practice in Supervision*. London: Jessica Kingsley.

Utting, W. (1992) (Foreword to) *The Right to Take Risks*. London: Counsel and Care.

Wynne Harley, D. (1991) *Living Dangerously. Risk Taking Society and Older People*. London: Centre for Policy on Ageing.

CHAPTER 5

RISK AND OLDER PEOPLE

Rosemary Littlechild and John Blakeney

INTRODUCTION

'Being at risk' is a term commonly applied to older people who are perceived as being in some way vulnerable or in potentially dangerous situations. Yet, despite its common usage by lay people and professionals alike, there has been surprisingly little written about the concept of risk and its use by social workers with older people. A bibliography compiled in 1993 by the Centre for Policy on Ageing (Jackson 1993) found only 17 references to the general nature of risk-taking in work with older people compared to many more on specific issues such as dangers in the environment, risks of falling and self-neglect.

During the 1980s, the issues of the rights of older people began to come to the fore. Norman (1980) published a key document raising issues on civil liberty issues for older people and many local authority social services departments published documents of intent about the rights to which older people who used their services would be entitled. In some cases these Charters of Rights caused heated discussion amongst staff about potential conflict between maintaining a person's rights and allowing them to take what they saw as unacceptable risks (for example see Baldwin, Harris, Littlechild and Pearson 1993, p.166). And yet it is only in recent years, since the implementation of the National Health Service (NHS) and Community Care Act, that many departments have issued explicit policies or guidance for their staff on undertaking risk assessments and identifying and managing risk. (For general guidance see Association of Directors of Social Services 1991). The increasing concern about elder abuse in the last decade (Eastman 1984; Pritchard 1992) has prompted many Social Services Departments to publish for the first time comprehensive adult protection procedures.

This chapter will examine the situations when older people are generally deemed to be at risk, who is most likely to be involved in their assessment and what factors will affect their perception and recommended course of action. It will discuss how the concept of risk must be considered in the assessment and management process, with particular reference to older people with dementia. Finally it will identify some key points for good practice.

WHEN ARE OLDER PEOPLE DEEMED TO BE AT RISK?

The vast majority of older people in Britain live in their own homes and make arrangements for any necessary care with no recourse to formal sources of help. The 1985 Household survey indicated that 75 per cent of people aged 75 and over received no help at all from either Social Services or domiciliary health services (OPCS 1988). It is usually when, for some reason, those arrangements are interrupted or cease to be available that they come under the scrutiny of helping professionals and a 'risk assessment' may be undertaken. In these situations, a risk analysis could be defined as balancing the potential gain from an action or decision against the potential danger of another action or decision or *vice versa*.

When is that most likely to happen? One of the most common situations is when older people are living in the community and are seen, usually by others, as needing residential or nursing home care. A study of a thousand applications for local authority residential care (Neill, Sinclair, Gorbach and Williams 1988) found that four-fifths of the application forms identified the older person as being 'at risk'.

Older people who come to the attention of social workers in hospital are also likely to undergo a risk assessment before being discharged. With the introduction of the NHS and Community Care Act 1990 and the transfer of social security funds to local authority social services departments, the number of older people undergoing an assessment by hospital social workers has increased considerably. The anticipated move from 'service-led' assessments to 'needs-led' assessments (Department of Health 1991) should encourage good practice by the thorough examination of all options available. However, monitoring information from the first year of the community care legislation Henwood (1994) indicates that hospital social workers in particular feel under considerable pressure as they experience the tension between the two competing notions of good practice from the health service (speedy throughput of patients) and social services (thorough assessment).

However, in any situation where a risk assessment is undertaken, there is rarely one generally accepted definition of what the risks might be and how they could attempt to be overcome. The perception of those people involved will be affected by a number of complex personal and social factors.

Who then in these situations might be the principle players involved in an assessment of risk and what might be the factors affecting their judgements?

CONTRIBUTORS TO A RISK ASSESSMENT

(1) Professionals

In Neill *et al.*'s (1988) detailed study of 60 referrals for residential care, social workers identified risk as an important factor in their decision-making in nine out of ten cases. Clearly, in some cases there is a fear of being held responsible if a serious accident takes place, deemed to have occurred through lack of professional surveillance or intervention. There is an element of protecting one's own professional interests if an internal or external scrutiny or extensive media coverage is likely to ensue.

Following the NHS and Community Care Act, local authorities are obliged to publish eligibility criteria for the allocation of services. A process of rationing must therefore necessarily take place and practitioners must undertake a thorough assessment of people's needs in order to maintain an equitable distribution of resources to meet them. Problems arise, however, when eligibility criteria are not made explicit, when central or local government policies affect the local prioritization of resources with the result that significant sums of money and resources are no longer accessible part of the way through the financial year.

The Department of Health (1991) guidelines on assessment and care management acknowledge that an evaluation of risk is central to any assessment but warn that 'Agencies and professionals tend to vary in their perceptions of risk and crisis' (p.59). Whilst some social workers may consider the older person's right to self-determination and independence as central to decision-making, other professionals may be more concerned about the person's physical health safety.

(2) Service Users

In Neill et al.'s study (1988) outlined above, the older applicants to residential care identified risk as an important factor in their decision in only 40 per cent of cases compared to in 90 per cent of cases by social workers and 75 per cent by the care-givers. This difference in perception is replicated in a small study of eight older women entering very sheltered housing (Lawrence 1992). In all cases the families identified their concerns about the physical risks their relative ran in remaining in their own home whilst seven of the eight women identified reasons such as the house or garden being too large, the changing nature of the local community and loneliness as being the key factors. Similarly, in Neill's (1988) study the worry about risk from the older people themselves was unrelated to their physical health but associated with either the previous experience of a dangerous event (for example a fall, burglary or fire) or the feelings that they were experiencing because of the anxiety of others!

Norman (1980) highlights the anomalies that exist in the ways that certain groups in society are free to take risks and decide what level of danger they expose themselves to compared to the over protectiveness to which older people are often subjected. She and other writers (Norman 1987; McEwen 1990; Bytheway 1995) have written extensively on the ageism that older people experience both at the hands of professionals and others, often well-meaning rather than malicious in their intentions but with the result of the older person's wishes being ignored or at best given token attention. Allen, Hogg and Peace's study (1992) of 103 older people who had recently entered residential care found that at least 20 per cent of them experienced pressure either from their families or professionals to do so. A third of the people interviewed said that the decision to move had not been their own and that generally the move had been as a result of a breakdown in either their own health or living situation or that of a main carer.

It is of concern that such recent research continues to confirm that older people are often not central to the decision-making about their own lives and that decisions are made at a time of crisis or turmoil in their lives. Too often assessments concentrate on what it is older people *cannot* do whereas, if asked, they themselves will stress both their own strengths and abilities and their need for independence and reluctance to be dependant 'on the welfare'.

(3) Carers

It is not always those who are closest at hand to the older person who are most concerned about the risks they encounter. Neill's (1988) research and anecdotal evidence suggests that the greatest anxiety is often shown by those 'absentee' relatives who are geographically separated from the older person and cannot share in their practical care. Their anxiety is likely to be based on the physical or mental well-being of the older person whereas carers who are more closely involved are also likely to be concerned about their own health and well-being, the changing needs in their own family or an exhaustion with their role as a carer.

(4) Advocates

Clearly, the right of the older person to make decisions about their lives is less straightforward when the older person has a mental impairment which prevents or impedes their decision-making. In that situation the use of an advocate may be necessary to represent and argue for what might be in the person's best interests. Whilst advocacy schemes are developing all the time, they are in most areas by no means an established resource that an older person may call upon. It is much more likely that a relative, friend, social worker or other professional will need to take on that role. However, the discussion above has indicated that with such diverse agendas, those people may not be in a position to do so. For example, in a research study on people's experiences of social workers (Littlechild 1993) a man caring for his wife with Huntingdon's Chorea and wanting to discharge her from hospital explained,

> I said I was going to have another go and I asked for a meeting. They were all telling me 'You won't cope'. I was a bit disappointed the social worker didn't stick up for me. But I'd asked the head of Crossroads to come along and I said to her 'Do you think your ladies will cope?' She was the only one on my side. She said to me afterwards, 'I don't know how you kept your rag'. (p.14)

He felt let down that the professionals did not share his judgement about his ability to care and to take the risk to 'have another go'.

As social workers become responsible for the budget that controls resources at their disposal, it will become increasingly difficult for them to act as an advocate for the older person. Indeed some independent advocacy schemes would say it was an impossible task for a statutory social worker to undertake (Pilling 1988). Likewise, some local authority social services departments are clearly stating that the role of advocate is an inappropriate one for care managers to undertake.

If there are so many potential stake-holders in decisions that are made about the lives of older people, how can a social worker effectively tread that very fine line between upholding the principle of allowing older people to take decisions about their own lives whilst not being seen to be negligent in their duties and taking action which is regarded as interfering or excessively intrusive?

ASSESSMENT

Integral to appropriate assessment is the process of information gathering. For the process of assessment to be effective, the information gathered needs to be as comprehensive and as accurate as possible. In the assessment of risk and older adults it is necessary, as in all assessments, to be aware of the influence of the various 'isms' (e.g. sexism, hetero-sexism, racism, ageism, ableism), and their related stereotypes, on the information given and on how that information is then processed. As part of this awareness it is also necessary to differentiate as to whether the information given is related to actual risk, anticipated risk or exaggerated risk.

Case Example 1

A distraught carer informs you that his mother, who is just out of hospital following a fall, continuously falls and cannot be left alone; he informs you that the last fall was caused by her passing out so an alarm would not sufficiently guarantee her safety. Finally he needs to return to work after taking time off to look after her following discharge from hospital.

Taking this information at face value would preclude most of the resources available to you, the assessor, and to the service user, leaving little to look at outside the provision of physical monitoring, either in the home or elsewhere. But what other information is available to you?

The older person herself informs you that she has only fallen three times in the last twelve months – once on some ice when shopping, once when having had too much to drink at a birthday party, and finally when she had been ill with a chest infection that had left her incapacitated and in hospital.

This puts a completely different light on things. Which pieces of information from which provider of information are accurate, which anticipates and which exaggerates the risk or lack of risk?

The example above not only highlights the problems involved in evaluating information as part of the assessment process, but also illustrates some of the issues discussed earlier about who is involved in the assessment process. For an assessment to be appropriate as a process of information gathering, evaluation and planning then it must involve all those involved at all stages. If an assessment as a process has not been appropriate then how can the assessment as product be?

The assessment of an individual and their environment requires the recognition of the different realities impacting on that environment. This is particularly so when considering the assessment and management of risk, the focus being individuals and how they relate to, and interact within, their environment. This sounds fine in principle but how accurately can risk be predicted? It is made more difficult by the fact that an assessment often takes place in unfamiliar situations or locations, such as a time of crisis or in a hospital setting. This information can illustrate how well an individual operates outside of their normal environment, but it can also mislead. It is necessary to look at the individual and at the environment separately as well as together. Has the service user been ill or are they now? Have they just had a bereavement? Have their physical or mental abilities been impaired and if so was this recent? Has their financial situation changed? And so on. All these things may contribute to a changed ability to manage and a changed level of risk, but this may be a short or long term contribution to increased or decreased risk; it may be real or it may be perceived, all of which is part of the assessment.

What about the environment? Maybe the local shop has closed or the bus service has been re-routed; perhaps the access to the house is no longer appropriate. Has there been a recent spate of burglaries? Have the neighbours changed? Is the house safe? What's the weather going to be like and is the house appropriately heated? Again things that can have a temporary or long term effect on a person's ability to manage and to their level of risk.

There are also issues around the other people involved. What about levels of stress within the family? Are carers burning out? What family changes are taking place? Is there a history of abuse or violence? Is abuse taking place now? Who manages finances, and how well? How friendly/unfriendly are the neighbours, and what's the history there? Again all affective on ability to cope short or long term, on changed risk or on interpretations and perceptions of risk.

An assessment is often made at a critical time in a service user's life and is a snapshot of that time – often there will be recent changes that have a temporary or long term effect. However there may also be an underlying cause to someone's apparent increase in risk, or inability to cope, which may not be readily apparent. Such a situation may provide an opportunity to effect change to either negate or minimize the risk.

Case Example 2

Mrs A arrives at your office identifying herself as a full time carer for her husband. He was knocked over crossing the road three years ago causing head and spinal injuries. He uses a wheelchair all through the day, he needs assistance with all self care tasks. At present Mr A receives day care once a week and goes into respite care for two weeks in every eight. Mrs A is suffering from an agitated depression, this being the third occurrence in the last 18 months, there being no previous history of depressive illness. The present care package resulted from the assessment subsequent to Mr A's accident three years before. It transpires that Mr A does not like leaving his wife and on the last two occasions has refused to go for respite care. Mrs A wishes to return home to look after her husband who today is at the day centre.

On the surface it would appear that the care package that has been in effect for the last three years has been operating effectively, but Mr A's refusal to go into respite care on the last two occasions have led to it now failing to meet Mrs A's needs. This would appear to be a temporary problem only and fairly easily rectified. However Mrs A's depression had appeared on 2 previous occasions over the last 18 months. Could there be an underlying problem?

It subsequently transpires that prior to his accident Mr A was a perpetrator of domestic violence, and though no longer physically violent he is still abusing. Mrs A has experienced many years of violence from Mr A and now has the role of full time personal carer for him. This is a role she hates but feels is her duty.

The risk then is not Mrs A's ability to care for Mr A but the return to what remains for her an abusive environment. The change needs to be made not in the support of Mrs A's caring role but in the environment that she lives in, perhaps enabling her to withdraw from the role of carer, perhaps in counselling for both Mrs and Mr A.

The process of risk assessment needs to evaluate what is actual and what is anticipated risk. Also what is someone's real and their perceived ability to cope. When assistance or intervention is identified as needed, then is that assistance short term or long term? Also where does change need to be effected, if at all to manage or minimize the level of risk?

MANAGEMENT

As with assessment, so the management of risk should be recognized as involving all those people concerned. For the social worker or care manager the management of risk is part of the professional task of care management. For the service user and service provider the emphasis is on the management of risk and its effect on the quality of life for both the service user and their carer(s).

Central to the management task is regular monitoring and review which can be formal or informal. A formal review, as well as being part of the processes of both assessment and management, should form a dynamic link between the two. These can be held as required, and part of the review process is to set the timescale between that review and the subsequent one. On an informal basis the management of risk can be monitored on a day-to-day basis as required. This monitoring does not have to be conducted by the social worker/care manager. It is often best undertaken by an identified key worker. As monitoring evaluates any changing ability to cope, or changing level of risk, so the management of risk must be adaptable also.

Within the new era of 'community care' and the mixed economy, the management of risk will involve input both by the community and in the community. Support by the community can involve statutory sector input, for example social worker, community nursing, home care, mobile meals and private and voluntary sector input, for example domiciliary care, day care, visiting services. Care in the community can involve input from family, friends and neighbours. All of these may have a role in the management of risk, and this should be recognized and valued in the assessment and management process and product. This product is reviewed, monitored and re-produced.

Throughout the processes of assessment, management and review, the role of the service user, or the person at risk, is central as contributor and as part of the ongoing process of evaluation and planning. But what of those who lack insight into their levels of risk, those less able to assess their risk taking behaviour?

ISSUES OF PEOPLE WITH DEMENTIA

There are some very important questions when assessing someone who has a dementia. How well is the person able to assess their level of risk? How much insight do they have into their illness and their ability to cope? Are they capable of exercising informed choice? These questions are often self-evident. However, there are some equally important questions for the assessor to ask about the assessment process itself. Does it empower or disempower? Does it deskill or devalue? What is being assessed – inability and weakness or ability and strength?

Case Example 3

As a duty social worker you receive a call from a distressed individual who informs you that their elderly next door neighbour, Mrs B, has been wandering in and out all day dressed only in night clothes. It is the middle of January and has been snowing. Mrs B lives alone and has no known family.

The assessment process has already started. What are your concerns and are you considering actual, anticipated or exaggerated risk?

You arrive to find Mrs B with the neighbour. She is very agitated, wanting to go home. She is unable to tell you where home is. Mrs B is very disorientated. Mrs B is quite unable to look after herself, and there is no one to take on that role. Her disorientation and agitation is such that she will continue to wander whilst inappropriately dressed for the weather.

What are the questions going through your mind at this time? If you question Mrs B's ability to self determine and make informed choice then an assessment leading to a product involving residential care to ensure safety seems appropriate. But what about questions about cause, disempowerment and devaluing? What is the cause of the dementia? Is it short or long term? Could Mrs B exercise informed choice if the circumstances can be changed?

You call out the GP who arranges a hospital admission. It transpires that Mrs B has a chest infection and is also malnourished and dehydrated. When you visit her in hospital two weeks later, she is totally lucid and orientated. With the hospital occupational therapists, she has demonstrated herself fully capable of self-care tasks, requiring no assistance or prompts. Mrs B does not remember you, but is that surprising?

Mrs B was in an acute confusional state caused by physical ill health, which could have been wrongly assessed as dementia. There are a number of physical problems that, with older adults, can cause similar symptoms to dementia such as a chest infection, constipation or a urinary tract infection. Disorientation can therefore be functional and curable.

An individual with an organic dementia should not be assumed to lack insight or the ability to make informed choices. The assessment process may take longer. For example, the gathering of information may require getting the timing right, finding alternative ways of communicating, repetition and familiarizing the service user with the assessor and the assessment.

Case Example 4

Mr C/D has a dementia. He has not been taking his medication and has shown a marked deterioration over the last few days. He has been admitted to hospital for an assessment. Tests show a recent stroke and further damage within his brain. On the ward he is clearly disorientated – after two weeks he still cannot find his way round. Mr C/D is also very agitated and continuously attempts to leave the ward. The consultant informs you that the medical assessment is completed and asks you to assess for placement and discharge.

C

You have spoken with Mr C on the ward on two occasions – he still fails to recognize you. You attempt to elicit information from him but all he says is he wishes to return home. He shows no insight as to his dementia. An occupational therapist's assessment on the ward has shown that Mr C is unable to manage in the kitchen, not even being able to make a cup of tea without prompts. Family members tell you that Mr C is now much worse and they feel could no longer cope at home alone. A discharge planning meeting decides that, in the interests of Mr C's safety, a residential placement is the only solution. Mr C is not happy with this but the assessment has demonstrated his inability to make informed choice or assess risk.

D

You have spoken to Mr D on a number of occasions about who you are and your role in planning with him for his discharge. Mr D has been adamant throughout that he wishes to return home. A kitchen assessment in the hospital showed Mr D as unable to cope. However, on a home visit, after some initial disorientation, Mr D was able to find his way around and make tea. Family members tell you that Mr D is now much worse and they feel could no longer cope at home alone. You are able to reassure that Mr D was shown in better light in his home environment. He is disorientated on the ward which exaggerates his problems. A discharge planning meeting discusses various options. Mr D's disorientation within a strange environment precludes the use of external resources such as day care and, at this time, residential care. His own coping mechanisms within a known environment suggest that a return home is viable. However, his memory and recognition problems suggest that the fewer strange faces the better; the home care organizer will try to get the seven mornings covered by only two home care assistants to check his medication. A graduated discharge is discussed but felt inappropriate as this would disorientate Mr D. Mr D is to be discharged home after visits from the home care assistants. The home care organizer will be the key worker. The placement will be reviewed after one week.

The two scenarios in Example 4 are the same at the point of referral. The differences are in how the multi-disciplinary teams work. Example 4C assesses Mr C's weaknesses and inabilities; example 4D recognizes Mr D's weaknesses and inabilities but assesses and plans to his strengths and abilities. There are two very different outcomes.

KEY POINTS FOR GOOD PRACTICE

- To deny someone the right to exercise informed choice and take risks, on the basis of their age alone, is ageist.
- When choosing between safeguarding the right to an older person's self-determination and their physical well-being, the balance between the two should be the product of a full multi-disciplinary team assessment.
- An effective multi-disciplinary team recognizes the 'discipline' of the service user and their carer(s).
- Whenever an older person is deemed to be at risk, a number of people may have their own differing agendas, interests and perception of that situation.
- Is then the risk being assessed actual, anticipated or exaggerated? What evidence supports any of these claims?
- An assessment may take place when, for whatever reason, the older person is lacking confidence in their own abilities. The assessment process involves encouraging, informing and valuing the service user and recognizing where it is appropriate to provide advocacy.
- Good assessment involves recognizing inabilities and weaknesses whilst building on abilities and strengths.
- What is the least disruptive change that will appropriately manage the risk/ Must you remove the person or can you adapt the environment?

REFERENCES

Allen, I., Hogg, D. and Peace, S. (1992) *Elderly People, Choice, Participation and Satisfaction*. London: Policy Studies Institute.

Association of Directors of Social Services (1991) *Adults at Risk*. Available from Social Services Division, Metropolitan Borough of Stockport, Town Hall, Stockport SK1 3XE.

Baldwin, N., Harris, J., Littlechild, R. and Pearson, M. (1993) *Residents' Rights: A Strategy in Action in Homes for Older People.* Aldershot: Avebury.

Bytheway, B. (1995) *Ageism.* Buckingham: Open University Press.

Department of Health (1991) *Care Management and Assessment, Practitioner's Guide.* London: HMSO.

Eastman, M. (1984) *Old Age Abuse.* London: Age Concern.

Henwood, M. (1994) *Fit for Change? Snapshots of Community Care One Year On.* Leeds: Nuffield Institute/London, King's Fund Centre.

Jackson, W. (1993) *Risk-taking, Safety and Older People, Selected Bibliographies on Ageing 3.* London: Centre for Policy on Ageing.

Lawrence, M. (1992) *The Effect on Family Relationships when an Elderly Person moves to Sheltered Accommodation.* M.Soc.Sci. Dissertation, University of Birmingham, unpublished.

Littlechild, R. (1993) 'Consumer and carer study – Kenilworth care management project.' *Social Services Research 4,* 6–19.

McEwen, E. (1990) *Age, The Unrecognised Discrimination.* London: Age Concern.

Neill, J., Sinclair, I., Gorbach, P. and Williams J. (1988) *A Need for Care? Elderly Applicants for Local Authority Homes.* London: Gower.

Norman, A. (1980) *Rights and Risks.* London: Centre for Policy on Ageing.

Norman, A. (1987) *Aspects of Ageism: A Discussion Paper.* London: Centre for Policy on Ageing.

Office of Population Censuses and Surveys (1988) *General Household Survey.* London: HMSO.

Pilling, P. (1988) *The Case Manager Project: Report of the Evaluation.* London: City University.

Pritchard, J. (1992) *The Abuse of Elderly People.* London: Jessica Kingsley.

CHAPTER 6

RISK FOR WHOM? SOCIAL WORK AND PEOPLE WITH PHYSICAL DISABILITIES

Liz Ross and Jan Waterson

INTRODUCTION: NEGOTIATING AN ABLE-BODIED WORLD

The inadequate and frequently patronising responses of social service organizations to people with disabilities are well documented (Connolly 1990). Even where policies are conceived in non-discriminatory and empowering language there is no knowing how far this affects planning, management, recruitment or training initiatives, let alone service delivery. The introduction of care management has failed to resolve the fundamental issue of a disabling environment or to empower people with disabilities (Oliver 1991), but they are now empowering themselves (Oliver 1990). The crucial issue for social workers is not what specific roles and tasks they should perform, but that those roles and tasks should be shared with people with disabilities. Thus the focus becomes one of searching for new ways to engage people with disabilities more actively in their own affairs and to change or eliminate the barriers and negative risks they face, rather than simply one of functional assessment (Sapey and Hewitt 1991).

People with physical disabilities are frequently trapped in other people's perceptions of how they should live and thus may be seen to be a risk not only to others but also to themselves. Disability and people with disabilities are viewed negatively (Finkelstein 1993). Situations like the theatre manager who claims that Health and Safety legislation prevents him from admitting someone in a wheel chair, overheard 'whispers' that 'people like that shouldn't have children', the denial of their sexuality and professionals who assess their needs by listing only what they are unable to do, not what they can do, are enough to encourage denial of the reality of disability, particularly if, as in the case of visual disability, it is not obvious (French 1993a).

For a person with a physical disability the possibility that a particular action, or lack of action will have an undesired outcome becomes an everyday part of life. If, as Alaszewski et al. (1994) suggest, risk is 'the possibility that a given course of action will achieve an undesired outcome or some undesired outcome will develop' and 'vulnerability is the extent to which a person is likely to experience damage', then people with physical disabilities are vulnerable in ways that are significantly different from those for able bodied people.

If, on the other hand, risk is defined as also having potentially positive connotations, then they should be entitled to take risks. In other contexts this would be described as empowerment. Indeed, as we will describe later protection from undesirable risks may frequently conflict with rights to empowerment.

This chapter does not set out to give detailed guidance on all the potential risks that people with physical disabilities face and may require social work assistance in negotiating. For example, we do not do full justice to the risks associated with sensory disabilities (see Corker 1993; Woolley 1993; Williams, Waterson and Willetts 1994). Rather, it seeks to provide frameworks in which risks may be viewed. Good practice involves balancing apparently conflicting factors.

The next section outlines some of these key considerations: what do we mean by risk and do different people define it differently? That is, does a social worker view potential risk in the same way as a service user or their carer? Do social workers and their managers always agree? We then examine what risk means to people with physical disabilities, their carers and social workers and their managers. The following two sections look at what choices can be made and how these choices are reflected in assessment models. The final section mentions some of the 'sharp edges' of this work which will continue to be the tightropes that social workers will need to negotiate.

Points for Practice: *Negotiating an able-bodied world*
- Specific tasks and roles are less important than working jointly with people with disabilities in an empowering way.
- People with disabilities are entitled to take risks, especially those which may be beneficial to them.

FRAMEWORKS FOR ACTION

Assessment of risk can be both objective and subjective. Both are important. Even assessment of objective risk is far from straightforward. Considering whether a particular action or non-action is risky means estimating the likelihood of an undesirable outcome occurring and the alternatives, breaking down a complex situation into its component parts (Wharton 1992). Environmental, social, physical and emotional aspects need considering and the analysis should allow for alternative beneficial as well as harmful outcomes (Brearley 1982). Risk assessment then becomes the task of estimating the probability and size of known possible outcomes resulting from a complex interaction of known and unknown factors. Sometimes, all the possible outcomes of a situation may be identifiable, but the likelihood is not all will be. In some cases of uncertainty 'you realise (what) you do not know' (Green, Tunstall and Fordham 1991). In others 'you do not know (what) you do not know'. It follows that to be 'at risk' is a situation where a person is exposed to opportunities, hazards and dangers, of which they may or may not be aware.

Management of risk can be even more problematic (Hood *et al.* 1992). Decisions have to be made on the basis of the assessment (Flood and Carson 1993). In the social services context it is likely that all the potential outcomes are uncertain and decisions are likely to be made against an uncertain background rather than a situation where exact risk measurement is possible. Risk management thus involves devising and implementing strategies to handle such situations.

For many people with physical disabilities, despite increasing user involvement, this may well be an exercise over which they themselves have limited control and input. Whilst the person with physical disabilities may be the main character in the action, s/he may not be the most active player. Much of the legislation surrounding people with disabilities gives other people, notably professional social workers and medical personnel, the responsibility for assessing their needs and by implication the risk of undesirable outcomes from acting or not acting. Despite suggestions that some users might become their own care managers (Audit Commission 1992) recent changes under the 1990 National Health and Community Care Act and the attendant changes in the way the Independent Living Fund is administered have if anything increased the control of the professionals. Some authorities have attempted to circumnavigate this regressive step by allowing users to be their own key worker if not care manager. In this situation the risk is one of unnecessary dependence and service control.

Information may be dispersed among the players, with each one knowing, or not knowing, what they do not know. Thus an assessment of the risks involved in particular actions may be made in different ways by different players, each of whom will be assessing risks to the main character and to themselves, and possibly other players and wider 'society'. Each uses a different set of objective and subjective criteria to come to a decision. Each will use a different set of objective and subjective criteria to assess the nature of risk in a particular situation. Thus an objective assessment needs to be integrated with social perceptions (Renn, Burns, Kasperson and Kasperson 1992) and the capacity of each individual actor to assess his or her own exposure to risk taken into account.

For example, if a young person with physical disabilities wishes to live independently, s/he may underestimate the likelihood of an accident in the new home while estimating the outcomes of continued dependence within her parental home as highly undesirable (Oliver 1983). Jo had lived with her parents for 20 years. She had recently decided that she wanted to live with a friend, who was also confined to a wheelchair. Despite needing intensive physical help with personal care both young women were convinced that with appropriate support they would not only survive but thrive. Jo's mother had never worked but had spent her time looking after Jo and her father, who had died three years previously. She insisted that she would always support Jo in whatever she wanted to do but continually pointed out that Jo might fall, be confined to bed if help to get her up failed to come one morning and so forth. The social worker was also aware of the potential physical problems Jo and her friend might encounter if help proved unreliable and how dependent they would be on it. She was also aware of the financial costs of adapted accommodation and providing 24-hour support (Fitton, O'Brien and Wilson 1995), and knew that her department was cutting back its expenditure. She pointed out the potential costs that Jo would have to pay for such support (RADAR 1994). In the end Jo 'saw sense' as her mother put it.

Points for Practice: *Frameworks for Action*
- Positive and negative aspects of risk need assessment.
- Subjective and objective aspects of risk are important.
- Risks affect others as well as the person with physical disabilities.
- Everybody has their own viewpoint.

WHAT RISK AND FOR WHOM?

This section outlines some specific examples of risks that people with physical disabilities and their carers may face. Movement into any new or changing situation is a social risk for all of us, but particularly for those whose disability is physically obvious or one which is likely to impact upon those around them. A person with epilepsy knows that he risks social alienation if he has a fit in a social environment.

> It is not only physical limitations that restrict us to our homes and those whom we know. It is the knowledge that each entry into the public world will be dominated by stare, by condescension, by pity and by hostility... Our disability frightens people. They don't want to think it is something which could happen to them. So we become separate from common humanity, treated as fundamentally different and alien. (Morris 1991, p.25).

In such a climate people with disabilities are expected to be uncomplaining and grateful for any service they receive. To consider complaining about services may be seen as a very risky business indeed (RADAR 1994).

The person with physical disabilities rarely experiences situations which have been designed with his/her abilities in mind. Thus movement and access to every sort of social situation or facility may be problematic in a number of ways. The decision to undertake a particular action depends on a pre-assessment of the risks involved, such as accidents arising from uneven surfaces, awkward kerbs or steep ramps. Embarrassment and loss of dignity can occur all too frequently. They can be blamed for this by suggestions that *they* should have made a better assessment of the difficulties of access and risks involved before starting and not put themselves *and others* into embarrassing and frustrating situations.

Tangible access is however, only one part of the equation. The physical world is generally conceived and thought about in terms of the able bodied.

Information about facilities is given by people who are able bodied. Details may not be available or may be misleading because they are filtered by people without personal experience. Thus, a well planned journey may be fruitless because access is not as information suggested. That risk may be sufficient to give up attempting to go – it is not worth it.

The importance of involving the users of services in gathering and assembling information in the form that is most useful for them cannot be overestimated as the following example indicates. As part of a project to design maps which would aid mobility and access for people in wheel chairs (Vujakovic and Matthews 1994), able bodied and people in wheelchairs were each asked to draw a map of the area around their meeting place, showing how they could get to another building. Able bodied people drew detailed maps of roads, footpaths and key buildings such as banks, shops and other facilities. The people in wheelchairs drew very simple maps showing one way of getting between the buildings. They had no information about other routes which they knew were inaccessible to them in wheelchairs. Consequently, they did not know what they did not know about that area. This project has now developed maps of the city centre of Coventry on which roads are classified according to a mobility index and major barriers to mobility are marked.

People with physical disabilities are regarded as having special housing needs (Morris 1993a). In general, special housing and support services resemble a lottery rather than a co-ordinated and widely available option (Fiedler 1988). Even where social service departments and housing departments work together, people with physical disabilities risk problems of stigma and 'ghettoism' (Robinson 1987) often having little choice about location. However, we are all at risk of chronic illness and disability. Thus creating special facilities becomes not only discriminatory but irrelevant. Zola (1989) argues for 'adaptable' rather than 'special needs housing'.

The current disability bill sets out to 'prohibit discrimination against disabled people on the grounds of their (not society's) disability' (Barnes and Oliver 1995). It may go some way to tackling discrimination in the areas of access to goods and services, employment and transport. At the moment risk of unemployment is high, higher the more severe the disability, and people with physical disabilities risk lower wages even when employed (Martin and White 1988). Indeed, the majority (54%) of working age disabled adults live in households where there are no earners (Abberley 1991). This coupled with probable extra expenditure arising from the particular needs of the disability means that the risk of poverty is very real (Oliver and Barnes 1991).

We now move on to the question of who defines what is a risk. 'Throughout the post 1945 period the expansion of health and social services for disabled people has been constructed on the erroneous belief that disabled people are not competent to make basic decisions about their individual service needs' (Barnes 1991). Control over one's own life does not mean doing everything for oneself. Nobody, however able bodied, does that. However, taking control is likely to mean making decisions which involve assessing risks. It is the ability of the person with physical disabilities to assess and evaluate the risk involved in a particular action, both to him or herself and to others, that will determine the level of his/her autonomy throughout their 'disability career'

(Carver 1982). Moreover, as French (1993b) has argued, narrowly defined independence may lead to inefficiency, isolation and stress. After all, able-bodied people have limitations and need to ask for help. The only difference is that those situations are defined as acceptable, whereas help with a disability-related need may not be if independence is narrowly defined and insisted on. The choice of how far to go is for the person with the disability.

Because for people with physical disabilities independence itself may be highly dependent upon the support and assistance of others, they may not be able to risk ignoring the perceptions of others. The risk of personal care and support systems breaking down is significant. The alternative may be residential care, a reduction in services or having no choice in who provides the care. Some people with disabilities have received payments allowing them to make their own arrangements for personal care assistance, offering greater choice and control and higher levels of satisfaction (Zarb and Nadash 1994). Such arrangements tend to be more reliable, thus reducing the risk of being left without care. However, in taking on the responsibility of choice and control the person with physical disabilities also takes on the risks involved in choosing and employing a personal carer. Recent research shows that the best run schemes include support and advice for the person with physical disabilities from an independent living scheme worker or local disability organization (Zarb and Nadash 1994).

Carers too can experience alienation, stigma and loss of social and financial support, and personal independence through their association with disability. Having taken the risk of becoming a carer they may seek to retain the person for whom they care in a state of dependence and thus view anything which threatens this as a risky enterprise. As we saw with Jo, they may emphasize the physical dangers of independent action on the part of the person with physical disabilities and underestimate potentially beneficial outcomes. The person with physical disabilities may be aware that in taking certain actions she risks losing the support and essential care of a parent or carer by taking action which is disapproved of or thought to be putting herself at risk. At a personal level it is reciprocity that is frequently denied to people with disabilities (Morris 1991). The social work task is to minimize the risks of isolation and maximize social integration. At an organizational level the need is for carers organizations to combine with disability organizations rather than compete (Parker 1992).

Points for Practice: *What risks, for whom?*
- Social barriers are frequently more disabling than physical ones.
- Having choice, autonomy and control does not mean doing everything for oneself, particularly if it is isolating, stressful and inefficient.
- Ensuring safe physical access includes comprehensive, intelligible information as well as a safe and accessible built environment and transport.
- Adaptable housing is preferable to special needs housing.

- Poverty is a widespread risk. Check all entitlements.
- Independence can involve chosen assistance, but people with physical disabilities need support with employing carers.
- Provide channels for complaint.
- Balance and integrate carers and users needs as far as possible.

MAKING CHOICES: ASSESSING AND MANAGING RISKS

'The problem for disabled people in all this is that other people historically have had and still have, the power to define, decide and provide for our needs.' (Oliver 1993). Few medical personnel or social workers understand the experience and perceptions of people with disabilities and they impose their own assessment both of need and of the risks involved in certain actions upon them (Morris 1993b) although they are 'often the best assessors of their own needs and solutions' (Social Services Inspectorate 1990). The implementation of community care and its desirability has been largely unquestioned but the assessment of needs and the meeting of those identified is much more contentious, set as it is within the framework of the service user experiencing personal choice, maximum independence, dignity, respect and control (Department of Health 1989). Achieving that may involve risk taking in situations where both the social worker and the person with physical disabilities are aware of potentially undesirable outcomes and accept that potential outcome in anticipation of other potentially greater rewards. Such risk taking is now generally seen as acceptable and indeed a right (Norman 1980; Brearley 1982; Oliver and Barnes 1991).

Although risk assessment as such is barely mentioned in the official care management guidance (Department of Health 1991) this clearly forms part of a needs assessment (Hughes 1993). Whilst assessment is usually described in terms of social need, implicit within this is an indication of what will happen if a particular social need is not met. In other words social need assessment is about the identification of risks or hazards and estimating the likelihood of an undesirable outcome (Stevenson and Parsloe 1993). Disability groups themselves have defined risk as unmet need, highlighting the damage done by lack of resources when people with disabilities cannot afford the equipment they need to be independent. The legality of leaving identified needs unmet will shortly be tested in court and social workers and social work managers may be risking action against themselves, despite protestations about inadequate funding. As Oliver (1983) has remarked it is hardly credible that doctors would fail to diagnose illness simply because of a shortage of resources to treat them.

Many departments are currently allocating services, including initial assessments, in terms of the degree of potential individual risk, where situations are highly volatile or where users are very vulnerable. Referral to prevent further deterioration or enhance quality of life, such as increasing social support, social activity and opportunity, risk to morale or needs for advice and information, are unlikely to feature very highly. It is noteworthy that those needs which are likely to receive a low priority are precisely those that individuals with disabilities would perceive as protecting them from harmful risks and enabling them to take positive risks (Hunter 1988). Such needs might include occasional and flexible household assistance available at short notice (Beardshaw 1988). The frustrations and feelings of insecurity and anxiety experienced due to being unable to control such help is a very real risk for people with physical disabilities, particularly as they age (Zarb 1991).

Hughes (1993) suggests that the purpose of assessment (of older people) is an assessment of quality of life and risk. She lists ten areas for assessment, personal characteristics, attitude to self, functioning, health, environment, finance, recreation, family, community, relationships and support networks and suggests a framework within which each dimension can be examined 'not only in terms of deficits, i.e. needs and risks, but also in terms of the strengths and resources which enhance quality of life and reduce risk or which can potentially be mobilised to do so' (p.355). This list demonstrates the complexity of assessing quality of life and balancing the favourable and unfavourable risk outcomes.

Social workers are likely to find it particularly difficult in situations where they have serious concerns about physical or emotional risk to a person with physical disabilities. The nature, prognosis and treatment of the disabling condition provides the framework within which assessment of social needs are made. Many physical disabilities are defined in medical terms by a disease or condition and with each goes a set of medical criteria to assess the degree of limitation associated with the condition and a set of requirements in the form of treatment or constraints to keep the condition in a stable state. Thus when medical personnel are assessing the needs of a physically disabled person they may be using a different set of risk criteria from those used by the person with the disability themselves and their carers (Harrison 1993).

There is a concern to protect from harm any who appear particularly vulnerable through mental ill health or uncertainty about the progression of the person's condition. It may be hard to 'allow' genuine choices. Biehal (1993) notes that whilst some social workers she studied, having explored with the users the risk their choices would entail, made it clear that they had the right to make their own decisions about risk. However, when

> working with situations of risk where there may be a high degree of uncertainty about outcomes and a desire to manage that uncertainty by taking decisions on behalf of the person concerned, advice and guidance may slide into coercion in order to persuade an individual to take a particular course of action. (p.453)

In other situations practitioners may be involved in balancing potential gains from intervention, including an assessment of need versus the risks associated with doing nothing. In others they may be crucial in developing the skills of user self-assessment.

Whilst prognosis and treatment may be important influences on social needs they are only part of the whole picture and need to be assessed in the terms of the user's perception. Smale and Tuson (1993) very usefully distinguish between questioning and exchange models of assessment. Many of the features of the exchange model reflect earlier discussion in this chapter. The basic assumption is that users are expert in themselves, but that the social worker brings expertise in the process of problem solving, including a willingness to share perceptions of problems, to negotiate with others about tasks and responsibilities in providing support. In this way workers can aim to move towards a model in which needs are user defined, support can be provided flexibly, in terms of amount, timing and type, under maximum user control. Listening to users' views would entail moving from a reactive crisis management service to a proactive crisis prevention service, in which help would be provided in case of unforeseeable crisis and as circumstances change (Zarb 1991).

Jo's social worker had information to impart about the risks of being dependent on possibly unreliable carers and she could estimate the financial costs of Jo moving into her own accommodation. Whilst Jo needed this information and it may appear to be objective, it has to be set within the social worker's own subjective perceptions of Jo's situation and the services for which she, as a social worker, was 'gatekeeper'. In addition to this information Jo needed help in problem solving, in weighing up the positive and negative risks, in acknowledging the unknown and in recognizing the needs of her mother. A social worker who recognized that she, herself, is using both objective and subjective perceptions of risk and was able to share these and negotiate with the other participants could have helped Jo to develop her own risk estimating skills. The discussion between the various actors could then have come under Jo's control and the focus could move to addressing the risky situations rather than avoiding them.

Points for Practice: *Making Choices*

- Achieving personal choice, maximum independence, dignity and control may involve risk taking where there are possible undesirable outcomes as well as possible rewards.

- Needs-led assessment involves risk assessment, including unmet needs.

- Advice and guidance can very easily slip into coercion when workers are anxious about the effects of mental ill health on users' ability to to make appropriate judgements about risks.

- An exchange model of assessment assumes that the worker has expertise in problem solving. The user has expertise about the problem.

CONCLUSION: THE SHARP EDGES

Concepts of empowerment to which we have constantly referred sharply focus the long running and familiar debate in social work between protection and autonomy. In this case, it is protection from the negative consequences of risk taking and autonomy in maximizing the positive potentials of risk taking, rather than neglect simply reclothed as empowerment (Kemshall, personal communication 1995). As Stevenson (1994) has remarked, how these debates are negotiated 'will be critical in establishing social work's claims to credible status as a distinctive occupation, with a sound ethical basis and a reasonably secure body of knowledge and skills, which is not dominated by political imperatives and populist influences' (Stevenson 1994, p.170).

Risk is unlikely to disappear from the social work agenda. Proposals for post-qualifying training clearly give it importance (CCETSW 1992). Moreover, social workers will continue to be at the sharp end of reconciling policy with practice, especially in the shape of issues of documenting unmet need. Skilful supervision will remain crucial in helping practitioners resolve boundary issues, concentrate on their helping role, embody professional values and implement agency strategic purposes.

We have attempted to give some indications of the way risk may be defined in this context, in both objective and subjective terms. The identification and recognition of hazards and potential dangers to users, carers and social workers, the differences between acceptable and reasonable risk and the need for protection are not peculiar to people with physical disabilities. For, as Lonsdale (1990) warns social workers should guard against the assumption the risks arising from disability are isolated from other issues.

REFERENCES

Abberley, P. (1991) 'The significance of the OPCS disability surveys.' In M. Oliver (ed) *Social Work – Disabled People and Disabling Environments.* London: Jessica Kingsley Publishers.

Alaszewski, A., Harrison, L., Manthorpe, J. and Walsh, M. (1994) *Risk and Social Welfare.* Institute of Health Studies: Hull, University of Hull.

Audit Commission (1992) *The Community Revolution: Personal Social Services and Community Care.* London: HMSO.

Barnes, C. (1991) *Disabled People in Britain and Discrimination: A Case for Anti-Discrimination Legislation.* London: Hurst.

Barnes, C. and Oliver, M. (1995) 'Disability rights: rhetoric and reality in the UK.' *Disability and Society 10,* 1. 111–116.

Beardshaw, V. (1988) *Last on the List: Community Services for People with Physical Disabilities.* London: Kings Fund.

Biehal, N. (1993) 'Changing practice: Participation, rights and community care.' *British Journal of Social Work 23,* 5, October 1993, 443–458.

Brearley, P. (1982) *Risk and Social Work.* London: Routledge and Kegan Paul.

Carver, V. (1982) *The Individual Behind the Statistic.* Milton Keynes: Open University Press.

CCETSW (1992) *Post Qualifying Education and Training: A Framework.* London: CCETSW.

Connolly, N. (1990) *Raising Voices: Social Service Departments and People with Physical Disabilities.* London: Policy Studies Institute.

Corker, M. (1993) 'Integration and deaf people: the policy and power of enabling environments.' In J. Swain, V. Finkelstein, S. French and M. Oliver (eds) *Disabling Barriers – Enabling Environments.* Milton Keynes: Open University Press.

Department of Health (1989) *Caring for People.* London: HMSO.

Department of Health (1991) *Care Management and Assessment, Practitioners Guide.* London: HMSO.

Fiedler, B. (1988) *Living Options Lottery: Housing and Support Services for People with Severe Physical Disabilities.* London: The Prince of Wales' Advisory Group on Disability.

Finkelstein, V. (1993) 'The commonality of disability.' In J. Swain, V. Finkelstein, S. French and M. Oliver (eds) *Disabling Barriers – Enabling Environments.* Milton Keynes: Open University Press.

Fitton, P., O'Brien, C. and Wilson, J. (1995) *Home at Last: How Two Young Women with Profound Intellectual and Multiple Disabilities Achieved their own Home.* London: Jessica Kingsley Publishers.

Flood, R.L. and Carson, E.R. (1993) *Dealing with Complexity.* New York: Plenum.

French, S. (1993a) 'Can you see the rainbow? The roots of denial.' In J. Swain, V. Finkelstein, S. French and M. Oliver (eds) *Disabling Barriers – Enabling Environments.* Milton Keynes: Open University Press.

French, S. (1993b) 'What's so great about independence?' In J. Swain, V. Finkelstein, S. French and M. Oliver (eds) *Disabling Barriers – Enabling Environments.* Milton Keynes: Open University Press.

Green, C.H., Tunstall, S.M. and Fordham, M. (1991) 'The risks from flooding: which risk and whose perception?' *Disasters 15,* 227–236.

Harrison, J. (1993) 'Medical responsibilities to disabled people.' In J. Swain, V. Finkelstein, S. French and M. Oliver (eds) *Disabling Barriers – Enabling Environments.* Milton Keynes, Open University Press.

Hood, C., Jones, D.N.C., Pidgeon, N.F., Turner, B.A. and Gibson, R. (1992) *Risk Management. Risk, Analysis, Perception and Management: Report of a Royal Society Study Group.* London: The Royal Society.

Hughes, B., (1993) 'A model for the comprehensive assessment of older people and their carers.' *British Journal of Social Work 23,* 345–364.

Hunter, D. (ed) (1988) *Bridging the Gap.* London: Kings Fund.

Lonsdale, S. (1990) *Women and Disability.* Basingstoke: Macmillan.

Martin, J. and White, A. (1988) *Report 2. The Financial Circumstances of Disabled Adults in Private Households.* London: HMSO.

Morris, J. (1991) *Pride against Prejudice.* London: Women's Press.

Morris, J. (1993a) 'Housing, independent living and physically disabled people.' In J. Swain, V. Finkelstein, S. French and M. Oliver (eds) *Disabling Barriers – Enabling Environments.* Milton Keynes: Open University Press.

Morris, J. (1993b) *Community Care or Independent Living?* York: Joseph Rowntree Foundation.

Norman, A.J. (1980) *Rights and Risk: A Discussion Document on Civil Liberty in Old Age*. London: National Corporation for the Care of Old People.

Oliver, M. (1983) *Social Work With Disabled People*. Basingstoke: Macmillan.

Oliver, M. (1990) *The Politics of Disablement*. Basingstoke: Macmillan.

Oliver, M. (1991) 'From disabling to supportive environments.' In M. Oliver (ed) *Social Work – Disabled People and Disabling Environments*. London: Jessica Kingsley.

Oliver, M. (1993) 'Info: the voice of disabled people in Derbyshire.' In *Derbyshire Coalition of Disabled People and Derbyshire Centre for Integrated Living 10*.

Oliver, M. and Barnes, C. (1991) 'Discrimination, disability and welfare: from needs to rights.' In M. Oliver and C. Barnes (eds) *Equal Rights for Disabled People*. London: Institute for Public Policy Research.

Parker, G. (1992) *With This Body: Caring, Disability and Marriage*. Milton Keynes: Open University Press.

RADAR (1994) *Disabled People have Rights*. London: RADAR.

Renn, O., Burns, W.J., Kasperson, J.X. and Kasperson, R.E. (1992) 'The social amplification of risk: theoretical foundations and empirical applications.' *Journal of Social Issues 48*, 4, 137–160.

Robinson, I. (1987) *Re-evaluating Housing for People with Disabilities in Hammersmith and Fulham*. London: Borough of Hammersmith and Fulham and Brunel University.

Sapey, B. and Hewitt, N. (1991) 'The changing context of social work practice.' In M. Oliver (ed) *Social Work – Disabled People and Disabling Environments*. London: Jessica Kingsley.

Smale, G. and Tuson, G. with Biehal, N. and Marsh, P (1993) *Empowerment, Assessment and Care Management and the Skilled Worker*. London: HMSO.

Social Services Inspectorate (1990) *Assessment 'Getting the Message Across'*. London: HMSO.

Stevenson, O. and Parsloe, P. (1993) *Community Care and Empowerment*. York: Joseph Rowntree Foundation.

Stevenson, O. (1994) 'Social work in the 1990s: empowerment – fact or fiction?.' In R. Page and J. Baldock (eds) *Social Policy Review 6*. Canterbury: Social Policy Association.

Vujakovic, P. and Matthews, M.H. (1994) 'Contorted, folded and torn: environmental values, cartographic representation and the politics of disability.' *Disability and Society 9*, 3, 359–374.

Wharton, F. (1992) *Risk Management: Basic Concepts and General Principles*. Chichester: John Wiley.

Williams, P. Waterson, J. and Willetts, G. (1994) *Reaching the Needs of People with Visual Disabilities: A Community Care Training Package*. London: Royal National Institute for the Blind with HMSO.

Woolley, M. (1993) 'Acquired hearing loss: acquired oppression.' In J. Swain, V. Finkelstein, S. French and M. Oliver (eds) *Disabling Barriers – Enabling Environments*. Milton Keynes: Open University Press.

Zarb, G. (1991) 'Creating a supportive environment: Meeting the needs of people who are ageing with a disability.' In M. Oliver (ed) *Social Work – Disabled People and Disabling Environments*. London: Jessica Kingsley Publishers.

Zarb, G. and Nadash, P. (1994) *Cashing in on Independence: Comparing the costs and benefits of cash and services*. British Council of Organisations of Disabled People.

Zola, I.K. (1989) 'Towards the necessary universalizing of a disability policy.' *Millbank Quarterly 47*, suppl. 2, pt 2, 401–428.

CHAPTER 7

RISK MANAGEMENT AND PEOPLE WITH MENTAL HEALTH PROBLEMS

Tony Ryan

INTRODUCTION

Public concern over the safety of people with mental health problems living in the community has increased in recent years. This is the result of high profile incidents and subsequent inquiries into the deaths of Jonathan Zito (Sheperd 1995), Georgina Robinson (Blom-Cooper, Hally and Murphy 1995) and Frederick Graver (Heginbotham *et al.* 1994) among others. Media attention has also focused on the danger which the mentally ill pose to themselves. This was typified by the case of Ben Silcock who went into the lions' den at London Zoo. Along with such attention there has been a call for the effective assessment and management of risk in relation to the mentally ill living in the community. In the field of mental illness the term 'risk management' has become synonymous with the management of danger or threats of danger to the public. It has also been associated with the mentally ill self-harming and harming those carers and professionals who have the closest contact with them.

Whilst risk management can also have positive features, as in the case of carefully planned and monitored regimes of rehabilitation (Carson 1988; Ryan 1993), the primary concern here is with the management of harms and dangers. From the outset it should be noted that there can never be a risk free environment or situation. To talk of risk management in terms of risk removal is unhelpful and raises expectation to levels which are impossible to obtain in reality. From the outset it must be stressed that there will always be occasions where someone with a mental health problem is involved in a situation which results in harms. Consequently, for the purposes of this chapter, risk management will be defined as the minimization of dangers, both to and from, the individual with the mental health problem.

This chapter covers the nature of risk and factors which affect its management in this field. The range of risks which people can face as a consequence of mental illness is clarified and issues for practitioners and their managers are highlighted. The current framework for risk management provided by legislation, policy and practice is discussed and issues for practitioners and managers are also explored.

THE NATURE OF RISK

Research has shown that risk is a complex and multifaceted concept. However, there are several things known about risk which are useful to think of when working within the mental health field.

Perceptions of risk are individual and can be affected by a range of personal factors. The amount of information available about a particular risk will affect how people regard its likelihood (Kahneman, Slovic and Tversky 1982). The more information that is available on a potential risk event, the more it will be regarded as likely to occur (Tversky and Kahneman 1973; Combs and Slovic 1979; Kahneman et al. 1982). Thus, following widespread publicity of a murder or other violent act by a person with a mental illness, the public perception of the likelihood of the risk occurring will increase, even though the likelihood is no greater in reality than it was before the event. However, the possibility of a copycat phenomenon cannot be discounted from the resulting media publicity.

Factors which have been found to influence how people perceive risks include the degree of control they believe they have over the risk, whether or not it is voluntarily taken on, how evenly its affects are distributed, how time affects the risk and how familiar people are with the risk (Slovic, Fischhoff and Lichtenstein 1980). The perception of risk is also affected by whether the risk is regarded as an individual or societal risk (Green and Brown 1978), and if it is viewed as a public or private risk (Brun 1992). A risk can also be presented positively or negatively, as opportunity or threat, both of which can affect how the risk is perceived (Kahneman and Tversky 1984).

Risk perceptions are also affected by our interactions with others. Risks are rarely perceived in isolation and can be used as an expression of social solidarity (Douglas and Wildavsky 1982). This can be seen where NIMBY (not-in-my-back-yard) occurs in a neighbourhood when there is a proposal for a new mental health facility.

Within organizations risk is related to decision making processes. Many larger organizations operate on the premise that risk decisions are not made in isolation. Bureaucratic systems operate where one decision triggers another. In theory this means that the decision which triggered the undesired event can be traced and the individual who made it can be held to account. Security is gained from the knowledge that a number of people are involved in the risk decision. However, when the undesired event occurs it often leads to scapegoating rather than an analysis of the processes which the organization used to reach the risk decision. This can often be seen in cases which get to court or tribunal where the 'hindsight effect' is evident and particularly where it cannot be demonstrated that all the available information was fully utilized (Carson 1994).

In mental health care there is at present an increasing emphasis upon individual accountability which is likely to be followed closely by service accountability. Larger organizations must be seen to be doing everything to protect the public. After an undesired event they must take every precaution possible, no matter how remote the risk, to avoid the possibility of repetition. On the other hand smaller organizations have to embrace risks simply to survive. As a result they can be more flexible in the way they deal with risks (Luhmann 1993).

Risk, the Law and the Practitioner

The role of the law is to strike a balance between risk-takers, the prospective risks and the individuals who may be on the wrong end of the risk (Coleman 1992). The law makes people responsible for their behaviours, whether or not they were well intended.

Through contract law risks are allocated before the event, usually through insurance which spreads the risk. This is increasingly being used as a method of protection by practitioners through membership of professional bodies and by their employers through pooling schemes designed to spread the financial risk.

After undesired events occur the law allocates risks through tort law and liability. Individual practitioners can be held liable in several ways. These include negligence for which the practitioner can be placed at fault irrespective of their motive. The other form of liability which is most pertinent in this field is that of a breach of duty. Where a practitioner has a duty of care and fails to take the necessary care they can be deemed liable. The duty of care may extend beyond the practitioner's clients to a relative, a colleague or a member of the public. Whilst unintentional injury may lead to liability it should be stressed that intentional injury is even harder to defend in court! For a fuller exposition of these issues the reader is encouraged to refer to the chapter in this book by David Carson.

Many defence mechanisms are frequently employed by practitioners in difficult situations which need to be recognized and dealt with in order to avoid the possibility of liability. Table 7.1 covers a small but not insignificant sample of these mechanisms and associated issues.

Table 7.1 Practitioner issues which can lead to liability

Avoiding areas of work which are difficult

Not keeping updated with new practices and policies

Relying on other team members to cover up

Failing to acknowledge deficits in theoretical and practical skills

Being unclear about boundaries

'Burn-out' through being in a high stress role too long

'Rust-out' through being in a low stress role too long

Trusting to 'gut feelings'

Victim (service user/carer) blaming

By contrast there are only a small number of legal defences which can be used to avoid liability (Table 7.2).

Table 7.2 Legal defences
Where informed consent is freely given
Where the event was genuinely accidental
Where injury occurred as a result of a necessary act
Statutory authority
Acts of God

MENTAL ILLNESS RISKS AND PRACTICE ISSUES

Current policy relating to the mentally ill is concerned with those people whose illness is severe and disabling. A deliberate targeting of those at the 'heavy end' is now taking place. The three areas of highest concern are related to those people who present a risk of serious violence to others, risk of self-harm or risk of severe self-neglect (National Health Service Management Executive (NHSME) 1994). Virtuous though this may be it does not mean that mentally ill people, their carers, professionals and the general public do not experience other risks as a result of mental illnesses. Many of the everyday risks which the mentally ill face do not grab media attention in the same way which homicides and suicides do. Nevertheless they still have a dramatic impact upon those involved. Consequently, it is worth reviewing the range of risks from a practitioner perspective.

Social Risks

Often as a result of being diagnosed with a mental illness there comes a social stigma (Goffman 1963). Stereotypical images of mental illness learned from childhood and re-inforced through the mass media often contribute to people being socially isolated, scapegoated and suffering the effects of NIMBY (Philo, McLaughlin and Henderson 1993). For many practitioners this can be one of the most demoralizing aspects of mental illness as it can reduce the possibility of real integration and leave the client feeling rejected and unwanted by all but their professionals. Consequently, many of the most meaningful relationships for clients can be with their practitioners (Meeks and Murrell 1994) as the professionals and other service users become the major constituents of client social networks when they have been in services for a length of time (Holmes-Elber and Riger 1990).

Iatrogenic Risks

Once taken into the mental health care system people can experience many unintentioned yet unnecessary side-effects of the system. Not only does the mental health care system cause social effects but it can also leave lasting physical damage. Some of the effects are not immediately visible because of their insidious nature such as the long term side-effects of medications or electro-convulsive therapy. Other side-effects of the medications become apparent quicker as with tardive dyskinesia or oculogyric crisis which can be alarming to both the client and also those around them (British Medical Association and Royal Pharmaceutical Society of Great Britain 1992). Some of the involuntary movements which result from the medications can also be irreversible and reinforce stigmatizing (Rogers, Pilgrim and Lacey 1993).

For the practitioner this often means that their role includes advocating on behalf of those who cannot advocate for themselves because of their condition, albeit from a position of vested interest. The role of educator in relation to the effects of treatments is also important. Therefore, knowledge of the effects of treatments, or at least how to obtain such information is vital, particularly where unnecessary distress can be avoided.

Abuse Risks

People with mental illnesses have always been exposed to the risk of abuse from those around them. This has been as true of those who provide their services as those members of the public who regard the mentally ill as easy prey. Over the past 30 years there has been a series of inquiries into the institutions where they have been cared for (DHSS 1972; DHSS 1980; HAS and DHSS 1987; DoH and SHSA 1992).

Frequently it is clear to practitioners what actions need to be taken when abuse within the communities or even families occur. Usually this means involving statutory bodies and probably the criminal justice system. However, the issues surrounding professional abuse can be more difficult because the scope of the practitioner to be truly objective can be impaired by a range of factors. Whistleblowing is a stressful issue for all concerned but necessary if services are to become truly client-centred. Consequently, there is a role for professional bodies and service managers in handling these issues with sensitivity and in as confidential and supportive manner as possible. How such issues are dealt with the first time round can determine whether or not they are raised in the future. Being prepared to put the profession and the service under scrutiny always places the practitioner in a difficult situation. However, it was often because the rights of the client were placed second to those of the service and its staff that many of the public inquiries of the past took place. Whilst inquiries once focused upon institutions they now tend to focus upon individuals and in the future this will also mean practitioners as well as the mentally ill. It is possible that practitioners will increasingly become targeted for not disclosing bad practice or suspected abuse by their fellow professionals.

Homelessness

Debate continues on whether homelessness is a risk factor for mental illness or the reverse is the case. It is probably fair to say that one probably contributes to the other. Surveys have shown that between 25 and 45 per cent of homeless people have a mental illness (Leff 1993). A study in London showed that 30 per cent of people using a hostel for the homeless had been diagnosed as schizophrenic before they had become homeless (Timms and Fry 1989). While there is a strong belief among the general public that the closure of mental hospitals and homelessness are interlinked, only a small number of former long-stay patients end up homeless (Leff 1993). Many experience transinstitutionalization where they have been decarcerated from psychiatric hospitals to other forms of high level support such as residential and nursing homes (Brown 1985; Lamb 1989). It is probable that people who are now developing a mental illness are not getting into the services which at one time would have combined treatment with long term accommodation. Consequently it is important that practitioners recognize that risk management in this context can mean dealing with housing problems to assist with mental health problems.

Imprisonment

As with mental illness and homelessness, there is evidence to suggest that a link exists between mental illness and imprisonment. One large study found that over 38 per cent of all sentenced prisoners had a mental illness (Gunn, Maden and Swinton 1991). This has prompted suggestions that such figures have been swollen by people who previously would have resided on long stay hospital wards and who are now without appropriate alternatives (Murphy 1991).

A further point on the issue of imprisonment is that of length of custody. Where people have received a custodial sentence and are then transferred to forensic psychiatric services for treatment they often spend greater periods of time imprisoned because the time spent undergoing treatment does not count towards their sentence (Pilgrim and Rogers 1993). Consequently, they run the risk of losing their liberty because of their criminality and also because of their illness (Campbell and Heginbotham 1991).

A major issue in respect of the interrelationship between criminality and mental illness is the question of which process is better for the long term mental health of the client: hospital and possible extended incarceration or prison and less specialized treatment, if any? The practitioner needs to be clear about what the overall aim is. Is it to obtain liberty or treatment? Is public safety a priority over treatment? It will often depend upon the individual circumstances, the availability of services and the involvement of specialists who the practitioner can gain access to.

Suicide

The Department of Health estimates that up to 90 per cent of all suicides have some form of mental illness (DoH 1993) and have therefore made the reduction of suicide a target of future policy (DoH 1992). It is the leading cause of unnatural death for people suffering from depression (Charlton et al. 1993) and from schizophrenia (Gottesman 1991). In 1991 there were 5567 recorded suicides in England (DoH 1992) and it is probably fair to assume that the actual number was greater as many suicides may have been recorded as open verdicts. It is interesting to note that the number of in-patient suicides has steadily increased since the 1950s as the total in-patient population has decreased (WHO 1982). Between 1991 and 1993 there were 72 deaths from self harm by psychiatric in-patients (Mental Health Act Commission 1993).

There are a range of socio-demographic factors which relate to increased risk of suicide in the general population and are significant in relation to people with mental health problems (Table 7.3).

Table 7.3 Risk factors for suicide
Elderly
Male
Divorced, widowed or single
Unemployed or retired
Social isolation or living alone
Terminal illness
Other major physical illness
History of self-harm
Family history of suicide
Family history of alcoholism or mood disorder
Childhood bereavement
Social classes I and V
Psychiatric illness and personality disorder
(NHS Health Advisory Service 1994)

Access to the means of suicide such as firearms (Fischer, Comstock, Monk and Spencer 1993) and medications (Lester 1994) can also be significant factors in the accomplishment of the act.

Violence and Homicide

Until recently there has been a strong rejection of the link between mental illness and violence by many academics and advocacy groups with many choosing to focus upon the greater association with self-harm (Prins 1990). However, in recent years there has been an acknowledgement that mental illness may be one among several factors which increase the risk of violence. These factors include male gender, youth, drug or alcohol misuse and low socio-economic status. When these other factors are taken into account it would appear that mental illness as a risk factor for violence is minimal (Monahan 1992).

Despite much media attention on indiscriminate acts of violence by the mentally ill there is considerable evidence to suggest that this is not so. Victims of violence by the mentally ill are usually known to the attacker. There are certain groups where the risk of being attacked is higher than normal. Being a mother living with adult mentally ill children increases the risk of being attacked and this is further increased if there is no father present (Estroff and Zimmer 1994). The risk is also increased by being a carer with no contact with professional services (Estroff and Zimmer 1994). Other groups who are re-garded as being at a greater risk include those who are psychiatric in-patients, particularly females (DoH 1994), and health care professionals dealing with the mentally ill, particularly nurses (Whittington 1994).

Issues of personal safety are often foremost in the minds of practitioners who are working in isolated settings or dealing with people in their own homes. Good practice would suggest that practitioners do not undertake visits alone where they are dealing with people who have a history of violence or work at night in areas where there are known to be high levels of personal violence. Irrespective of whether or not the client is known to have a history of violence it is also good practice to ensure that practitioners know the daily movements of their colleagues and that they have a means of contacting them.

In relation to homicide there were 34 cases of homicide by people with a mental illness between 1991 and 1993 (Steering Committee of the Confidential Inquiry into Homicides and Suicides by Mentally Ill People 1994). Although the numbers concerned are low the early signs from the Confidential Inquiry suggest that males tend to kill adults who are known to them and females are most likely to kill their children. It is rare for homicides to occur at the hands of mentally ill people who are unknown to the victim.

Risk Management Strategies and Practice Issues

Historically, risk management of the mentally ill can be traced back to the Middle Ages where the mentally ill were managed by being driven from towns and cities or cast adrift on 'ships of fools' (Foucault 1971). There followed the period of the Enlightenment where risk management was a profit making industry with the principal method of management being confine-ment and incarceration in private jails and madhouses. The Victorian period saw a continuation of incarceration as a method of risk management but this occurred through separation of the asylums from the rest of the community rather than being placed within it. This allowed the development of psychi-atric treatments as a form of risk management to go virtually unchecked for around 100 years. Treatments of a physical, chemical and psychological basis were all tried and tested to manage the risks which the mentally ill posed to their charges, themselves and their fellow inmates. While some of the treat-ments which were developed by psychiatry had some effects upon symptoms they had little success with the causes. The anti-psychiatry movement her-alded the move towards community based alternatives in the 1960s and the process of decarceration commenced. This brought with it a greater awareness of the risks which the mentally ill posed and faced as they re-entered the spotlight.

Table 7.4: The history of risk management		
Period	*Risk management strategy*	*Risk management site*
Middle Ages	Expulsion	Banishment and Ships of Fools
Enlightenment	Confinement	Private Jails and Madhouses
Victorian Era	Incarceration	Asylums
Early 20th Century	Treatment	Psychiatric Hospitals
Mid 20th Century	Decarceration	Community
Late 20th Century	Integration	Community

Today the issue of managing these risks, whilst integrating the mentally ill into society, is one of the greatest challenges which society now faces. Consequently there are a range of different methods which have been developed to assist this integration.

Policy Driven Structures for Risk Management

Three key initiatives have taken place in recent years which are concerned with the management of the mentally ill. Case management is concerned with the assessment and delivery of care in the community and is the domain of health care professionals (Ryan, Ford and Clifford 1991; Onyett 1992). Care management is concerned with developing, monitoring and funding packages of social care in the community and is the domain of social services professionals (DoH/SSI and SWSG 1991a, 1991b). The Care Programme Approach is an overarching framework which ensures that all parties, including the person with the mental illness, are drawn together to agree a plan of care and applies chiefly to those who have the most severe problems. All three approaches are intended to remedy the problems associated with fragmented and frequently changing services. These are often features which are present in cases which resulted in serious incidents and which could have been avoided.

The 1983 Mental Health Act

The 1983 Mental Health Act is primarily concerned with how people come into contact with services and how treatment is provided. General psychiatry is concerned with the civil sections of the Act where the prime interest is with the treatment of the illness. Commitment can be voluntary, but the Act enables involuntary commitment of those who have not committed criminal acts but are deemed to be in need of treatment because they are a danger to themselves or others.

Forensic psychiatry is concerned with mentally disordered offenders who also come under the Act. Here the prime focus is with the safety of the public and treatment is secondary to safety. Discharge from hospital for mentally

disordered offenders can involve restrictions such as compliance with medication regimes and supervision arrangements. This is increasingly becoming
a feature of community care for the mentally ill who do not have a forensic
history through newly introduced measures.

Supervision Registers

Supervision registers (NHSME 1994) were finally introduced in September
1994 amid a high degree of scepticism and questioning about the ethics of
implementing such measures. The registers have been designed to keep close
scrutiny on people who have difficulty in maintaining contact with services
or who live itinerant lifestyles. Supervision registers are intended to ensure
that those most 'at risk' do not become lost to follow up.

Supervised Aftercare

This plank of community care for the mentally ill is intended to increase
compliance with treatment regimes. There are similarities with probation
orders as supervised aftercare arrangements can compel people to live in a
certain place, attend for treatment, training or education. Failure to do so can
mean that they could be recalled to hospital. The central notion here is that
people who need treatment will receive it before they deteriorate to a degree
whereby they have to be sectioned under the current Mental Health Act.

Clinical Practice as Risk Assessment

The recent spate of high profile incidents concerning people with mental
health problems and the dangers they pose to themselves and others has led
to an increased focus upon trying to predict such possibilities. On the issue of
violence it has been shown that professionals consistently over-predict and
get their predictions wrong 60 per cent of the time (Menzies, Webster and
Sepejak 1985). Professionals are slightly better at predicting in-patient violence but still over-predict (McNiel and Binder 1991). In a recent study in the
United States it was found that the accuracy of clinical predictions of violence
by men with a mental illness was modest, although better than chance, while
for women, clinicians were found to under-predict (Lidz, Mulvey and Gardner 1993).

There are three methods of assessment employed by mental health professionals. Clinical risk assessment is often based on interviewing the person
with the mental illness and some of the people in contact with them. Consequently it involves a strong element of subjectivity and is susceptible to the
biases of the clinician, their theoretical interests and previous experiences.
Actuarial risk assessments, through the use of psychometric scales have been
developed to assess dangerousness (see Campbell 1995) and potential suicide
(see Bowling 1991). Such tools can be dehumanizing, extremely positivistic
and subject to the biases of the developers. The third method of risk assessment is to combine both of these approaches (Carson 1990). This can be
particularly useful when risk-taking is used in rehabilitation or preparing
people for discharge but is limited to those people who are already engaged
with services.

Informal Controls

There are a range of informal methods of risk management employed by professionals and non-professionals alike. Coercion has been recognized as a method of controlling the mentally ill for a long time. Szasz (1963) has argued that voluntary commitment can never truly exist whilst there is involuntary commitment. Recently research has shown that many people regard themselves as having been coerced into hospital even though they were admitted as involuntary or informal patients (Rogers 1993). Several features of perceived coercion have been identified as being present in the process of hospital admission; persuasion, inducement, threats and force (Monahan *et al.* 1995). Many of the forms of coercion practised by professionals are also used by carers and relatives to control risks. Frequently relatives observe the practices of professionals and employ them, or they use the threat of involving professionals, to manage their ill relatives (Estroff and Zimmer 1994).

The practice of assertive outreach (Cohen 1991), a form of not taking no for an answer, which encourages people to engage with services and take medication could also be regarded as a form of coercion. This is primarily because many of the people it is aimed at usually do not want to engage with services.

A third form of informal control is that which operates through social sanctions. Parsons (1951) has suggested that people have a moral and social duty to get better when they are ill. They are expected to comply with anything which will free them from their sick role. Social pressure to admit that something is wrong even when the person disagrees or 'has no insight' can assist informally to control any risk associated with the illness as the person feels obliged to seek help.

CONCLUSIONS

Micro Issues: Individual and Organizational Risk Management

Risk perceptions are affected by a range of different factors which can influence practitioners and those with whom they come in contact. The perceived risk and its effects are worth considering when undertaking work in resettlement, rehabilitation, mental health promotion and service development in community settings. As highlighted previously, the management of risk is subject to a complex array of personal, group and organizational factors which can distort how risks are perceived and therefore how they are responded to. Like the risks which practitioners and managers are attempting to manage, the processes and strategies of risk management are also dynamic.

Organizational structure and culture can affect the way that risk management is carried out. Most larger organizations tend to be risk-averse while small organizations are inclined towards being risk-accustomed. Frequently this is reflected in the types of people they attract and risk management styles. The philosophy of empowering service users which is present in most health and social care arenas is often incongruous with the nature of larger organizations. Since a significant proportion of mental health services are provided by statutory organizations with risk-averse cultures this can create ambivalence for practitioners. It is here that managers of mental health services have the most significant part to play in risk management. Open acknowledgement that we can only strive towards, but never achieve, working within risk-free environments and with risk-free people is a useful basis for risk management. Support for practitioners through clear risk management polices and a commitment to system analysis rather than scapegoating is also a key component of effective risk management.

Macro Issues: Practice and Policy and Risk Management

A key feature which influences risk management is the nature of risk in mental health services where it is regarded in the negative. Rarely is it viewed as a method of empowerment which allows people to become independent of services. In recent years the practice of rehabilitation with therapeutic risk-taking (see Ryan 1993), has received less interest as prevention and crisis intervention services have been developed. This has resulted from a political rather than a clinical definition of risk in mental health care. The focus, whilst understandable, upon the 'big risks' as opposed to 'all risks' has meant that the conflict between philosophy and practice has been exacerbated as the defining of risk is not client or practitioner centred.

The thrust of the current approaches to risk management has been primarily administrative through centralized policy. However, the range of generally similar measures which have been introduced have almost certainly led to confusion among service users, their carers and probably among many practitioners. How case management and care management operate and fit with the Care Programme Approach can be hard to comprehend. Furthermore, the prime benefit of supervision registers in tracking people across boundaries would appear to have been lost as they have been set up locally without central coordination.

Finally, the 1983 Mental Health Act would appear to be in drastic need of revision. It is concerned mainly with hospital admission and treatment. Since the introduction of the Act there has been a significant emphasis placed upon the provision of care in community settings. Consequently, a new Act could address many of the issues which this redirection has thrown up. A new Act could cover the rights of the mentally ill, their carers and the general public, the treatment of people in alternative settings to hospital and liability issues relating to providers and purchasers of mental health services. It could also bring together the range of recent policy initiatives thereby increasing clarity for all concerned and reducing the accompanying risks both from and to people with mental health problems as a result.

Finally, and most important, a new Act could divert some of the emphasis away from engaging simply in risk minimization. A clear position on the role of positive risk taking as a therapeutic and empowering tool is critical. Without such a precise remit in legislation service managers and practitioners are likely to err on the side of conservative practice.

REFERENCES

Blom-Cooper, L., Hally, H. and Murphy, M. (1995) *The Falling Shadow: One Patient's Mental Health Care 1978–1993*. London: Duckworth.

Bowling, A. (1991) *Measuring Health: A Review of Quality of Life Measurement Scales*. Milton Keynes: Open University Press.

British Medical Association and Royal Pharmaceutical Society of Great Britain (1992) British National Formulary, No. 24. London, Pharmaceutical Press.

Brown, P. (1985) *The Transfer of Care*. London: Routledge and Kegan Paul.

Brun, W. (1992) 'Cognitive components of risk perception: natural versus man-made risks.' *Journal of Behavioural Decision Making 5*, 2, 117–132.

Campbell, J.C. (ed) (1995) *Assessing Dangerousness: Violence by Sexual Offenders, Batterers and Child Abusers*. London: Sage.

Campbell, T., and Heginbotham, C. (1991) *Mental Illness: Prejudice, Discrimination and the Law*. Dartmouth: Aldershot.

Carson, D. (1988) 'Taking risks with your patients – your assessment strategy.' *Professional Nurse 3*, 7, 247–250.

Carson, D. (1990) 'Risk-taking in mental disorder.' In D. Carson (ed) *Risk-taking in Mental Disorder; Analyses, Policies and Practical Strategies*. Chichester: SLE Publications.

Carson, D. (1994) 'Presenting risk options.' *Inside Psychology 1*, 1, 3–7.

Charlton, J., Kelly, S., Dunnell, K., Evans, B. and Jenkins, R. (1993) 'Suicide deaths in England and Wales: Trends in factors associated with suicide deaths.' *Population Trends 71*, 34–42.

Cohen, N.L. (ed) (1991) *Psychiatric Outreach to the Mentally Ill*. San Francisco: Jossey-Bass.

Coleman, J.L. (1992) *Risks and Wrongs*. Cambridge: Cambridge University Press.

Combs, B. and Slovic, P. (1979) 'Causes of death: biased newspaper coverage and biased judgements.' *Journalism Quarterly 56*, 2, 837–843.

Department of Health (1992) *The Health of the Nation. A Consultative Document for England and Wales*. London: HMSO.

Department of Health (1993) *The Health of the Nation. Key Area Handbook: Mental Illness*. London: Department of Health.

Department of Health (1994) *Working in Partnership: A Collaborative Approach to Care*. London: HMSO.

Department of Health and Social Services (1972) *Report of the Committee of Inquiry into Whittingham Hospital*. London: HMSO.

Department of Health and Social Services (1980) *Report of the Review of Rampton Hospital*. London: HMSO.

Department of Health Social Services Inspectorate and Scottish Office Social Work Services Group (1991a) *Care Management and Assessment: Practitioners' Guide*. London: HMSO.

Department of Health Social Services Inspectorate and Scottish Office Social Work Services Group (1991b) *Care Management and Assessment: Managers' Guide*. London: HMSO.

Department of Health and Special Hospital Service Authority (1992) *Report of the Committee of Inquiry into Complaints About Ashworth Hospital, Volume 1.* London: HMSO.

Douglas, M., and Wildavsky, A. (1982) *Risk and Culture: An Essay on the Selection of Technological and Environmental Dangers.* Berkeley: University of California Press.

Estroff, S.E., and Zimmer, C. (1994) 'Social networks, social support, and violence among persons with severe persistent mental illness.' In J. Monahan and H. Steadman (eds) *Violence and Mental Disorder: Developments in risk assessments.* Chicago: University of Chicago Press.

Fischer, E.P., Comstock, G.W., Monk, M.A., and Sencer, D.J. (1993) 'Characteristics of completed suicides: Implications of differences among methods.' *Suicide and Life Threatening Behaviour 23,* 2, 91–100.

Foucault, M. (1971) *Madness and Civilisation: A History of Insanity in the Age of Reason.* London: Tavistock.

Goffman, E. (1963) *Stigma: Notes on the Management of Spoiled Identity.* New Jersey: Prentice Hall.

Gottesman, I.I. (1991) *Schizophrenia Genesis: The Origins of Madness.* New York: WH Freeman and Company.

Green, C.H., and Brown, R.A. (1978) 'Counting lives.' *Journal of Occupational Accidents 2,* 1, 55–70.

Gunn, J., Maden, T., and Swinton, M. (1991) *Mentally Disordered Prisoners.* London: Report of the Home Office.

Health Advisory Service (NHS) and DHSS Social Services Inspectorate (1987) Report on the Services provided by Broadmoor Hospital: HAS/SSI(88)SH.

Heginbotham, C., Hale, R., Warren, L., Walsh, T. and Carr, J. (1994) The Report of the Independent Panel of Inquiry Examining the Case of Michael Robinson. London: North West London Mental Health NHS Trust.

Holmes-Elber, P. and Riger, S. (1990) 'Hospitalization and the composition of mental patients' social networks.' *Schizophrenia Bulletin 16,* 1, 157–164.

Kahneman, D., Slovic, P. and Tversky, A. (eds) (1982) *Judgement Under Uncertainty: Heuristics and Biases.* Cambridge: Cambridge University Press.

Kahneman, D. and Tversky, A. (1984) 'Choices, values and frames.' *American Psychologist 39,* 4, 341–350.

Lamb, H. (1989) 'Deinstitutionalisation at the crossroads.' *Hospital and Community Psychiatry 39,* 9, 941–945.

Leff, J. (1993) 'All the homeless people – where do they all come from?' *British Medical Journal 306,* 6879, 669–670.

Lester, D. (1994) 'Estimates of prescription rates and the use of medications for suicide.' *European Journal of Psychiatry 8,* 2, 81–83.

Lidz, C.W., Mulvey, E.P. and Gardner, W. (1993) 'The accuracy of predictions of violence to others.' *Journal of the American Medical Association 269,* 8, 1007–1011.

Luhmann, N. (1993) *Risk: A Sociological Theory.* New York: de Gruyter.

McNiel, D.E. and Binder, R.L. (1991) 'Clinical assessment of the risk of violence among psychiatric inpatients.' *American Journal of Psychiatry 148,* 10, 1317–1321.

Meeks, S., and Murrell, S.A. (1994) 'Service providers in the social networks of clients with severe mental illness.' *Schizophrenia Bulletin 20,* 2, 399–406.

Mental Health Act Commission (1993) Fifth Biennial Report 1991–1993. London: HMSO.

Menzies, R.J., Webster, C.D. and Sepejak, D.S. (1985) 'Hitting the forensic sound barrier: Predictions of dangerousness in a pre-trial psychiatric clinic.' In C.D. Webster, M.H. Ben-Aron and S.J. Hucker (eds) *Dangerousness: Probability and Prediction, Psychiatry and Public Policy*. New York: Cambridge University Press.

Monahan, J. (1992) 'Mental disorder and violent behaviour; Perceptions and evidence.' *American Psychologist 47*, 4, 511–521.

Monahan, J., Hoge, S.K., Lidz, C.W., Eisenberg, M.M., Bennett, N.S., Gardner, W.P., Mulvey, E.P. and Roth, L.H. (In press) 'Coercion in inpatient treatment: Initial results and implications for assertive treatment in the community.' In D. Dennis and J. Monahan (eds) *Coercion and Aggressive Community Treatment: A New Frontier in Mental Health Law*. New York: Plenum Publishing Corporation.

Murphy, E. (1991) *After the Asylums*. London: Faber and Faber.

National Health Service Health Advisory Service (1994) *Suicide Prevention: The Challenge Confronted*. London: HMSO.

National Health Service Management Executive (1994) *The Introduction of Supervision Registers for Mentally Ill people*. London: HMSO.

Onyett, S. (1992) *Case Management in Mental Health*. London: Chapman and Hall.

Parsons, T. (1951) *The Social System*. London: Routledge and Kegan Paul.

Philo, G., McLaughlin, G., and Henderson, L. (1993) *Mass Media Representation of Mental Health/Illness*. Report for Health Education Board for Scotland. Glasgow: University Media Group.

Pilgrim, D. and Rogers, A. (1993) *A Sociology of Mental Health and Illness*. Buckingham: Open University Press.

Prins, H. (1990) 'Dangerousness: A review.' In R. Bluglass and P. Bowden (eds) *Principles and Practice of Forensic Psychiatry*. London: Churchill Livingstone.

Rogers, A. (1993) 'Coercion and "voluntary" admissions: An examination of psychiatric patients' views.' *Behavioral Sciences and the Law 11*, 3, 259–268.

Rogers, A., Pilgrim, D. and Lacey, R. (1993) *Experiencing Psychiatry: Users' Views of Services*. Basingstoke: MacMillan.

Ryan, P., Ford, R. and Clifford, P. (1991) *Case Management and Community Care*. London: Research and Development for Psychiatry.

Ryan, T. (1993) 'Therapeutic risks in mental health nursing.' *Nursing Standard 7*, 24, 29–31.

Sheperd, D. (1995) *Learning the Lessons: Mental Health Inquiry Reports Published in England and Wales Between 1969–1994 and their Recommendations for Improving Practice*. London: Zito Trust.

Slovic, P., Fischhoff, B., and Lichtenstein, S. (1980) 'Facts and fears: understanding perceived risk.' In R.C. Schwing and W.A. Albers (eds) *Societal Risk Assessment: How Safe is Safe Enough*. New York: Plenum Press.

Steering Committee of the Confidential Inquiry into Homicides and Suicides by Mentally Ill People (1994) A Preliminary Report on Homicide. London: Steering Committee of the Confidential Inquiry into Homicides and Suicides by Mentally Ill People.

Szasz, T. (1963) *Law, Liberty and Psychiatry*. New York: Macmillan.

Timms, P.W., and Fry, A.H. (1989) 'Homelessness and mental illness.' *Health Trends* 21, 3, 70–71.

Tversky, A., and Kahneman, D. (1973) 'Availability: a heuristic for judging frequency and probability.' *Cognitive Psychology 5*, 2, 207–232.

Whittington, R. (1994) 'Violence in psychiatric hospitals.' In T. Wykes (ed) *Violence and Mental Health Care Professionals*. London, Chapman and Hall.

World Health Organisation (WHO) (1982) *Changing Patterns in Suicidal Behaviour*. Euro Report and Studies 74. Copenhagen: WHO.

ACKNOWLEDGEMENTS

I would like to express my gratitude to Keith Soothill and Janis Williamson for their encouragement and support throughout the preparation of this chapter.

CHAPTER 8

RISK WORK AND MENTAL HEALTH

Ann Davis

INTRODUCTION

Risk and risk taking are intrinsic to mental health social work practice. On a daily basis mental health practitioners and service users find themselves assessing, taking and managing risks. Risk work spans decisions about major life changes, moving into and out of relationships, judging the competence of individuals to exercise choice in their lives, assessing the degree of protection which an individual may require to live in safety. Risk work can influence the responses which workers and service users make to abuse, violence and physical threat in community and service environments. It is central to working with self-harm and self-neglect. Risk may play a part in assessments made by Approved Social Workers for possible admission under the Mental Health Act 1983. It is certainly part of the way in which decisions are being reached about the allocation of scarce resources in the mental health system. Indeed as Ramon has suggested for many people involved in the field of mental health 'dealing with the partially unknown: is part of the attraction of the work' (Ramon 1992, p.93).

Currently risk has a high profile in the mental health arena. It is an issue which is actively shaping debates about mental health policy, law and service response. Mental health practitioners are finding that concerns about risk minimization, assessment and management are playing an increasingly dominant part in determining their day-to-day practice priorities as well as their negotiations to obtain resources for service users. At the same time the agendas which have developed over the last decade around user involvement, empowerment and anti-oppressive mental health social work practice are suggesting that practitioners should view risk taking as a potentially positive element in working to extend the strengths and opportunities of people using mental health services (Braye and Preston-Shoot 1995).

The way in which risk is being defined in this field is embedded in differing, and at times conflicting, perceptions of mental health and illness. It is also shaped by a service context in which an increasingly complex and fragmented range of agencies are purchasing and providing treatment and care for people with mental health problems. Risk is, then, emerging as a key but contested concern in the mental health field. It is being discussed in a climate in which political, professional, organizational and service-users' interests and territories are being actively re-negotiated. It is thus important in considering risk work to take continuous account of the political, professional and resource interests which are influencing its development and direction.

This chapter argues that there are two main approaches to defining risk and operationalizing risk work which are currently on offer to mental health social workers – risk minimization and risk-taking. It outlines each and considers what they have to offer to mental health social workers practising in a range of health, social service and voluntary agencies providing services for people with mental health problems.

APPROACHES TO RISK WORK

Tilbury (1993) in his account of social work with people with longstanding mental health problems comments 'Risk in social work has not been given the attention it would appear to merit as a significant facet of the day-to-day experience of practitioners and managers' (p.62). Guidelines for action have been drawn up but little systematic work has been done to translate them into specific forms of practice which can be applied, evaluated and modified. The result is that scant attention has been paid to the complexity of tasks facing practitioners working with risk as well as the tensions and dilemmas which they are managing as a result of policy and legal requirements in this area. In looking in more detail at the way in which each of the two main approaches to risk work in mental health are beginning to be translated into practice the key components of each as well as possible future directions will be outlined.

THE RISK MINIMIZATION APPROACH

The risk minimization approach is evolving in the context of a framework promoted in mental health service policy guidelines. This guidance has, in the main, been developed as a response to the recommendations of several inquiries into incidents in which individuals with a history of mental health problems have fatally assaulted mental health workers, or other citizens or have taken their own lives. These events, the subsequent media attention, official inquiries and recommendations (see for example, Dick, Shuttleworth, and Charlton 1991; Blom-Cooper, Hally and Murphy 1995; Ritchie, Dick and Lingham 1994; Shepherd 1995) have all contributed to what has become the dominant framework for the development of risk work and risk training in the mental health field.

The key element in this framework is the Care Programme Approach (CPA). The Care Programme Approach has been developed as a means by which the support of people with mental health problems can be provided in what is, at an organizational level, an increasingly complex mix of workers and agencies involved in purchasing and providing services.

The Care Programme Approach has four basic elements:

- **systematic assessment** of the health and social care needs of the individual

- **an agreed care plan,** between service staff, the individual and carers and recorded in writing
- the allocation of a **key worker** whose job is to maintain close contact with the individual and monitor the care programme
- **regular review** of the service users progress and his/her health and social care needs. (DoH 1990)

This approach was introduced in 1991 to provide a range of mental health professionals, including psychiatrists, nurses, social workers and psychologists, with a common means of focusing their assessment and management skills on individuals who are designated as in need of care by virtue of their diagnosed and usually long term mental health problems. CPA is being promoted by policy makers as the primary way in which an individual with mental health problems receives the professional assessment, management and review he or she may require. Practitioners are encouraged to involve the user, his or her advocate, carers and/or interested relatives in this process so that the users' views of need are heard. Social Services Departments are encouraged to use CPA to fulfil their duties of care management under the NHS and Community Care Act 1990 (Schneider 1993; DoH 1994a; Audit Commission 1994).

As the issue of risk has risen on public, policy and professional agendas the Care Programme Approach has been extended to incorporate risk work. An assessment of risk has been identified as part of the care planning process. Risk is defined here as 'both risk to the patient him or herself, and risk to others' (DoH 1994a)

Some elaboration of what incorporating risk work into the Care Programme Approach might mean to practitioners has emerged from a number of sources. For example, it is given detailed consideration as part of the Blom-Cooper Inquiry Report. The authors of this report argue that it is important for mental health services to work with an 'ongoing assessment of risk and risk-management, assuming that risk will change over time and can be managed effectively' (Blom-Cooper, Hally and Murphy 1995, p.176). They suggest that all risk assessment and management strategies should comprise five basic components

- an assessment of mental state which thoroughly investigates potentially dangerous thoughts and actions held by an individual with mental health problems
- a decision made on the basis of the assessment about who might be harmed and how
- an evaluation of whether the arrangements being made for the care and treatment of the individual concerned adequately address the risk and if not what further measures might be taken
- a written record of what risks are thought to be present, the action to be taken and 'what level of risk is being accepted for an individual, bearing in mind the practical constraints, resources available and the rights of the individual to be treated in the least restrictive manner compatible with minimal risk'. (Blom-Cooper, Hally and Murphy 1995, p.176)

- a regular review system to revise, if necessary, the evaluation and action in the light of more recent information.

Work has also been undertaken to guide service providers in determining priorities in CPA risk work. Guidelines written for those purchasing and providing services have suggested that a 'tiered' approach to the Care Programme Approach might be adopted. This provides 'minimal' CPA to individuals with 'low support needs which are likely to remain stable'. A more 'complex' CPA to those needing support from more than one type of service whose needs are 'less likely to remain stable'. A full, multi-disciplinary CPA for individuals 'suffering from severe social dysfunction, whose needs are likely to be highly volatile, or who represent a significant risk' (DoH 1994b).

Within the CPA framework practitioners have been advised to take particular account of situations where an individual's psychiatric diagnosis combined with his or her legal and service status indicates a high risk potential.

Individuals whose behaviour has been characterized by violence and or self-harm in the community and who have, as the result of hospital admission, acquired a status as detained patient under the Mental Health Act (1983) have been identified as requiring a thorough, multi-disciplinary risk assessment followed by the establishment of a clear, agreed risk management plan subject to regular review (DoH 1994a).

Individuals due to be discharged from hospital into the community have been identified as another priority group in relation to risk work. Guidance here suggests that hospital discharge should only be agreed when a judgment is made 'that any risk to the public and patients themselves is minimised and managed effectively' (DoH 1994a). The work required to reach this judgment should be based on a full assessment of 'needs and capabilities' and 'Those undertaking individual decisions about discharge have a fundamental duty to consider both the safety of the patient and the protection of other people. No patient should be discharged from hospital unless and until those taking the decision are satisfied that he or she can live safely in the community, and that proper treatment, supervision, support and care are available' (DoH 1994a, p.2). Discharge from hospital brings with it an increased risk of suicide and staff are advised to assess possible suicide intent at this time (Morgan 1990; Blom-Cooper; Hally and Murphy 1995).

Some individuals due to be 'followed up in the community' have also been identified as a priority for risk work. Here risk management and reduction are highlighted as essential ingredients of the ongoing support required for those individuals with a past history of violent, harmful or suicidal behaviour.

While work of this kind has begun to provide some notion of the focus, procedures and activities involved in risk work it has become clear that this risk-orientated, multi-disciplinary development of the Care Programme Approach is not viewed as sufficient for the purpose. Evidence from inquiries and research have suggested that the coordination being achieved through the Care Programme Approach is very patchy (see Shepherd 1995; Audit Commission 1994). Partly in response to this a requirement was placed on all health authorities in April 1994 to 'set up registers which identify and provide information on patients who are, or are liable to be, at risk of committing serious violence or suicide, or of serious self neglect' (NHS Executive 1994). These supervision registers have been described as 'a means of identifying those who should be a priority for the allocation of professional time and resources' (Blom-Cooper, Hally and Murphy 1995). They have also been seen by some as a first step towards the introduction of the compulsory supervision of people in the community with 'serious mental disorder' who are deemed to be 'high risk'.The proposed introduction of 'supervised after care' would place requirements on individuals in relation to their treatment, residence and service use with failure to comply resulting in possible recall to hospital (House of Commons 1995).

The operationalization, then, of the risk minimization approach has taken the form of centrally generated guidelines offered for local adoption and adaptation. These guidelines use a narrow definition of risk. They focus professional activity and organizational coordination on a small minority of 'high risk' individuals identified as such because of a combination of the severity of their psychiatric diagnoses, their past behaviours, legal status and service positioning. As a direct consequence of their risk rating such service users may find themselves entered on supervision registers. In the future, this group of service users may find themselves legally compelled through after care orders to fulfil the requirements of risk minimization programmes.

This approach has been shaped by reactions to media, public and professional concerns about the consequences of the violence, self-harm, suicide and serious self-neglect of a small minority of people with severe and longstanding mental health problems. As an orientation to the complex practice issues which surround inter-agency and multi-disciplinary work the risk minimization approach is limited in several important respects.

It defines risk in very specific ways which exclude consideration of the majority of people using mental health services. Its prime method of risk assessment combines a thorough clinical interview with the matching of an individual to a list of risk factors derived from clinical or forensic psychiatry (see for example Crichton 1995; Whittington 1994; Morgan 1990; 1994). This method, acknowledged as one which is very unspecific and insensitive when applied to individuals, cannot accommodate the complex social and interpersonal factors which are relevant to understanding risk in the context of an individual's life. In relation to risk management and review this approach offers little beyond exhortation about the need for communication and co-ordination across services and disciplines in order to maintain contact with the service user (Ritchie, Dick and Lingham 1994; Blom-Cooper, Hally and Murphy 1995).

In effect the risk minimization approach locates risk in a deficient and potentially dangerous minority of individuals who need to be identified, registered and managed by medication and surveillance. It rarely moves beyond a consideration of immediate environmental factors which might trigger violent behaviour in an individual. As a consequence it fails to engage adequately with issues of risk as they affect the majority of service users. Questions of individual rights, competence and autonomy are rarely addressed. It cannot adequately accommodate consideration of the way in which social, economic, cultural and interpersonal environments influence vulnerability as well as a potential for violent, harmful and self neglectful behaviour.

THE RISK TAKING APPROACH

The risk taking approach has been developed by practitioners working with an explicit agenda to involve and empower mental health service users. This approach starts with a definition of risk which is positive and normalizing. Taking chances which may have unfortunate or dangerous consequences are viewed as taken for granted facts of life for the majority of autonomous, self-determining adults. As Mosher and Burti (1994) frame it in their list of practice guidance for community mental health services 'Take risks; if you don't take chances nothing ever happens.' (p.101).

Risk-taking is therefore an essential element of working with mental health service users to ensure autonomy, choice and social participation. It is a means of challenging the paternalism and over protectiveness of mental health services. It has a part to play in questioning and transforming established structures which reward user dependency, incompetence and passivity. It is part of the delivery of normalizing experiences to those who are at risk of being segregated and marginalized by their use of mental health services (Ramon 1991). It is a means of engaging with the stigmatization and social exclusion which people with mental health problems describe as part of their daily lives (Barham and Hayward 1991).

The starting point of the risk-taking approach is not a service framework or set of practice procedures. It is a set of shared values which inform practice. These values are committed to the notion that people with mental health problems are first and foremost people. As Braye and Preston-Shoot (1995) have usefully identified there are choices to be made here.

> On the one hand are values located in a long tradition of social care. These urge practitioners to 'treat people better' in the context of allotted roles and place in the social structure. On the other hand are values calling for radical change to, and renegotiation of, existing roles and social structures, to create a fairer society. Thus the traditional agenda is to bring about the adjustment of service users to existing conditions in society, a focus on personal problems. The radical agenda emphasises the structural context in which problems are produced and reproduced (pp.35–6).

In practice, of course, pure forms of the traditional and radical positions are rare. Risk work is more likely to be informed by a synthesis of value positions shared by practitioners. On a traditionally-biased agenda risk work is likely to be viewed as part of a practice which counters discrimination, respects persons, attempts to equalize opportunities and provides normalizing experiences and valued environments. On a radically-biased agenda risk work is likely to be part of a practice which works with service users as citizens, counters oppression by recognizing and engaging with the structures which contribute to powerlessness and strives to achieve equality. In other words. risk is firmly located in its social, cultural and political contexts. It becomes part of working for change in the relationship between the individual and the social structure.

Because of its orientation the risk taking approach connects directly with user literature and campaigns for service and/or societal change. (see, for example, Barker 1991; Hastings and Crepaz-Keay 1995; Read and Wallcraft 1994). It does this by considering the limiting and oppressive nature of some of the community located service environments in which people with mental health problems find their autonomy restricted or denied. In this way it questions the decisions that are taken by service providers to protect individuals from risk. It asks on what basis such decisions are being made and what consequences they have for people's rights and opportunities for full participation. It also has the potential to open up debates about the risks which arise for people with mental health problems as a direct result of service use; for example, the risks to health and functioning which can result from physical treatments and the risks to self-esteem and personal wellbeing which contact with mental health professionals may engender (MIND 1986; Barker 1991; Rogers, Pilgrim and Lacey 1993; Read and Wallcraft 1994).

It also begins to open up a dialogue between mental health service users and service workers about the way in which people with mental health problems perceive and define risk in their lives. As several studies have demonstrated, when people using mental health services are asked about the elements which contribute to hazard and risk in their own lives they are likely to point to the part that poverty, poor housing, unemployment, crime, stigma and social exclusion play in making their lives hazardous – a perspective which contrasts sharply with the diagnostically and service-driven perspectives of many mental health practitioners (Rogers, Pilgrim and Lacey 1993; Barham and Hayward 1991). As Onyett (1992) has pointed out 'Diagnosis is a neat way of creating social order in our chaos, but cannot represent the experience of the users.' (p.94).

The risk taking approach operates at a level of generality which leaves the detail of the relevant knowledge base, methods and skills development to be worked through by practitioners and service users in the context of the organizations which provide mental health services. It indicates that critical to this work are the ways in which conflict, power and competence are addressed in practice. As Braye and Preston-Shoot (1993) suggest

> empowerment practice here can involve the quite minute dissection of areas of decision making to maximise autonomy in those areas where competency can be established rather than operate a blanket disqualification and providing safety for developmental and incremental risk-taking in less well established areas (p.127).

This approach raises a number of questions about strategies for working across organizations and disciplines to establish shared service values which widen definitions of risk work to apply to the majority of service users.

RISK WORK AND MENTAL HEALTH SOCIAL WORK

The two approaches which have been considered in this chapter offer social workers contrasting orientations to risk work. They also suggest that there are some common features to good practice in this area. In developing risk work practice mental health social workers can profitably use the general frameworks provided by both of these approaches to reflect on the balance which they want to achieve in their practice. This balance will have to take account of a number of personal, professional, organizational and legislative factors. But all should be considered in a manner which gives due consideration to the following essential components of risk work:

- practice principles
- practice locations
- interpersonal encounters
- organizational support.

The practice principles informing risk work should take as their starting point the fact that 'psychiatric diagnosis remains a major disqualifier from the otherwise broad assumption of autonomy in decision making enjoyed by citizens' (Braye and Preston-Shoot 1993, p.125). Across the range of mental health services it needs to be acknowledged that it is all too easy for the recognition of individuality, self-determination, personal responsibility and autonomy to be lost as reactive over protectiveness and control are triggered in situations which practitioners consider to be risky. At the same time detailed attention needs to be paid to the way in which competence and its limits are understood and worked with. There is a range of potentially useful practice principles which can be considered for this purpose (e.g. Hoggett 1993; Braye and Preston Shoot 1995; Mosher and Burti 1994). What must not be forgotten is that the process of debating, adopting and reviewing principles needs to be one which involves service users, practitioners and managers. It is a process of individual and collective commitment.

Practice locations must provide an environment for users and practitioners which seek to both minimize the negative risks of harm and harassment and maximize the opportunities for positive risk taking for change and empowerment. Balancing risk work in this way will involve a range of policy and practice measures which reflect agreed practice principles. These will include, for example, policies in relation to harassment and clear procedures for service users and practitioners to use in relation to complaints. They will also include opportunities for service users to share information about the risk taking they are faced with in their own lives in forums where support from others – service users and practitioners is readily available. Parallel to this is the need to make provision for staff, individually and collectively to share and find support for difficulties which they are working with as a result of the stress and uncertainties of risk work. Training in relation to dealing with risky and unpredictable situations arising in service locations needs to be provided for practitioners and service users in ways which address both their separate and their shared concerns. From this work clear procedures need to be devised which sensitize and empower people working with difficult and potentially dangerous situations.

Interpersonal encounters lie at the heart of risk work. What practitioners bring to these encounters must reflect the principles they are committed to as well as the range of established practice skills which are part of the repertoire of experienced social workers. As many recent commentators in this field have pointed out (Blom-Cooper, Hally and Murphy 1995; Ritchie, Dick and Lingham 1994) the quality of risk work is linked directly to the establishment of relationships of trust and empathy and these require time. There are no short cuts to this in relation to risk assessment or management which seeks to minimize as well as encourage risk taking. Aids to risk work such as risk minimization checklists are only adjuncts to lengthier more detailed and time consuming work which is focused on getting to know an individual and building trust and confidence over time. The work involved in risk taking is not a matter of handing all decisions over to the service user(s) involved. It requires detailed attention, planning, identifying supports and review. It may also involve allowing the time for individuals to make mistakes, fail and return to the task.

Of course not all risk work engages with known individuals. Practitioners operating in crisis services, engaged in assessments as Approved Social Workers and working in drop-in services are being called on to make quick responses to and decisions about people who they do not know. Personal encounters are still critical to this kind of intervention. The time scale means that practitioners must take responsibility for clearly communicating their concern for the individual service user, their reasons for being in the encounter, what the outcomes may be and what steps that will involve them and the service users in (DoH and Welsh Office 1993; Sheppard 1990).

Advice to Approved Social Workers (ASWs) from people who have been subject to sectioning under the Mental Health Act 1983 indicates that

> ASW's need to listen to people in distress and crisis. Even when the person appears unable to talk rationally and coherently, professionals must listen to them. Constant communication needs to be maintained, and can only be achieved if the ASW involved is prepared to spend time listening to the person, trying to empathise with them and to enter their experience. The person's account of what is happening to them should be respected and taken seriously' (Hastings and Crepaz-Keay 1995, p.14).

In situations where there is a risk of danger to others because of the disturbing behaviour of an individual the interpersonal encounter remains central. It is the means of establishing a connection with the individual which acknowledges feelings, allows for expression of feeling and maintains with calm purpose the work required to minimize risk to self and others.

Organisational support is essential for risk work to be balanced and effective. Organizations provide the mandate for work undertaken by mental health social work practitioners and they also have responsibilities in relation to the fulfilment of that mandate. Practitioners who are anxious and defensive because of their perceptions that they need to act in ways which protect them from organizational blame are unlikely to meet the requirements of good practice in this area. The provision of regular and sound supervision for staff is therefore essential. The Blom-Cooper Report commended the 'well established practice' of regular supervision provided within social work to other mental health practitioners involved in maintaining a balance in risk work. The Association of Directors of Social Services' (1991) guidance on work with Adults at Risk talk about a strong system of supervision as being

> fundamental, to ensure that the social worker is supported adequately, that the authority's responsibilities are discharged properly and ultimately that the appropriate service is provided to the user. Work in this area is often difficult and demanding emotionally and it is essential for line managers to be aware of their role in ensuring its effective completion (p.5).

This suggests that managers need to identify the areas of organizational support that are critical to successful risk work. This needs to be achieved through dialogue with practitioners and service users and review of success and failure in situations requiring risk minimization and risk taking. Acknowledgement also needs to be made of the complex interagency and interdisciplinary agendas which generate dilemmas and tensions in risk work (Audit Commission 1994; Ritchie, Dick and Lingham 1994). Organizational support which proactively sustains risk related decision making and practice is difficult to build in the mental health services. But without it and a resourcing of it risk work will remain underdeveloped. Support such as this must include work at policy and staff development levels.

Work on service and practice principles which reaffirm the practice of experienced practitioners and provide primary orientation and direction for new practitioners is part of the investment in risk work which mental health organizations need to make. Again this is an area where work with service users is vital (Barker 1991; Read and Wallcraft 1994; Hastings and Crepaz-Keay 1995).

CONCLUSIONS

In the current climate of debate around risk work in the mental health services the challenge to social work practitioners is to identify, develop and reaffirm the distinctive contribution they can make to risk assessment and risk management. Recent Department of Health guidelines have noted that social workers along with probation officers have particular expertise in the area of risk assessment and management on which other members of multi-disciplinary teams might usefully draw (DoH 1994a). This expertise reflects a perspective which strives to work with the complexity of risk and risk taking as it applies to the majority of people using mental health services. It acknowledges and investigates the social, cultural and psychological factors which shape the experiences of people with mental health problems. It is influenced by a commitment to working with service users in identifying the sources of stress which can trigger difficult and risky situations. This socially informed user-centred perspective can serve to extend and rebalance the diagnostically and behaviourally focused approaches to risk minimization which is currently dominating this area.

REFERENCES

Association of Directors of Social Services (1991) *Adults at Risk: guidance for Directors of Social Services*. Stockport: ADSS.

Audit Commission (1994) *Finding a Place: A Review of Mental Health Services for Adults*. London: HMSO.

Barham, P. and Hayward, R. (1991) *From Mental Patient to the Person*. London: Routledge.

Barker, I. (1991) *Power Games*. Hove: Pavilion.

Blom-Cooper, L.; Hally, H. and Murphy, E. (1995) *The Falling Shadow: One Patient's Mental Health Care 1978–1993*. London: Gerald Duckworth and Co.

Braye, S. and Preston-Shoot, M. (1993) 'Empowerment and partnership in mental health'. *Journal of Social Work Practice 7, 2*, 115–28.

Braye, S. and Preston-Shoot, M. (1995) *Empowering Practice in Social Care*. Buckingham: Open University.

Crichton, J. (ed) (1995) *Psychiatric Patient Violence: Risk and Response*. London: Gerald Duckworth and Co.

Department of Health (1990) *Care Programme Approach. Health Circular (90)23/Local Authority Social Services Letter(90)11*. London: Department of Health.

Department of Health (1994a) *Guidance on Discharge of Mentally Disordered People and their Continuing Care in the Community. Health Service Guidelines. Local Authority Social Services Letter LASSL(94)4*. London: Department of Health.

Department of Health (1994b) *Draft Guide to Arrangements for Inter-agency Working for the Care and Protection of Severely Mentally Ill People*. London: Department of Health.

Department of Health and Welsh Office (1993) (2nd edition) *Code of Practice, Mental Health Act 1983*. London: HMSO.

Dick, D., Shuttleworth, B. and Charlton, J. (1991) Report of the Panel of Inquiry appointed by the West Midlands Regional Health Authority, South Birmingham Health Authority and the Special Hospitals Service Authority to Investigate the case of Kim Kirkman. Birmingham: West Midlands RHA.

Hastings, M. and Crepaz-Keay, D. (1995) *The Survivors Guide to Training Approved Social Workers*. London: CCETSW.

House of Commons (1995) *Mental Health (Patients in the Community). Bill 122. 51/3*. London: HMSO.

Hoggett, B. (1993) Changing needs and priorities in Mental Health Law. Paper read at Conference of the Law Society, Institute of Psychiatry and the Mental Health Act Commission. 'The Mental Health Act 1983. Time for Change?' November.

MIND (1986) *Finding our own Solutions*. London: MIND.

Morgan, H.G. (1990) *Persons at Risk of Suicide; Guidelines on Good Clinical Practice*. The Boots Company.

Morgan, G. (1994) 'Assessment of risk.' In R. Jenkins *et al.* (eds) *The Prevention of Suicide.* London: HMSO.

Mosher, L. and Burti, L. (1994) *Community Mental Health: A Practical Guide.* New York: W.W. Norton and Company.

National Health Service Executive/ Department of Health (1994) Introduction of Supervision Registers for Mentally Ill people from 1 April 1994. Health Service Guidelines HSG(94)5.

Onyett, S. (1992) *Case Management in Mental Health.* London, Chapman Hall.

Ramon, S. (ed) (1991) *Beyond Community Care: Normalisation and Integration Work.* London: Macmillan.

Ramon, S. (ed) (1992) *Psychiatric Hospital Closure: Myths and realities.* London: Chapman and Hall.

Read, J. and Wallcraft, J. (1994) *Guidelines for Empowering Users of Mental Health Services.* London: MIND/COHSE.

Ritchie, J., Dick, D. and Lingham, R. (1994) *Report of the Committee of Inquiry into the Care of Christopher Clunis.* London: HMSO.

Rogers, A., Pilgrim, D. and Lacey, R. (1993) *Experiencing Psychiatry: Users' Views of Services.* London: Macmillan.

Schneider, J. (1993) 'Care programming in mental health: assimilation and adaptation.' *British Journal of Social Work* 23, 4, 383–403.

Shepherd, D. (1995) *Learning the Lessons: Mental Health Inquiry Reports Published in England and Wales between 1969–1994 and their Recommendations for Improving Practice.* London: The Zito Trust.

Sheppard, M. (1990) *Mental Health – the Role of the Approved Social Worker.* Sheffield: Joint Unit for Social Services Research, Social Services Monographs: Research in Practice Series, University of Sheffield.

Tilbury, D. (1993) *Working with Mental Illness.* Basingstoke: Macmillan.

Whittington, R. (1994) 'Violence in psychiatric hospitals.' In T. Wykes (ed) *Violence and Health Care Professionals.* London: Chapman and Hall.

CHAPTER 9

FACTS, FANTASIES AND CONFUSION
RISKS AND SUBSTANCE USE

Ronno Griffiths and Jan Waterson

INTRODUCTION: BREAKING THROUGH THE BARRIERS

Most people use substances. Many have taken risks with them. Some substance use is highly stigmatized and illegal, whereas other uses are legal and socially approved (Robinson, Maynard and Chester 1989). So, it is not surprising that not only do those involved hold different perceptions about what constitutes risk, but that those perceptions also change throughout the life course. Given the sensitive nature of some substance use it is not surprising that myths, fantasies and confusion about the subjective and objective meanings of risks abound. Consequently, it is important for workers to try to take account of others' starting points, distinguishing fact from fantasy.

We do not attempt to deal with all potential risks arising from substance use. There are many existing accounts of the problems that can arise and their impact on the lives and families of those involved (Griffiths and Pearson 1988; BASW 1989; Baldwin 1990; McMurran 1993; Paton 1994). Although risk reduction or avoidance is a central theme in recent practitioner texts, apart from risk of relapse or 'at-risk' groups the word is rarely explicitly mentioned (BASW 1989; Collins 1990; Velleman 1992). We look at the dynamics of risk taking which are rarely addressed, but which arise from the ambiguous nature of substance use, and outline some transferable strategies or ways of thinking for the worker to utilize as they assess and manage substance related risks. Unusually, we link drugs and alcohol use which have traditionally have been viewed as separate issues and fields of service delivery (Plant and Plant 1992; Ettorre 1992).

The next section deals with the need for all concerned, user, informal and formal carers, to share their pictures of what is going on and its implications. In other words, to try and establish shared and 'owned' pictures of the physical, emotional, legal and social risks of use and non-use. Analysing any risk behaviour means assessing competing rewards and costs. Sometimes the balance sheet is clearly one-sided. At other times it is more evenly balanced. A shared definition and interpretation of the balance sheet is crucial.

For practitioners the initial concerns are risk to the user, their significant others and the risks the user poses to society. Equally significant but less frequently admitted, are the risks the user may pose to the worker, both in a personal physical sense with unpredictable violence resulting from intoxication, withdrawal or frustration at not being able to find a way out of their chaos or even express that chaos. For managers the allocation of resources and providing professional supervision for the worker are likely to be the main issues. Supervision is essential, given the social complexity of substance-associated risk taking. Wary workers are unlikely to take on inappropriate 'rescuing and saving' roles when clarification and support would be more helpful and realistic even if less comfortable.

Having addressed some of the difficulties of sharing pictures particularly when they conflict, we move on to problem definition. Assessment necessarily involves predictions and models and theories. We lay out a sequential framework for assessing use as well as a threefold typology of substance use – experimental, recreational and chaotic/dependent. A summary section indicating considerations for practice concludes the chapter.

SHARING PICTURES

The key to assessing and managing risk lies in an open and honest dialogue around respective perceptions and fears. The major hurdle with people who use substances are differing – and often conflicting – perceptions of risk. Family members and professionals may assume or predict potential risk or recognize actual risk but feel powerless in the face of the users continued resistance to change. This often results in increased antagonism and breakdown in communications between those involved, which in turn may exacerbate the risk if dialogue becomes impossible.

Facts not Fantasies

Assessment should be based on facts. Onlookers, including professional workers often assess and rank risks on the bases of myths, preconceptions, personal experience (or lack of it) and their own understandable fears which are often fuelled by the media, rather than on factual appraisal. For example, if a worker believes that cannabis use will inevitably lead to the injecting of heroin and certain death, then they will overestimate risk quite inappropriately (Griffiths and Pearson 1988). The client may quite accurately recognize that the only risk that they face is a legal one. Conversely, if the worker used cannabis for a prolonged period in their carefree youth and encountered no problems, they may fail to detect problematic cannabis use by their client who has in fact developed a psychological dependence on the drug. The same process is even more common with regard to alcohol use. How many youngsters have experimented with solvents to the horror of their parents? How many parents have gone on to breathe a sigh of relief when those children made the transition to daily alcohol consumption exceeding the limits recommended by the Health Education Authority? The impact of such personal attitudes, along with their cause, should be explored in supervision in order to assess risk accurately, to ensure that clients needs are recognized and that the worker has not imposed their own ranking.

Workers need to be aware that family members may also base their assessment of the situation on the understandable attitudes and fears that they hold. These should be respected but explored and opened up by the worker. They may need to be challenged sympathetically with a view to them understanding the real nature of the drug or alcohol use and the objective and subjective role that it plays both for the user' and for themselves. This could ultimately help them all make sense of the situation, deal with their guilt, anger, hurt and a vision of the future narrowed by the overwhelming certainty that their loved one is lost to them for ever.

Drug users and drinkers have biased pictures too. Like everybody else, they are influenced by prejudices, attitudes and misinformation, but they may also have a vested interest in keeping the picture out of focus. There are many reasons why substance users are resistant to acknowledging the full extent of the risks that they may be facing. For a start, to openly admit to a problem is to contemplate change which represents hard work, loss and the possibility of failure and further damage to self-esteem. In other words, to lay themselves open to new risks.

Accepting and Informed Help

However well intentioned help is, unless it is accepting and informed it may misfire. For example, Sam had used solvents for over three years before it came to light. He then felt confused by his parents, teachers and social worker saying that 'If you use solvents you will be dead within a year'. How could he trust the message or the messengers when he was living proof that they were wrong? He did not want to tell them. Such dissonance between the user's actual experience and simplistic if well intentioned prophecies can have negative and far reaching qualities. Initially, Sam dug in his heels, determined to continue his heavy solvent use to 'show them they are wrong, that they're liars who know nothing'. Later, when he began to acknowledge that his health and future were being threatened, he had no-one to turn to because he felt that all the adults had been moral, misinformed and unsympathetic. At a loss, he increased his solvent use, thus increasing the potential for physical and psychological harm and the risk of further alienation and isolation from his support network.

It is interesting to note how many drinkers or drug takers may internalize a sense of powerlessness as a result of well intentioned interventions. Jess was one of many teenagers who became involved with heroin use in the early 1980s. On the basis of the information available to her she believed that she was making sensible decisions about her drug use, reducing the risks. She was indignant when a youth worker asked how much heroin she was taking. 'I wouldn't touch that filth. I just do scag' (scag is a street name for heroin). On learning that she was using heroin, Jess was still able to justify her use: 'I don't jack up, I only chase the dragon'. She believed that as she wasn't injecting, but merely inhaling the fumes of the drug, she was immune to its addictive properties. The youth worker was at pains to point out how misguided she was. In fact, at that point her use was so sporadic that she was not physically or psychologically dependent.

When the high level of heroin use amongst young people became a matter of national concern, Jess and her peers began to receive a new set of messages. She was told – by the press, her parents and peers – that you only had to use heroin once to become an addict and that the withdrawal from the drug was dangerous, painful and difficult. The fear of withdrawal became so great that Jess felt that she could not take the risk. With that and more pressure from her frightened parents to stop, she increased her use until she did become physically dependent.

Eventually, Jess did agree to a medically supervised detoxification. When drug-free she felt isolated, vulnerable, anxious and 'weird'. Normality for her had become a drug-induced state and the impact of her psychological dependence was more compelling than an understanding of the risks involved in continued heroin use. But at the age of 15 she did not have the maturity or resources to deal with these contradictions (as is true for so many problem drinkers and drug takers several years her senior). Her drug use escalated, she went on to inject, to use a cocktail of drugs and to become involved in prostitution and crime to support her habit. She resisted all attempts by her drugs worker to explore the risks until she was hospitalized following an overdose. She then acknowledged that her behaviour was life threatening but she spoke for hundreds when she said 'If I'm up front about what's going on, I'll have to do something about it. And I can't. Just thinking about it does my head in. So whatever happens, whatever I do, I'm fucked. It just makes sense to use again.'

Pluses and Minuses

Few people can make value free decisions in the face of risk and having knowledge about potential harmful effects is not enough to make people change their behaviour. We can see this in the numbers of people who are involved in potentially dangerous sports, who smoke tobacco, drink to excess or drive too fast. It is more a matter of gains and losses arising from particular behaviour. These are not necessarily obvious to onlookers, but it is clear that when risk behaviour continues users see their gains outweighing their potential losses.

For some users the risks involved form part of the attraction and 'buzz'. Risk whether belonging to a dangerous group, pursuing a dangerous activity or simply flaunting authority can be attractive. In this instance whether it be the ultimate risk of death or of simply of being found out, it heightens the drug experience. Risk taking, and pushing out the boundaries of behaviour is inextricably bound up with the process of adolescence. However, it is frequently the norm in a society where fast adrenaline enhancing activities are promoted in work and leisure contexts. The excitement on the faces of such people is tangible when they look back on the experience and relive the risks that they took, thus eclipsing any downside. Unless the worker acknowledges this in the balance sheet of gains and losses arising from substance use, any other assessment they make is likely to be discounted.

Others, whilst not emphasizing the gains, deny any risks almost completely. We have met numerous heavy drinkers and drug takers who have developed and internalized the belief that they are immune to any costs. They survive psychologically by exerting power and control – not over the substance but over the risk itself.

Others feel so undervalued by society and other people that their internalization becomes a rational reason for continuing their misuse. Sonja was only 20 when she voiced the kind of fatalism all too common amongst disaffected people with no future or attractive alternatives in the present. 'I've got to die sometime. I might as well die happy than live unhappy. Do you know what I mean?' Or Jamie: 'I've got AIDS. Nobody has ever given a damn about me before. It won't change now. If they care at all it will be that they are glad I'm dead. I might as well carry on sharing works (infecting equipment).'

Some users know that they are involved in risky behaviour but survive by adopting a 'better the devil you know' attitude. For those involved in heavy compulsive dependent use, the risk or cost of stopping may be far greater than that of continuing. A life of oblivion is far more attractive than one without the buffer of intoxication. Without the substance the user will have nothing to soften the blow of past and present traumas, their failures and losses (family, friends, childhood, love, employment, esteem, health and hope). They risk losing their identity (albeit an identity as an addict or alcoholic, but nevertheless with all the attachments of certainty, purpose and belonging) and the loss of a strong relationship – even though they are aware that they both love and hate the substance.

Finkelhor with Araji, Baron, Browne, Doyle Peters and Wyatt (1986) refers to a number of studies which demonstrate a link between past sexual abuse and problem alcohol or drug use in later life. This research evidence is borne out by practitioners who are increasingly working with women and men who are disclosing sexual abuse. The risks of their often chaotic and heavy substance use pale into insignificance in comparison to the functions served by the drug. It helps to dull the pain of the abuse, to avoid the memory, the guilt and anger. It can also play a part in the self-harm inflicted to expunge or control the pain or to maintain the overwhelming sense of worthlessness. As Pam said 'If I stop using, I might be a little girl again and my little girl was hurt, hurt, hurt. And I probably don't like her because she didn't stop me from hurting.'

Mickey was all too aware that his continued alcohol use was causing havoc in his life, leading to breakdown in his marriage, loss of access to his children and much more. But alcohol could still provide escape and refuge. On balance he could not let go – the loss and risk were too great. What was the point of stopping if the only other thing to gain was the awareness of pain – emotional, psychological and physical? He knew that his alcohol use could kill him – and it did.

Many individual problem drinkers and drug takers are aware of the risks but as we have seen are – or believe themselves to be – powerless to make changes. In a bid to deal with the negative feelings of poor self-esteem that arise from this sense of powerlessness, the individual may resort to intoxication to avoid acknowledging the risks and the consequent feelings (Peele

1985). This process is exacerbated if a group is involved. The group protects its identity and existence by encouraging denial. It cannot afford for one member to recognize and act upon their personal risk taking behaviours because other members may be forced to do the same and also become vulnerable to facing up to their powerlessness and threat of failure.

Balancing Acts

Research evidence from studies of drug users and HIV underlines the importance of social and situational influences (Stimson 1991; Rhodes and Stimson 1994). Whilst drug users are largely willing to adapt their injecting practices because of their perceived risk of contracting HIV through shared injecting equipment, they are less willing to amend their sexual practices (Stimson 1991; Rhodes et al. 1994). They identify themselves as drug users – not as homosexuals, the group they perceive to be most at risk from HIV through sexual contact. Similarly, drug users are more likely to use condoms when engaged in commercial sex transactions than they are when engaged in private sexual encounters with regular or casual sex partners (Rhodes et al. 1994). Like all of us, drug users have a set of priorities which they need to juggle according to their circumstances and world view. This juggling act may not fit the stereotypes, assumptions or simplistic analyses and dictates of some professionals involved. So, in ordering their concerns substance users are no different from the rest of the population – they just tend to be admonished because they choose alternative priorities.

A dependent substance user needs to be skilful in order to survive in a system when all the odds are stacked against them. They are frequently described as manipulative people who continually change their story and views. This label does not take into account that lack of consistency of lifestyle, experiences and substance use is inevitable if that lifestyle and/or substance use is erratic. Powers of recall are affected by past and present states of abstinence and intoxication. Indeed, as we have already noted some people take drugs precisely to forget.

WHAT PROBLEM, IF ANY?

In 1982 the Advisory Council on the Misuse of Drugs put forward a definition of the problem drug taker. Although alcohol was outside of the terms of reference the definition can also be usefully applied to problem drinkers. 'A problem drug taker (drinker) is any person who experiences psychological, physical, social or legal problems in relation to intoxication, and/or regular excessive consumption and/or dependence as a consequence of his/her own use of drugs or other chemical substances' (ACMD 1982).

This definition not only moves away from emotive labels such as 'addict/alcoholic' thereby enabling a more holistic view of the individual. It also allows for the fact that somebody may be involved in risk related behaviours prior to the development of problems.

Workers are often faced with seemingly contradictory questions. Is there a problem? Is it a drug or alcohol problem? Who is it a problem for? Not only will perspectives differ as to the risks faced by the individual, but there will also be a variety of views about who is at risk: the individual user; their partner, parents or children; other service users; the worker; the community. In seeking an honest answer, workers should remember that it does not necessarily follow that if substances are involved that there are necessarily problems. Also, if there are problems there can be no certainty that they are substance related.

Workers and users alike may be so overwhelmed by confused stories that it can be helpful to break them down into their component parts. The following models can be used by workers to clarify and make sense of situations.

Apart from the fact that they are available in the first place, people usually start using because of subcultural factors: social expectations and fashion – it's the thing to do. Parents often desperately seek reasons for their child's substance use and blame themselves for it, thinking that they must have created some sort of problem (Plant and Plant 1992). However, people rarely choose drugs as a solution to their problems in the first instance. They first become accustomed to using/drinking as they move from experimenting to using drink and drugs in a recreational manner. Only later is there a chance that use will become dependent/compulsive.

Although a variety of types of problems may be encountered with any stage of use, specific problems tend to be associated with types: experimental use with physical harm; recreational use with management problems for others; dependent/compulsive use with often severe and intractable personal and social difficulties. Thus, if the substance user can be identified with a particular point along this continuum, worker and client can concentrate their efforts on the most pertinent risk areas, so as to reduce those risks and slow, stop or reverse progress towards potentially increasingly problematic patterns of use. 'You may feel that you do not have problems now, but let's see in the kind of risks that you may be vulnerable to in the future.'

Experimental Use

This is a short-lived phase where new users are experimenting with a drug. Since they cannot know in advance whether or not they will enjoy the experience, which substance is selected is to an extent random; choice depends upon factors such as fashion and availability and whim. Increasingly, substance use has become enmeshed with growing up (Plant and Plant 1992). Taking the risks that authority figures, parents, teachers or social workers took is meaningless, thus experimentation becomes the norm.

Experimental use is often a group activity, carried on with friends or acquaintances, perhaps at parties or dances, or perhaps in riskier secret situations. Inexperienced users may find the drug affects them in ways that they had not anticipated and which they find unpleasant or frightening. Lack of knowledge and skills may increase the dangers of administration, the likelihood of overdose and the possibility of dangerous behaviour and accidents. Most drugs are used with far greater control by regular, experienced users (Zinberg, Harding and Apsler 1978).

If their experiences are negative or neutral, they will stop, perhaps switching to another substance, unless their use is sustained by other considerations, such as a need for group membership. If, however, their experiences are on the whole positive, they will probably move onto recreational use.

Recreational Use

Recreational users have found a drug(s), whose effects they enjoy and use it regularly, but discriminatingly and in a controlled way. For example, most drinkers or users of cannabis would probably place themselves in this category. Any difficulties they may experience as the result of use – hangovers from drinking, or the comedown from stimulant use – are generally dismissed as the price one has to pay for having a good time.

Nevertheless, their use and behaviour may well present management problems for others: parents, the local community, youth workers, social workers, the criminal justice system. Recreational use covers a wide spectrum of behaviour. In the case of alcohol, for example, it extends from the most sedate drinking patterns to drink driving to the wildly immoderate consumption and behaviour characteristic of some football fans.

Dependent/Compulsive Use

Recreational use is essentially hedonistic. Most people stay in this stage (with use declining with age and increasing responsibilities), but some find that drugs or drink can also serve as a way of coping with, or avoiding problems (Waterson 1992). Their lives tend to become increasingly focused around drinking or drug use, as it becomes the antidote to all problems, including those due to its use. Aspects of life which are not drug-related become peripheral. Dependent use is often a solitary or small group activity, increasing social isolation from family and other friends. In time, however, the substance use may exacerbate rather than solve those problems. For example, the client runs the risk of becoming further alienated in an already difficult relationship, job and so on. Some dependent users may succeed in keeping their lives more or less on an even keel; others may spiral down into chaos.

This continuum is not meant to suggest an inevitable progression from experiment to dependent use. Individuals may stop using at any point, or regain control over chaotic use, or remain as problem-free recreational users. Each category includes a range of behaviours and the boundaries, particularly between recreational and dependent use, sometimes merge into each other. The probability of individuals moving from experimental to dependent/compulsive patterns of use relates to a number of factors, such as the wide availability of a range of highly potent mood-altering substances, the greater acceptance of drug use among young people, cultural developments such as the 'rave scene', and economic factors such as high rates of unemployment.

Separating Antecedent Factors from Consequent Issues

Anthony Thorley (1987) shows how a sequential framework, which distinguishes issues and factors which predate problem drug or alcohol use and what results, can be used to assess substance use (Figure 9.1).

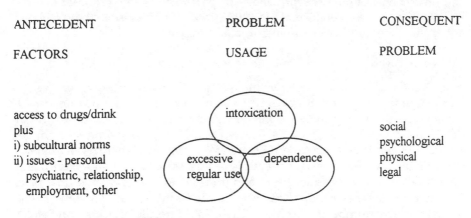

ANTECEDENT	PROBLEM	CONSEQUENT
FACTORS	USAGE	PROBLEM

access to drugs/drink
plus
i) subcultural norms
ii) issues - personal
   psychiatric, relationship,
   employment, other

social
psychological
physical
legal

Source: Thorley 1988

Figure 9.1 Sequential framework for assessing alcohol/drug problems

These resulting problems may be associated with specific types of substance use, excessive regular use, intoxication or dependence, singly or in combination. Such interrelationships need unpicking to identify or predict where risks may lie. The following matrix suggests how the distinct risks associated with specific types of use can viewed and risks ranked (Figure 9.2). Readers can generalize from this example of heroin use to other situations and substances.

Type of use	*Risks*		
	Physical	*Social*	*Legal*
Intoxication	O.D. Accident	Violence	Driving under the influence Possession
Excessive regular use (+4 days a week)	Increased likelihood of injecting/cocktails	Isolation	Theft
Dependence	Withdrawal if supply disrupted	Breakdown of relationships Homelessness	Supplying Prostitution

Figure 9.2 Type of use and associated risks

Only when this stage of clarifying the links between antecedent factors, type of consumption and consequent issues is completed can worker and client embark on a programme of risk reduction or elimination. This involves dealing with such questions as how can excessive consumption be avoided? Can alternative ways be found to deal with antecedent factors? How can the user minimize the problems associated with use? For example, if they become aggressive when under the influence – or paranoid when with other people. What steps can be taken to avoid the situations that give rise to these feelings when the client has been drinking or taken drugs?

Choosing Goals

This broad definition of problems that we have been using allows for a range of treatment goals. The concept of risk reduction or harm minimization in the drugs field has gained credence and government backing since the advent of HIV (Advisory Council on the Misuse of Drugs 1988). Following on from the concept of controlled drinking (O'Hare *et al.* 1992), it recognizes that abstinence may not be necessary, or feasible – at least not in the short term, and that it is preferable to reduce harm and improve the prospect and quality of life than to run the risk of alienating people from services altogether. The growth in the number of needle exchanges, outreach projects and health promotion programmes advising on safer use of drugs and drink has brought harm reduction into the mainstream of policy and practice. Nevertheless there are still critics of risk reduction approaches, and workers face more and more ethical dilemmas about providing advice to young people that may be construed as encouraging substance use. Supervisors should be aware of any potential and actual dilemmas and offer appropriate support. Managers may need to publicly defend such approaches.

The choice of goal needs to be negotiated with the client. Workers need to focus on breaking up the overall process of choosing into component parts, encouraging confidence. The actual goal may also need to be broken down into achievable parts or stages. Sometimes, the worker and client may get caught up in an interdependent cycle of helplessness and hopelessness. Neither party can break this interlocking cycle and often a complete collapse in communication or a confusion of boundaries results. A worker may feel so deskilled and involved that they 'just want to take them all home with me'. Another worker, feeling resentful at the time they have devoted to a client to no avail, may label them unmotivated and manipulative withdrawing all emotional and even practical support. Such adjectives may be true but are damaging and unhelpful. As we have seen the lack of motivation to change seems a sensible option in the short and even very long term for users and workers need to recognize this. Indeed, as workers feel increasingly powerless and frustrated in the face of apparent self-destruction, users may recognize their capacity to provoke, and escalate their behaviour thus gaining another pay-off or distraction from the real issues.

CONSIDERATIONS FOR PRACTICE

Good practice is so often a matter of balancing apparently conflicting factors and thus depends on clear conceptual frameworks and analysis. We summarize the points made in this chapter:
- All workers, users and carers make judgements based on attitudes and experience. These need exploring and sources identifying.

- Judgements about substance use need grounding in facts about the substance and the circumstances involved in any given case. Drug users and drinkers do not form homogenous groups.
- Substance associate risk taking needs to be seen in terms of losses and gains (internal and external).
- Risk itself can be attractive, particularly if linked with group membership.
- Contemplating change can seem more risky than to continue using.
- The ability to change depends on some self-esteem. Many people with drug or alcohol problems have very low self-esteem.
- Substance use does not necessarily mean problems, nor are all problems substance related
- Stages (experimental, recreational and dependent) and type (intoxication, excessive regular use, dependence) of use tend to be associated with different problems.
- Goals need to be negotiated with the client. Harm reduction may be the desirable or only feasible aim.
- Workers need supportive supervision to deal with potential moral and boundary issues.

REFERENCES

Advisory Council on the Misuse of Drugs (1982) *Treatment and Rehabilitation: Report of the Advisory Council on the Misuse of Drugs*. London: HMSO.

Advisory Council on the Misuse of Drugs (1988) *AIDS and Drug Misuse, Part 1*. London: HMSO.

Baldwin, S. (1990) *Alcohol Education and Offenders*. London: Batsford.

BASW (1989) *Dealing With Alcohol Problems – Practice Guidelines*. Birmingham: BASW.

Collins, S. (1990) *Alcohol, Social Work and Helping*. London: Routledge.

Ettorre, E. (1992) *Women and Substance Use*. Basingstoke: Macmillan.

Finkelhor, D., with Araji, S., Baron, L., Browne, A., Doyle Peters, S. and Wyatt, G.E. (1986) *A Sourcebook on Child Sexual Abuse*. London: Sage Publications.

Griffiths, R. and Pearson, B. (1988) *Working with Drug Users*. Basingstoke: Wildwood.

McMurran, M. (1993) *Young Offenders and Alcohol Related Crime – a Practitioner's Guide*. Chichester: John Wiley.

O'Hare, P.A., Newcombe, R., Matthews, A., Buning, E.C. and Drucker, E. (1992) *The Reduction of Drug-Related Harm*. London: Routledge.

Paton, A. (1994) (3rd edition) *ABC of Alcohol*. London: British Medical Journal.

Peele, S. (1985) *The Meaning of Addictions*. Lexington, M.A.: Lexington Books.

Plant, M. and Plant, M. (1992) *Risk-takers: Alcohol, Drugs, Sex and Youth*. London: Tavistock/Routledge.

Rhodes, T., Donoghoe, M., Hunter, G., Souteri, S. and Stimson, G.V. (1994) 'Sexual behaviour of drug injectors in London: implications for HIV transmission and HIV prevention.' *Addiction 89*, 1085–1096.

Rhodes, T. and Stimson, G.V. (1994) 'What is the relationship between drug taking and sexual risk? Social relations and social research.' *Sociology of Health and Illness 16*, 209–228.

Robinson, D., Maynard, A. and Chester, R. (1989) *Controlling Legal Addictions*. Basingstoke: Macmillan.

Stimson, G.V. (1991) 'Risk reduction by drug users with regard to HIV infection.' *International Journal of Psychiatry 3*, 401–415.

Thorley, A. (1987) 'Some practical approaches to the problem drug taker.' In T. Heller, M. Gott and C. Jeffrey (eds) *Drug Use and Misuse: a Reader*. London: John Wiley.

Velleman, R. (1992) *Counselling for Alcohol Problems*. London: Sage.

Waterson, J. (1992) *Women and Alcohol: The Social Context of Changing Patterns of Use During Pregnancy and Early Motherhood*. Unpublished PhD thesis, London School of Economics.

Zinberg, N.E., Harding, W.M. and Apsler, R. (1978) 'What is drug use?' *Journal of Drug Issues 8*, Winter, 9–35.

CHAPTER 10

OFFENDER RISK AND PROBATION PRACTICE

Hazel Kemshall

INTRODUCTION

Criminology has become increasingly concerned with risk, predominantly with questions of risk distribution, perception and management (Box 1987; Clark, Fisher and McDougall 1993; Cornish and Clark 1986; Farrington and Tarling 1985; Flynn 1978; Hay and Sparks 1993.) These studies have concentrated upon either the production of risk indicators for specific offender groups in particular settings, or upon offender calculations of getting caught. Whilst prediction of both dangerousness and re-offending has traditionally exercised the thoughts of parole boards (Flynn 1978), the applicability of criminology's prediction studies to the work of probation has remained under developed.

Traditionally the Probation Service has espoused a welfare ethic, concerned with the humanitarian rehabilitation of offenders (McWilliams 1987, 1992), and the identification and alleviation of offender need. Beginning with the imposition of the Statement of National Objectives and Priorities (Home Office 1984) in the mid 1980s the Probation Service has been subject to a 'reforming' process in which both values and objectives have been largely re-constituted. By the end of the decade this process had gained momentum culminating in the Audit Commission Reports (1989a, 1989b), the Criminal Justice Act 1991, and National Standards for the work of the Service (Home Office 1992a). By the time the Criminal Justice Act 1991 was implemented, the Probation Service was no longer the rehabilitative arm of the criminal justice system. Rather, it had taken its place as one of the five agencies of an increasingly centralized and managed justice system (Raine and Wilson 1993), (along with the police, courts, crown prosecution service, and prisons), with a brief to administer tougher community penalties, protect the public, and assist courts in targeting serious offenders for incarceration.

This new agenda was reiterated by the Home Office Three Year Plan for Probation (Home Office 1992b) which outlined the main tasks of the service as: crime reduction, diversion, Pre-Sentence reports, community supervision, work with prisoners, accommodation, child welfare, equality of opportunity, management of staff and other resources, partnership and quality of service. It is important that the Plan placed service to the courts and to the public before the rehabilitation of the offender. The shift, from the humane response to offender need and aberrant behaviour, to the effective management of a growing offender population without threatening public safety had begun. Within this newly prioritized objective the accurate assessment and prediction of those who pose a risk to public safety, and who therefore require either greater community surveillance or incarceration is vital. As a consequence risk assessment and effective risk management are likely to become the main preoccupations of the Probation Service.

In its response to offender risk the Service will have to develop new assessment tools, intervention strategies, management processes, train its staff, and deal with the complex nature of risk and the difficulties of prediction. The latter is central to risk assessment, as such assessments are concerned with predicting whether a particular harmful event or action will occur in the future, and most important for Probation what they might be and who will enact them. It is important, therefore, to consider prediction issues in some detail before moving on.

THE QUEST FOR PREDICTION

Prediction, or the art of foretelling that an event, behaviour or action will occur has preoccupied those working with the mentally ill, dangerous or violent for sometime (Limardi and Sheridan 1995). The purpose of prediction is to seek to control, and if possible prevent the future occurrence of harmful behaviours to self or others. It is important to know with some certainty who to treat, who to release, who to incarcerate and whom to protect. The concept of 'danger-ousness' (in particular who is and who is not) has dominated much of the mental health literature since the 1970s, particularly in relation to mentally dis-ordered offenders (Floud and Young 1981; Prins 1986; Reed 1992; Wood 1988). The accurate prediction of who will be a danger and when has been central to the allocation of resources, the imposition of either residential/cus-todial or community care, and the balancing of individual rights against the protection of the public.

The concern to accurately predict dangerousness has spread from the largely clinically based decision making of mental health to the arena of penal policy and sentence decision making. In an important work, Bottoms (1977) noted the role played by the concept of dangerousness in the penal policy changes of the 1970s. This concept, and more important its accurate predic-tion, offered a seemingly reliable and objective system for selecting out certain individuals for increased surveillance and control. In effect, the 'bifurcation' policy noted by Bottoms offered a mechanism for allocating lesser and cheaper penalties to the 'ordinary offender' whilst reserving tough measures for the 'really serious offender' (p.88).

This classification system has been exacerbated by the increased 'commer-cialization of crime control' (Christie 1993) in which cost-benefit analyses, market forces, privatization, economy, efficiency and effectiveness have all impinged upon the management of criminal justice including Probation (Raine and Wilson 1993; Statham and Whitehead 1992). This approach to criminal justice has been labelled the 'new penology' (Feeley and Simon 1992) and it exhibits the following three key features: the management of justice and thereby the management of offenders, the targeting of increasingly limited resources at those most risky to public safety, and a policy of selected surveillance of those deemed to be 'less risky' in order to diminish both prison over-crowding and prison costs. The effective, and to a large extent the economic implementation of these policies depends upon the accurate prediction and safe management of risk.

The trend towards more accurate classificatory systems and increased targeting has been reflected in recent Probation practice. Most notably in the identification of those 'at risk of custody' by using the Cambridge Risk of Custody scale in the 1980s to complete Social Inquiry Reports, the post 1991 Criminal Justice Act focus on 'seriousness' and gravity scores in order to prepare Pre-Sentence Reports, and most recently the HMIP thematic inspection on 'dangerousness' and those deemed to pose a risk (Home Office 10/94).

Criminological studies have also engaged with the issue of prediction, primarily through the use of statistical methods and an actuarial approach to the possibility of risk (e.g. Farrington and Tarling 1985). This type of prediction is based upon predicting an individual's behaviour from how others responded in similar circumstances, or from the individual's similarity to others who have proved to be risky in the past. This is in sharp contrast to the clinical method which is based upon observation of the individual, a clinical assessment, knowledge, experience, and professional training. Where it has begun to concern itself with risk, predominantly sex offenders, lifers, and parole releases, the Probation Service has predominantly applied the clinical model of prediction. Cases tend to be individualized, with officers bringing their own theoretical perspectives, knowledge base and experience to the assessment process with often little reference to existing empirical data or the relevant actuarial studies (Kemshall 1995a). With its roots in individualized therapeutic case work the Service has found it easier to adopt the clinical method from the mental health arena than the actuarial model from criminological studies. Earlier studies of parole decision making have noted the resistance to the use of actuarial information with a tendency for decision makers to rely upon past experience and case studies (Flynn 1978; Glaser 1973). In its urgent need for predictive methods the Probation Service is in danger of uncritically accepting the heritage of clinical inference without giving full consideration to the role actuarial studies of offender risk could make to assessment. It is also in danger of placing too much faith in the possibility of accurate prediction.

THE PROBLEMS OF PREDICTING RISK

The dictionary definition (Oxford Dictionary 1989) identifies the following components of risk:

> the (mis)chance component, the exposure to hazard or danger, and the damage or loss component.

In essence, a risk calculation is one where there is uncertainty as to whether a loss or damage will occur. It is an unpredictable event and down to 'chance', and the actor must calculate the relative loss or damage likely if 'things go wrong' before proceeding to act or not. In an article on worker risk decisions,

Brearley (1979) described this calculation as 'gambling' because of the difficulties of accurate prediction and the costs to worker and client if things go wrong. In the United States workers have been subject to litigation for just such mis-calculations (Tarasoff vs Regents of the University of California 1974, 1976).

Clinical prediction, particularly in the mental health field has a poor record of accuracy (Convit *et al.* 1988; Gondolf, Mulvey and Lidz 1990; Miller and Morris 1988; Steadman and Morrisey 1982). Such clinical inference methods are affected by the subjective views of the clinician, the reactions of the respondent, and the interaction between them as well as by the restricted applicability of the predictive instruments used which are often limited to a few discrete behaviours or one section of the population (Milner and Campbell 1995). The technique is dependent upon observation which can be subject to value-judgements (Kemshall 1993), and interviewing in which both interpretation by the interviewer and the willingness of the respondent to disclose will impact upon the reliability of the information subsequently gained. These issues have affected child abuse work as evidenced by the Beckford Inquiry (London Borough of Brent 1985), and Parton (1986) has suggested that risk assessment pre-Beckford is best characterized by optimism, exaggeration of parental co-operation and skill, and judgements 'to the good' which were not based on evidence. Probation practitioners and service managers should be wary of over reliance on a risk assessment method which is open to such bias. In addition, the method is heavily dependent upon the past experience, values and beliefs of the practitioner which may carry stereotypical views and discriminatory attitudes. There is a potential for mis-classification, with the possibility of further stigmatization and alienation for those already on the margins of society.

Statistical, or actuarial methods are noted to have greater accuracy (Milner and Campbell 1995) than clinical methods although a number of difficulties still remain. Any contribution to risk prediction can only be in general terms about groups of people or types of actions. A range of probable outcomes is articulated, but uncertainty over which outcome, where, when and by whom still exists. Again there is the potential for mis-classification with severe consequences for those who may lose their liberty at point of sentence or parole, and where disclosure to third parties takes place in order to protect potential victims. Civil liberties may be infringed, and there are considerable ethical issues involved in the classification of offenders based upon assessment and prediction methods which may turn out to be inaccurate. There are also severe difficulties for agency, practitioner and victim if risk is under-predicted, not least the possibility of harm to victims and blame to agency and worker.

Monahan (1981) in an important work on violence prediction has stated that prediction (especially clinical) is wrong about 95 per cent of the time, and that the safest prediction is to state that no-one is a risk as this is likely to be the most accurate. In effect, despite a plethora of predictive measurements and screening tools risk assessment and prediction is at best a 'good guess'. To enhance the 'guess' to a judgement of reasonable credibility information and data from a number of sources should be compared, and actuarial methods should be utilized to increase the accuracy of clinical assessments. The latter, if well supported, can have an important role in identifying who is most likely to become risky from the range of probable outcomes suggested by actuarial data. However, it is doubtful that causal connections will ever be satisfactorily proved, and an agency involved in the delicate job of balancing personal rights against statutory responsibilities, and offender rehabilitation against public safety, may well do better to talk of risk markers rather than risk indicators.

The Probation Service cannot guarantee to prevent risk, only to credibly identify the possibility of risk and take adequate steps to diminish it. A risk assessment can only identify the probability of harm, assess the impact of it on key individuals, and pose intervention strategies which may diminish the risk or reduce the harm. Assessments cannot prevent risk.

THE PROBATION SERVICE RESPONSE AND ITS LIMITATIONS

The main Probation Service response has been the Association of Chief Officers of Probation document *Guidance on the Management of Risk and Public Protection* (ACOP 1994). This document correctly recognizes that the Criminal Justice Act 1991 and National Standards for Probation require 'a more active recognition of responsibilities for assessing risk to the public and its subsequent management' (p.1). Whilst predominantly a management perspective focusing on systems and procedures, it does recognize some of the inherent difficulties in dealing with risk. It warns that the Service has a 'limited ability to protect the public' (,p.1), and that systems in themselves do not solve the problem of risk. Potential victims of risky offenders are identified as staff, children and the public. These definitions reflect the legislative concerns of the Criminal Justice Act 1991 in respect of both violent and sexual offenders as expressed in section 1 (2) (b) of the act (Wasik and Taylor 1991), and the overall concern to protect the public from continued offending as outlined in National Standards (Home Office 1992a).

Whilst the ACOP document urges Services not to focus exclusively on risk to staff, it does acknowledge that Services are pre-occupied with 'extreme cases of potential dangerousness, with a concentration on particular offence categories' (ACOP 1994, p.1). With the exception of Hereford and Worcestershire, Services focus upon dangerousness, and use offence type as the main indicator of risk. Risk is viewed primarily in terms of the possibility of physical violence, sexual offending, and mental ill health.

The public may have other risk concerns beyond that of physical harm from violence. The public may perceive greater risks in respect of burglary, car crime and other property offences, and in respect of offender types other than the physically dangerous (Kemshall 1995b). Particular communities may perceive themselves to be at greater risk from some groups and offence types more than they are from others. For example, those in poverty fearing property crime even of a small value, ethnic minorities fearing racial crime, and older people fearing burglary. However, some of the Service risk assessment models referred to in the ACOP document would not place these offences or offenders in a risk category. These fears of crime, and hence perceptions of risk, are specific to the situations of the people concerned, to the impact that such offences would have on their lives, the losses they would sustain, the lack of control they could exert on events, and the uncertainty and unpredictability of whether such events would occur again. This highlights the complex nature of risk, and the important distinction between objective risk and subjective perceptions of that risk. The Service's view of acceptable risk may not be that of the public. There can be enormous diversity in what people perceive as risky to them, and hence what they want managed for them. It is simplistic to assume that there is a uniform public craving freedom from the sole risk of dangerous offenders. Rather, there are many 'publics' daily making decisions about what and who is risky to them and how they will respond to and manage that risk. It is important to recognize this, as the perceptions of risk held by the Home Office, the Probation Service, and the public may not necessarily coincide or remain static over time.

Further analysis of the ACOP document reveals that the Service's understanding of prediction and its predictive instruments are somewhat embryonic in form. Whilst the guidance suggests a number of questions for officers to ask as part of a risk assessment, it is not clear how they have been arrived at, whether they have any predictive validity, or how officers should evaluate the information subsequently gained. The exemplars attached to the document from various Services present risk indicators as though causal connections had been proved and as if prediction were not plagued by unreliability. The empirical evidence for the risk indicators is not presented, and clinical and actuarial methods are combined in an haphazard fashion. Only one Service (Warwickshire) notes the unreliability of prediction, and the tendency for practitioners to underestimate risk due to ethical considerations, personal bias, beliefs and attitudes.

Classification of risk primarily upon offence type presents a number of difficulties. Not every offender in the offence category will present a risk; some serious offending is never repeated and the general public is not at risk. A number of life licensees who have committed murder would fall into this category. However, repeated thefts from vehicles, thefts, and some burglaries might be classed as low risk but present a significant source of both distress and risk to those subject to them especially if they occur frequently within a particular neighbourhood. Classification as risky is bound to commit additional resources; can the Service afford to 'over target' either practically or financially? Where Services intend to label cases and pursue computer registration the implications of the Data Protection Act for registrations that cannot be proved should be considered. Mis-classification when applied to sentencing or parole decisions can have consequences for the liberty of the individual which must have some basis in evidence and credible decision making. Liberty can not always be restricted on the basis of 'just in case'. Even within a serious offence category risk will change over time. The important question is who will change and how will we know? Individuals may only become risky if certain very specific situations or factors occur. The Confidential Inquiry into Homicides and Suicides by Mentally Ill People (Steering Committee 1994) noted the link between mentally ill patients in the community who failed to take their medication and subsequent acts of violence. A key question is how can individuals whose circumstances may change be adequately targeted, and will officers act upon new and relevant information when it is presented? (e.g. the Clunis report, Ritchie, Dick and Lingham 1994). Services need to develop sound risk assessment procedures and supervisory practice if officers are to do more than 'take a gamble' (Brearley 1979).

AN ALTERNATIVE RISK ASSESSMENT MODEL

Two questions need to be urgently addressed. The first is how can we be more certain that the feared outcome will occur? The second is, once we are more certain what do we do? The pursuit of greater certainty must involve an informed analysis of situational and behavioural factors as well as of offence type. This shifts attention to the identification and assessment of *risky situations* rather than of risky offence types, and begins to alleviate some of the difficulties noted above. It also has the potential to identify courses of action for the officer.

Brearley (1982) has developed a useful framework for understanding and assessing risk which assists workers in recognizing the complexity of factors in a risky situation. In essence, his model assists workers in identifying the 'hazards' which may lead to the 'danger' resulting. A hazard is defined as 'a condition which introduces the possibility that loss, damage, or diminution will result from danger'. The 'danger' is the resulting event which, if it occurs, loss and so forth, will be caused to be suffered. According to Brearley hazards can be split into two important categories: generally predictive, and the specific. The generally predictive utilize actuarial assessment methods and the specific are dependent upon clinical inference. In the general predictive category of offender risk would fall information known to have relevance to the class of offence or offender, for example known reconviction rates, age, length of criminal career. This is information well explored in reconviction studies, particularly in the work of Farrington and Tarling (1985), and in the reconviction predictor work of Humphrey, Carter and Pease (1992). In the specific category would fall information specifically relevant to that individual offender, for example, personal characteristics, attitudes, situational factors of his or her immediate environment, past history, and known patterns of behaviour including offending. The danger would be the impact of another offence, upon whom and with what consequences to the victim, the officer and the offender. In all situations, however, there are also particular strengths which may serve to reduce the hazards and limit the danger. For example, gaining employment, leaving a peer group, undergoing a specific intervention or therapy. The worker has to 'weigh up' the hazards against the strengths and decide upon the level of risk present and whether this is tolerable. Part of the toleration calculation is an estimate of the costs of responding or not responding to the risk, and the costs to all involved if the harmful event takes place. Some risks will not be worth the cost of intervention. Intolerable risk will require further action, either to reduce the hazards by action which will remove them, or by action which increases the presence of strengths. Workers could apply the following checklist (adapted from Brearley 1982) to their cases to determine the presence or level of risk in case situations:

(1) General predictive hazards:

(2) Specific hazards:

(3) Strengths in the situation, either of the person, of others, or of the environment:

(4) Danger(s):

(5) Level of risk present: 1 2 3 4 5. (1 = low risk).

(6) Risk of what?

(7) Risk to whom?

(8) Consequences of the risk, to whom?

(9) Costs of acting/not acting? To whom?

(10) Action required to minimize the hazards:

(11) Action to enhance the strengths:

(12) Consequences of no action, to whom?

(13) Recommendation (to include case plan reflecting work proposed on hazards and strengths, and including evidence for level of risk determined.

(14) Date for review:

This checklist offers a systematic approach to risk assessment in which probabilities of risk, its nature, to whom, and why it might occur can be identified. The source of the risk markers (rather than causal indicators) can be made explicit, and it combines the greater accuracy of actuarial methods with the clinical observation and personal knowledge of the officer. It can be applied within a reasonable time span to all cases at commencement as part of the supervision plan, or used to consider risk probability for the purposes of Pre-Sentence reports, Temporary Release and Parole reports.

Officers using the model will need to pro-actively seek information and ask questions of the offender and significant others in order to complete the checklist. The offender's situation and immediate environment will also require investigation. In this way data from a number of sources can be compared and evaluated. Ethical issues of disclosure and infringing liberty will also become more explicit as strengths have to be considered in addition to hazards, and classification has to be evidenced. The views of the officer have to tested against the available information and the presenting evidence, in this way bias, stereotypical views and the potential for discrimination can be counter balanced. Whilst no judgement will ever be 100 per cent accurate or 100 per cent objective, this model offers the possibility of consistency, open decision making based upon available knowledge of offender risk taking and behaviour, and a systematic testing out of views which can otherwise remain idiosyncratic and unsupported by evidence.

GUIDANCE FOR PRACTITIONERS IN THE USE OF THE MODEL

In applying the model officers will need greater knowledge of actuarial information on offender behaviour and to diminish their belief in clinical inference as the sole, reliable method for assessing offender behaviour and subsequent risk. In addition, officers must recognize that structured interviews have a limited capacity for revealing reliable information due to the respondent's ability to manipulate answers and their own interpretive value-judgements (Milner and Campbell 1995). This requires that information gathered through such interviewing should be validated by other sources, compared and contrasted. Officers must develop techniques for evaluating what they are told, asking 'what does this mean?', 'what has changed?', 'is this a new hazard?'. Both the Clunis report (Ritchie *et al*. 1994 and the Beckford Inquiry (London Borough of Brent 1985)) showed that relevant information on risk was available but was not recognized, communicated or acted upon.

Officers may need to curtail their natural belief and natural optimism about the behaviour of offenders. These have been necessary tools in the formulation and maintenance of humane and rewarding relationships with clients. In risk assessment officers will need to be more outward looking to other sources of information and knowledge bases in order to validate externally, rather than internally accept, what offenders present in terms of their own risk. It is important to bear in mind that behaviour and situations interact to present a risk. Officers will need to know about both, although the latter in terms of the offender's immediate environment and significant networks is often under explored. Such networks, proximity to offending opportunities, pressure of others, and disintegration of community bonds may all be important factors in the exacerbation of a risk. Finally, risk changes in both nature and frequency over time. Cases will need to be subject to constant review, and most particularly in the light of new information.

TRAINING AND MANAGEMENT ISSUES

Training will need to be more sophisticated than the identification of the 'dangerously' violent or the 'dangerously' mentally ill. Officers will need to understand the complex nature of risk, the issues involved in predictability, problems of risk perception, potential for mis-classification and issues of civil liberties, the role of risk in current penal policy, the potential for discrimination, how to develop and use risk markers, applying a risk assessment model, and risk management strategies. An introductory course with at least the following objectives is recommended for all officers and their immediate line managers:

Specimen Three Day Risk Training Course

(1) To provide officers with an understanding and knowledge of current definitions of risk, including the place of risk in present penal policy.

(2) To provide officers with an understanding and knowledge of the applicability of risk definitions to their work with offenders.

(3) To provide officers with an understanding and knowledge of the variability of risk, and how this applies to their work, including cultural and gender differences in both perceptions and toleration of risk.

(4) To provide officers with knowledge of the discriminatory issues which may affect risk perception and its subsequent management.

(5) To provide officers with an understanding of the issues involved in risk prediction, including knowledge of differing predictive methods and how to achieve a greater degree of accuracy.

(6) To provide officers with an understanding and knowledge of applicable risk markers, including the formulation of a risk assessment model to apply to their own practice.

(7) To provide officers with some strategies for risk management in their work, to include an examination of the factors which hinder risk perception and responses to it.

(8) To provide a follow-up day to assess the impact of training to officer practice.

Training and practice guidance will need to be supported by adequate management systems and appropriate supervision of officers. Systems for the registration of offenders as risky are not a response to risk in themselves, and managers and officers should not over-rely upon administrative procedures as a way of responding to risk. This may give both officers and managers a false sense of security, leaving practice little changed. Systems need to ensure that risk assessments regularly take place, are based upon a sound knowledge base, and are free from attitude bias and discriminatory practices. This requires more than an administrative check that the relevant forms have been completed. Rather, it requires purposeful supervision of officers which can both check and facilitate that assessments are appropriate and that intervention strategies to limit risk are followed through. Supervisors have an important role in testing out officers' views against the information and evidence provided, and in checking that changes in either behaviour or situation are thoroughly considered. This will require supervisors to improve their own knowledge base, to develop techniques for case evaluation which they can systematically apply, and to guard against overly subjective or collusive processes in supervision.

CONCLUSION

Offender risk is set to become the Service concern of the late 1990s and beyond. The Probation Service can either pursue a simplistic response based upon offence categorization and largely unproven predictive indicators, or it can acknowledge the complex nature of risk and the variability of public perceptions of it. The former response will no doubt quickly fulfil the present penal policy desire effectively to target who can safely be de-carcerated without significant risk to public safety. However, its accuracy may prove more illusory than real and this will have severe consequences for the treatment of offenders and the credibility of the Service. The latter response will take more time but may prove to have greater efficacy in the long run. The Service must not appear to promise what it cannot deliver. It should avoid an expectation of wholly accurate prediction or public safety from any risk. The real task for the Service may well be the articulation of the range of probable risks facing the public and how limited they already are rather than the uncritical application of supposedly objective indicators of risk.

References

Association of Chief Officers of Probation (1994) *Guidance on the Management of Risk and Public Protection. Position Statement.* ACOP.

Audit Commission (1989a) *Promoting Value for Money in the Probation Service.* London: HMSO.

Audit Commission (1989b) *The Value for Money Audit Guide.* London: HMSO.

Bottoms, A. (1977) 'Reflections on the Renaissance of Dangerousness.' *Howard Journal 16,* 2, 70–96.

Box, S. (1987) *Recession, Crime and Punishment.* London: Macmillan.

Brearley, C.P. (1979) 'Gambling with their lives.' *Community Care* Nov 8, 289, 22–23.

Brearley, C.P. (1982) *Risk and Social Work: Hazards and Helping.* London: Routledge and Kegan Paul.

Christie, N. (1993) *Crime Control as Industry.* London: Routledge.

Clark, D.A., Fisher, M.J. and McDougall, C. (1993) 'A new methodology for assessing the level of risk in incarcerated offenders.' *British Journal of Criminology 33,* 3, 436–448.

Hazel Kemshall and the University of Birmingham wish to confirm that the model of risk assessment suggested in this chapter is merely one possible method of assessing the risk of an offender and no guarantees can be given that such a model of assessment is infallible. Those officers using the model must consider each individual case on its merits.

The author is currently a holder of an Economic and Social Research Council grant to investigate 'Risk in Probation Practice' under the ESRC initiative 'Risk and Human Behaviour'. Grant number: L211252018. The sponsorship of the ESRC is gratefully acknowledged.

Convit, A,. Jaeger, J,. Lin, S.P,. Meisner, M. and Volavka, J. (1988) 'Predicting
assaultiveness in psychiatric in-patients: A pilot study.' *Hospital and Community
Psychiatry 39*, 4, 429–434.

Cornish, B. and Clarke, R. (eds) (1986) *The Reasoning Criminal: Rational Choice
Perspectives on Offending.* New York: Springer Verlag.

Farrington, D.P. and Tarling, R. (1985) *Prediction in Criminology.* Albany, NY:
Albany State University Press.

Feeley, M. and Simon, J. (1992) 'The new penology: Notes on the emerging
strategy of corrections.' *Criminology 30*, 4, 449–475.

Floud, J. and Young, W. (1981) *Dangerousness and Criminal Justice.* London:
Heinemann

Flynn, E. (1978) 'Classifications for risk and supervision.' In J. Freeman (ed)
Prisons Past and Future. Cambridge Studies in Criminology.

Glaser, D. (1973) *Routinizing Evaluation.* Rockville Maryland, National Institute of
Mental Health.

Gondolf, E.W., Mulvey, E.P. and Lidz, C.W. (1990) 'Characteristics of perpetrators
of family and non-family assaults.' *Hospital and Community Psychiatry 41*, 2.

Hay, W. and Sparks, R. (1993) 'Vulnerable prisoners: Risk in long-term prisons.' In
K. Bottomley (ed) *Criminal Justice: Theory and Practice.* British Criminology
Conference 1991, British Society of Criminology/Institute for the Study and
Treatment of Delinquency, London.

Her Majesty's Inspectorate of Probation (1994) *Thematic Inspection: Dealing with
Dangerous People: The Probation Service and Public Protection.* Home Office 10/94.

Home Office (1984) *Statement of National Aims and Objectives.* London: Home Office.

Home Office (1992a) *National Standards for Supervision in the Community.* London:
Home Office.

Home Office (1992b) *Three Year Plan for the Probation Service 1993–1996.* London:
HMSO.

Humphrey, C., Carter, P. and Pease, K. (1992) 'A reconviction predictor for
probationers.' *British Journal of Social Work 22*, 33–46.

Kemshall, H. (1993) 'Assessing competence: Scientific process or subjective
inference? Do we really see it?' *Social Work Education 12*, 1, 36–45.

Kemshall, H. (1995a) *Risk in Probation Practice.* Unpublished research sponsored
under the Economic and Social Research Council programme: Risk and Human
Behaviour.

Kemshall, H. (1995b) 'Risk in probation practice: The hazards and dangers of
supervision.' *Probation Journal 42*, 2.

Limardi, B.J. and Sheridan, D.J. (1995) 'The prediction of intentional interpersonal
violence: An introduction.' In J. Campbell (eds) *Assessing Dangerousness:
Violence by Sexual Offenders, Batterers, and Child Abusers.* Interpersonal Violence:
The Practice Series. Sage.

London Borough of Brent (1985) *A Child in Trust: the Report of the Panel of Inquiry
into the circumstances surrounding the death of Jasmine Beckford.* Presented to the
Brent Borough Council and to Brent Health Authority by members of the Panel
of Inquiry, London Borough of Brent.

McWilliams. W. (1987) 'Probation, pragmatism and policy.' *Howard Journal 26, 2,* 97–121.

McWilliams, W. (1992) 'Statement of purpose for the probation service: a criticism.' *NAPO News 39,* 8–9.

Miller, M. and Morris, N. (1988) 'Prediction of dangerousness: An argument for limited use.' *Violence and Victims 3, 4,* 263–283.

Milner, J.S. and Campbell, J.C. (1995) 'Prediction issues for practitioners.' In J. Campbell (eds) *Assessing Dangerousness: Violence by Sexual Offenders, Batterers, and Child Abusers.* Interpersonal Violence: The Practice Series. London: Sage.

Monahan, J. (1981) *The Clinical Prediction of Violent Behaviour.* Beverley Hills, CA: Sage.

Oxford English Dictionary (1989) Prepared by J.A. Simpson and E.S.C.Weiner. Vol.xiii, Clarendon Press, Oxford.

Parton, N. (1986) 'The Beckford report: A critical appraisal.' *British Journal of Social Work 16, 5,* 531–556.

Prins, H. (1986) *Dangerous Behaviour, The Law and Mental Disorder.* London: Tavistock.

Raine, J. and Wilson, M. (1993) *Managing Criminal Justice.* Hemel Hempstead: Harvester Wheatsheaf.

Reed Report (1992) *Review of Health and Social Services for Mentally Disordered Offenders and Others Requiring Similar Services.* London: Department of Health/Home Office.

Ritchie, J.H., Dick, D. and Lingham, R. (1994) *Report into the Care and Treatment of Christopher Clunis.* London: HMSO.

Statham, R. and Whitehead, P. (1992) *Managing the Probation Service: Issues for the 1990s.* London: Longman.

Steadman, H.J. and Morrisey, J.P. (1982) 'Predicting violent behaviour: A note on a cross validation study.' *Social Forces 61,* 475–483.

Steering Committee of the Confidential Inquiry into Homicides and Suicides by Mentally Ill Persons. (1994) *A Preliminary Report on Homicide.* London: Steering Committee of the Confidential Inquiry into Homicides and Suicides by Mentally Ill Persons.

Tarasoff versus Regents of the University of California. 118 Cal. Rpt. 129, 592, P.2d, 553 (1974)

Tarasoff versus Regents of the University of California. 17 Cal. 3d, 425, 551, P2d (1976)

Wasik, M. and Taylor, R.D. (1991) *Blackstone's Guide to the Criminal Justice Act 1991.* London: Blackstone Press Ltd.

Wood, D. (1988) 'Dangerous offenders and the morality of protective sentencing.' *Criminal Law Review* 424–433.

CHAPTER 11

SEX OFFENDER RISK ASSESSMENT

Sue McEwan and Joe Sullivan

INTRODUCTION

Until relatively recently the issue of risk has been dealt with by focusing almost entirely upon the perpetrator. However, through work with perpetrators, practitioners have developed a greater understanding of sexual offending and have recognized the need to become involved with the family, not only to enable work with the perpetrator, but also to help in the protection of victims.

When trying to break the pattern of offending, it is crucial that practitioners are aware of the collusion or 'grooming' of families and how this affects the motivation to change of all those involved. The realization that risk does not simply apply to 'hands on' abuse (Salter 1988) has increased agencies' awareness of risk and caused greater concern.

We recognize the gaps in the provision of services to victims and non offending family members where work often ends at the point of disclosure or with 'self-protection' work.

This chapter introduces an integrated approach. It is an ideal and we recognize that it has numerous implications for all those involved. The chapter is, however, practice based using 'tried and tested' exercises. It gives a full account of an assessment programme using groupwork although it could be easily transferred to 2–1 work.

The chapter also contains an outline of the relevant points for risk assessment from recent literature and focuses on some of the issues for agencies managing risk.

HOW RISK IS DEFINED

Risk is defined by a victim, a perpetrator, a third party, or an agency, based upon an observation, allegation, admission or suspicion of sexually abusive behaviour. It can also be defined as a potential risk, based upon previous sexual offending; for example, when a Schedule 1 offender moves in with a new partner and there are children in the home.

The definition is subjective at this point, being based upon a victim's disclosure of an 'allegation' of abuse; a perpetrator's 'admission' of abuse; a third party's 'observation' or 'suspicion' of abuse, or the 'potential' for abuse being recognized. Once defined, the local social services department will become involved in investigation and, usually, a case conference will be convened.

WHAT IS RISK?

Regarding sexually abusive behaviour, the risk is undoubtedly, 'what danger does this person pose to others?'

In relation to the perpetrator the questions to be answered are:

> Is it likely to happen? Has it happened? What is the extent and nature of the abuse? Will it happen again?

These questions need to be answered at the investigation stage and more fully once other agencies such as police, courts, CPS, probation and psychological services become involved in the post-investigation assessment period. For assessment purposes the minimum required from a perpetrator is an acknowledgement that the abuse has happened. Absolute denial raises a number of issues which require different responses and these will not be addressed here.

In relation to the victim living in the family home, the questions are likely to be:

> Will it happen again? What's going to happen now?

For the victim it is not just about 'hands on' abuse. They are likely to have been subjected to behaviours by which the perpetrator isolated them within the household, making them feel different or special. The removal of the perpetrator from the home is likely to have both positive and negative effects for the victim – their place within the family will need to be re-established. This may lead to thoughts such as:

> 'I wish I hadn't said anything,' or, 'It's my responsibility to put things right.'

The non offending partner's questions are likely to be:

> Is it likely to happen? Has it happened? Will it happen again? What do I do? What should I do? What should I have done? What could I have done? What will be imposed? How do I put things right?

For agencies, the most important questions in relation to the non offending partner will be:

> How able is this person to protect the victim and other children? Are they willing to accept the abuse has happened and the consequences? Are they colluding with the perpetrator?

For the siblings in the family the questions are likely to be:

> How do I fit into all of this? Do I tell (if it has happened to me)? Will it happen to me? Why did s/he have to say anything?

In cases where the abuse occurs outside the family home, the victim's experience may be very different. However, the questions outlined above will still apply to non offending partners and children within the home.

HOW ACCURATELY CAN RISK BE PREDICTED?

Over the years, the standard response within the Probation Service has been that all perpetrators remain a continuing high risk, with those in absolute denial seen as the greatest risk.

Perpetrators usually see themselves as low risk and falsely believe that disclosing further abuse or giving information increases their perceived risk. This, of course, is not the case. Practitioners in the field of child sexual abuse all concur that offences are planned, following on from a period of using abusive fantasies during masturbation, and are never 'one-off' offences. Accordingly, perpetrators are viewed as high risk and this risk may only reduce by information gained over a period of time. The 'disclosure consequences calculation' taken by perpetrators can be observed in Figure 11.1.

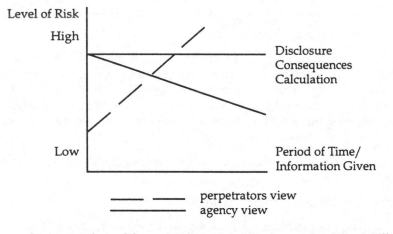

Source: Adapted from training material presented to West Midlands Probation Service by Ray Wyre (1988))

Figure 11.1

It may be that the perpetrator continues to be viewed as high risk, or that, with a highly motivated offender who discloses a great deal of information, the risk reduces. It is important that all agencies concur on the level of risk the perpetrator presents and that assessment is seen as an opportunity to evaluate 'real' risk as opposed to 'perceived' risk.

THE IMPORTANT FEATURES OF RISK

(1) Level and types of denial.

(2) Type of offences committed.

(3) Category of offender – extrafamilial, intrafamilial, sadistic, non sadistic.

(4) Target (victim) group. (Given evidence that perpetrators may have multiple paraphilias (Finkelhor 1986; Laws 1989) it is important to be careful about labelling).

(5) Duration of offence pattern. Age at onset of offending.

(6) Variation of offence pattern.

(7) Motivation to change. Experience of previous treatment and acceptance of worker assumptions.

(8) Presence of external factors affecting motivation, eg, a collusive or 'well-groomed' family will block a perpetrator's progress.

(9) Level of acceptance of responsibility for the abuse.

(10) Level of victim empathy (do not expect much at this stage!).

(11) Mental illness.

(12) Drug and alcohol misuse.

(13) Non-sexual offending. Previous convictions.

(14) Sexual aggressiveness (Malamuth 1994), Psychological testing, including penile plethmysnograph, cognitive scales and attitudes towards women and children.

(15) Abusive personality (Sullivan, McEwan, Hunt, Garrison, 1995)

(16) Seriousness of sexually abusive behaviour (often different from conviction or offence charged).

(17) Cultural issues – target group. It is important to note that the power base of most institutions is white and this may impinge on the ability of black victims to disclose.

(18) Learning disability – psychological testing required as many programmes are cognitive/behavioural. Relapse prevention techniques require direct consequences rather than victim empathy.

(19) Level of self-esteem/social isolation.

(20) Own victim experience.

(21) Links with other sexual offenders – co-defendants, paedophile rings?

ASSESSMENT PROCESSES

(i) The Preliminary Assessment

This is likely to be the preparation of a pre-sentence report if court proceedings are under way, or the work carried out following initial case conference. The requirements and format outlined below cover the work necessary at this stage.

In preparation, collate information, previous reports and depositions. The interview should last between one and a half and two hours. It should be conducted in a formal office setting, be video taped and requires three chairs of equal height in a triangular fashion in front of a flip chart. The two workers should be experienced in sex offender work, with a gender balance. One of the workers should take responsibility for leading the interview and writing an assessment or report.

(a) Start the interview by setting the scene, giving the reason for the interview and the aims and objectives (to give and collate information). Workers should then state the assumptions which underpin the work (e.g. all offenders use fantasy and masturbation, they plan their offending, sexual abuse is an abuse of power, there is no such thing as a 'one off' sex offence – and that perpetrators tend to deny all of this initially).

(b) Following a discussion and acknowledgement of denial tactics the perpetrator may use, it is useful to complete a family tree and gain as much information as possible about the perpetrator's life experience from childhood onwards including first awareness of sexual arousal to children.

(c) Then complete an abbreviated version of the Cycle of Offending (Wolf 1984) using fantasy, masturbation, grooming, abuse, guilt, as headings.

(d) Begin to collate information on the pattern of offending using the concept of the 'four hurdles' of motivation, overcoming internal inhibitors, overcoming external inhibitors and overcoming victims resistance (Finkelhor 1986).

(e) Collate the information gained from the interview.

(f) Decide if another interview is necessary.

(g) Decide on future action; e.g. pre-sentence report proposal, contact with social services department, the perpetrator's suitability for ongoing work.

(ii) Assessment Programme – Groupwork

There are a number of differing approaches to the duration of programmes. West Midlands Probation Service operates a model of a block week, full time for five days, followed by ten weekly half-day sessions. This service has large numbers of sex offenders and uses 'closed' groups of up to ten men in assessment. If they do not achieve, perpetrators must repeat the whole programme. Staffordshire Probation Service has smaller numbers to contend with, a steady trickle, and therefore operates an ongoing 'open' group, one day per week programme in which perpetrators continue until they complete or achieve the programme aims. The STEP programme (Beckett, Beech, Fisher and Fordham 1994), following evaluation of a number of community-based sex offender programmes, recently recommended the use of a 'block' element at the start of programmes.

Aims:	• To assist perpetrators to recognize the key components of their sexual offending cycle, to take responsibility for their offending and accept the continuing risk they represent.
Objectives:	• Collate information on pattern of offending.
	• Identify cognitive distortions used in rationalizing/denying behaviour.
	• Perpetrator to accept responsibility for behaviour.
	• Perpetrator to identify own cycle of offending.
	• Highlight the role of fantasy in planning of offending.
	• Identify level of victim empathy and facilitate development of victim empathy, if possible.
	• Introduce concepts of lapse and assist in the development of early start relapse prevention.

At this stage the aim is not to treat, simply to assess. It is inevitable that the perpetrator will change his language. Indeed, experience has shown that this change of language was problematic in early programmes when it was believed it signified change. This should not be seen as indicating a change of attitude or behaviour.

A number of programmes exist nationally which largely achieve the aims and objectives outlined. This is our version:

(1) Collate information on perpetrator and offending pattern:

- use the information gained in the preliminary assessment
- follow up with a sexual history, life history, and non sexual offending history, perhaps using checklists.
- videotape the perpetrator speaking for five minutes, alone to camera, on 'my offence'
- videotape a victim letter (this will not be shown to victim).

(2) Identify cognitive distortions used to rationalise/deny offending:

- use a variety of exercises including 'denial wall', Geese Theatre masks, complete offending analysis, walking through the offence, 'blame' cake, and an analysis of abusive/controlling techniques in sexual and non-sexual behaviour.

(3) Perpetrator acceptance of responsibility:

- this is closely tied with cognitive distortions: as distortions reduce, the level of acceptance increases.

(4) Offending Pattern – Cycles of Offending:

- use a non-abusive cycle to introduce the concept of fantasy and notion that we cannot act without having thought it through
- start with a storyboard – drawings of the offence, then move it backwards into planning and fantasy
- introduce pro-offending thinking and behaviours, together with seemingly irrelevant decisions and examine how the perpetrator overcame internal inhibitors
- examine motivation to offend and feeling states prior to triggers before completing a full inhibited cycle of offending.

(5) Fantasy and its role in offending:

- a continuum exercise is useful and can be used at any stage – asking perpetrators to place themselves along the continuum in relation to questions posed
- concepts of illegal/legal or non-abusive/abusive fantasies need to be explained and understood.

(6) Victim Empathy:

- examine the change of language from initial assessment to now.
- Have they moved? Do they recognise their victim(s) as such?
- the ripple effect of victimization exercise
- victim statements/victim drawings – what is the effect?
- repeat videotaping of victim letter – review (any change?).

(7) Lapse/Relapse:

- identify previous techniques of relapse prevention – why did they fail? Fragility of internal inhibitors?
- make 'stop' statements
- identify external inhibitors
- acknowledge PIG (the problem of immediate gratification).

It is important to note that the whole process is interlinked and no part is discrete.

All perpetrators will be expected to complete a transitional piece of work, using cycles and so forth formulated during the assessment period. This will be assessed by the staff and, although subjective, it is viewed in line with the growing experience of staff involved in the work. It is acknowledged that evaluation of the work produced and the programmes has been entirely practice based until recently. There are now some initiatives to evaluate programmes (the STEP Programme, Beckett et al. 1994) and some services are incorporating evaluation techniques into their programme, for example the Oxfordshire Probation Service Sex Offence Attitudes Evaluation Questionnaire (1993), and the employment of a PhD psychology student at the West Midlands Probation Service Regional Sex Offender Unit.

A common mistake in programmes is focusing predominantly on content and ignoring the process in groups. Sex offenders are usually extremely experienced in the art of manipulation and generally use every way they know to disrupt and unhinge the groupwork process. It is vitally important to engage them in process work to minimize manipulation at the start of the group and to deal with issues up front, and consistently throughout the programme. Ground rules set at the beginning of the group can help in the process, and regular trust exercises help to 'bond' the group. Also a clear contract on further admissions/disclosures helps to alleviate stress for both workers and perpetrators.

Clear statements about anti-discriminatory practice need to be made and particularly racism, sexism and homophobia challenged immediately and consistently.

Black perpetrators are very likely at present to find themselves in otherwise all white groups. We are not aware of any groups having been run specifically for black perpetrators and, for the present, there appears to be a consensus amongst practitioners that sexual offending is seen as the primary factor, with race and cultural issues being important in developing an understanding of the individual's offending pattern.

USING RISK MODELS TO DEVELOP A COMMON PHILOSOPHY FOR MANAGING CHILD SEXUAL ABUSE CASES

The well documented propensity to blame the victim for sexual attacks both inside and outside the family home has been exposed by numerous authors in recent years (Salter 1988; Adler 1987; Herman 1981). Particularly worrying is, however, the fact that this desire to lay the blame for sexual abuse with the victim or the family unit persists and while, as Salter (1988, p.33) points out, it is no longer the primary view, other authors in the 1980s (West 1981; Mohr 1981) have pointed to issues of the child's complicity in sexual offending and the benefits of dealing with child sexual abuse internally within the family.

Those who regularly attend case conferences in child abuse cases will be familiar with this philosophical view which persists and clearly reflects the needs of the offender rather than those of the victim or potential victims within a family unit. In the 1990s it is still not uncommon to attend case conferences where the issue of whether a child has actually been harmed by sexual abuse are being debated or where family reconstruction is being considered before any attempt has been made to assess the needs of the victim, non offending family members or even the perpetrator.

Clearly the first important principle in managing a response to dealing with sexual abuse is for a common philosophy to be established between the agencies and individuals involved in the decision making process. Salter (1988) suggests that the most effective response to child sexual abuse requires the co-operation of independent agencies unfamiliar with each other's structures and procedures.

> In responding to child sexual abuse such co-operation is not only desirable but essential, for without it attempts to provide quality services and protect children will certainly fail. (Salter 1988, p.68)

Although this observation was made with reference to the North American System the principle is equally applicable to Britain where the development of a common philosophy and protocol for dealing with child sexual abuse cases is still some way off.

ESTABLISHING A COMMON PHILOSOPHY

(1) Responsibility for Abuse

It will be important in developing a common philosophy to establish a number of core interagency beliefs, the most important of which should be the recognition that the responsibility for sexual offending lies exclusively with the offender. This principle should underpin all work with the offender, the victim and other non offending family members.

As noted previously, confusion on this issue still persists and generally contributes to many of the interagency disagreements about how to manage child sexual abuse cases. Such disagreements provide an easy target for sex offenders to manipulate in the decision making process.

Examples of these manipulations include projecting the problem of child sexual abuse as a problem with the family unit, which it is often proposed can be dealt with through the use of family therapy. This moves the focus away from the offender and can result in collusion with the secrecy which surrounds sexual abuse within the family and avoids a recognition of the cause of the problem. Sexual abuse causes family dysfunction, it is not brought about by problems within the family.

A further problem associated with not focusing on the sex offender as the cause of the abuse, is that the problem can be perceived as being with the victim, who will be even more vulnerable to blame in the early stages following disclosure, as they often experience feelings of guilt at a variety of levels in relation to the abuse.

While it is the needs of the victim which should be the primary focus of intervention following disclosure, it is the offender's responsibility for the abuse which should influence the decision about how the case should be managed. Hence, a philosophy which starts from the point of the offender being ultimately responsible for the abuse, inevitably points the way to a number of other procedures which should become 'core interagency beliefs'.

(2) Assessment Before Intervention

In proposing a protocol for dealing with child sexual abuse cases, most contemporary researchers suggest that the assessment process is vital in establishing what interventions are required in order to reduce risk. It is important that assessments are undertaken as quickly as possible on all members of the family in addition to the offender.

The offender's desire to have interventions completed quickly so that the family can return to 'normal', are often vocalized by the non offending family members or the victim and are often reinforced with an observation that the process of dealing with prosecution and case conferences feels more abusive than the actual sexual abuse 'might' have been. Where a standard protocol for dealing with child sexual abuse cases does not exist, the uncertainty about how to proceed allows offenders and distressed, yet groomed, victims and non abusing family members to urge time frames and courses of action which reflect the offender's rather than the victim's needs.

However, appropriate decisions about managing child sexual abuse cases can only be made following full and detailed assessments of the perpetrator, the victim and non abusing family members.

(3) Family Reconstruction is not an Aim of Assessment

All too often the precedent for family reconstruction is set before the assessment procedure has even begun. This precedent can be set in a number of ways; for example, by the removal of the child rather than the perpetrator from the home, or by the establishment of supervised contact before the assessment procedure has been completed. In some instances, case conferences respond to the family's anxiety to get the problem solved quickly by stating from the outset that the ultimate aim will be to reunite the family as soon as possible.

Such decisions will almost certainly lead to the perpetrator and all family members, including the victim, adjusting to the 'inevitable' return of the perpetrator in a way which is likely to impede the assessment process.

What we know about the power structures which sex offenders create in order to abuse within a family suggests that the issue of family reconstruction should not be addressed before full assessments have been completed – the phenomenon of 'the abuse continuing when the touching stops' (Salter 1992).

The extent of the grooming and 'hands on' abuse process needs to be recognized within a common philosophy as influencing how victims deal with the continuing crisis following disclosure.

As we can see from the research on the impact of child sexual abuse on victims and other family members (Salter 1988; Herman 1981; Browne and Finkelhor 1986) as well as the material on sex offenders (Finkelhor 1986; O'Connell et al. 1990; Morrison, Erooga and Beckett 1994), their patterns of offending and the risk they present to future victims, there can be little doubt that the problem presents highly complex issues which require an integrated response based upon a common multi-agency philosophy.

(4) Sex Offenders Cannot be Cured and do not Always Offend Against the Same Victim Group

Another important principle which needs to be incorporated into any common philosophy is that sex offenders do not necessarily offend against one type of victim, so men who have abused children outside the family may present a risk to their own children.

This debate has been informed by research which has found, albeit from self reports by sex offenders, that sex offenders commonly engage in a variety of different types of sexual offending.

> A brief review of selected studies in both of these areas appears to clearly show that some substantial percentage of rapist of adults have a sexual interest in children, particularly prepubescents and pubescents, and many of them have self-reported or been convicted of sexual involvement with these age groups. (Laws 1989, p.8)

ISSUES OF RISK MANAGEMENT

(1) Risk and Resources

One of the consequences of the increased work now being undertaken with sex offenders has been a greater understanding of the complexity of the issue and a realization of the inadequacy of our responses to the problem. The more our work informs our practice the more our practice has had to change. This has led to calls for greater resourcing, more co-ordination and better training not only within organizations working with perpetrators but within all agencies dealing with the issue of sexual abuse.

Some agencies have begun to develop policies and strategies based upon the work in the face of criticism about the disproportionate use of resources in an area which statistically forms only a small part of many agencies' overall caseload responsibility.

Within some probation areas sex offenders account for about five per cent of the overall caseload and yet developing principles for good practice have led to the establishing of specific groupwork initiatives, co-working of pre-sentence reports and recommendations for extended probation orders and licence supervision for sex offenders. Alongside this have grown practitioner forums and protocols for case conference involvement, all of which increase the time and resources expended on this one category of offender.

Social workers and child protection officers also report growing levels of involvement and greater time being spent on sexual abuse cases, with interventions becoming ever more intensive. Cases which have previously been dealt with by several home visits to discuss protection issues with victims and non offending parents are now requiring extensive and expensive external consultancy, groupwork and individual treatment programmes for victims and non offending family members.

In addition, some areas, for example, the West Midlands Probation Service, have established a 'risky adult' registration scheme, an extension of Schedule 1 registration, which can include perpetrators who have sexually offended against adult victims, recognizing that they may also represent a risk to children.

All these developments have important resource implications for managing risk in sexual abuse cases and give some insight into the reasons why decisions at a policy level have been slow to address the need for greater interagency co-operation and co-ordination.

(2) Monitoring and Reviewing

The argument which is often used to stem the flow of resources into an area such as this is the question of effectiveness, illustrated in the Audit Commissions Report on the Probation Service (1989).

> While there is a striking variety of probation schemes in operation involving much vision, creativity and imagination, schemes must be evaluated and their impact on offending behaviour assessed. It is unsatisfactory that, at present, considerable sums are spent with relatively little understanding of the effects achieved. (p.2)

If a situation is to be avoided where this argument is used to prevent the development of work in the area of sexual abuse, it will remain important for those managing agency responses to monitor and evaluate the effectiveness of policy decisions and programme developments.

This is particularly true for interagency initiatives which will inevitably rely for their funding on several funding bodies.

(3) Management Decision Making

The development of an interagency response to the issue of child sexual abuse will require the increased involvement of management in an area which until now has been largely practitioner led.

Resourcing issues will remain a key area for management attention as the anomaly of seemingly ever diminishing resources is measured against a growing need for new and improved services from all agencies involved in sexual abuse cases.

BIBLIOGRAPHY

Adler, Z. (1987) *Rape on Trial*. London: Routledge Kegan Paul.

Audit Commission. (1989) *Promoting Value for Money in the Probation Service*. London: HMSO.

Beckett, R., Beech, A., Fisher, D. and Fordham, A.S. (1994) 'Community based treatment for sex offenders: An evaluation of seven treatment programmes.' *The STEP Programme*. London: HMSO.

Browne, A. and Finkelhor, D. (1986) 'Impact of child sexual abuse, a review of the research.' *Psychological Bulletin 99*, 66–77.

Finkelhor, D. (1986) *A Sourcebook on Child Sexual Abuse*. Newbury Park CA: Sage.

Herman, J. (1981) *Father–Daughter Incest*. Cambridge MA: Harvard University Press.

Laws, D.R. (ed) (1989) *Relapse Prevention with Sex Offenders*. New York: Guilford Press.

Laws, D.R. (1994) 'Are rapists dangerous to children.' *NOTA Journal of Sexual Aggression 1*, 1.

Malamuth, N. (1994) Sexual Aggressiveness Paper presented at NOTA, (National Organisation for the Development of Work with Sex Offenders), Conference, Durham University.

Mohr, J.W. (1981) 'Age, structures in paedophilia.' In M. Cook and K. Howells (eds) *Adult Sexual Interest in Children*. New York: Academic Press.

Morrison, T., Erooga, M. and Beckett, R.C. (ed) (1994) *Sexual Offending Against Children: Assessment and Treatment of Male Abusers*. London: Routledge.

O'Connell, M.A., Leberg, E. and Donaldson, C.R. (1990) *Working with Sex Offenders: Guidelines for Therapist Selection*. Newbury Park CA: Sage.

Oxfordshire Probation Service (1993) Sex Offence Attitudes Questionnaire: Evaluation. Copyright: Oxfordshire Probation Service.

Salter, A.C. (1988) *Treating Child Sex Offenders and Victims*. Newbury Park SA: Sage.

Salter, A.C. (1992) Current Treatment Issues in Working with Sex Offenders. Conference paper delivered to NOTA Conference, Dundee.

Sullivan, J., McEwan, S., Hunt, S. and Garrison, K. (1995) The Abusive Personality, unpublished.

West, D.J. (1981) 'Adult sexual interest in children: Implication for social control.' In M. Cook and K. Howells (eds) *Adult Sexual Interest in Children*. New York: Academic Press.

West, D.J., Roy, C. and Nichols, F.L. (1978) *Understanding Sexual Attacks*. London: Heinemann Educational Books.

Wolf, S.C. (1984) 'A multi-factor model of deviant sexuality.' Paper presented at Third International Conference on Victimology, Lisbon.

CHAPTER 12

THE RISK OF VIOLENCE AND AGGRESSION TO SOCIAL WORK AND SOCIAL CARE STAFF

Brian Littlechild

INTRODUCTION

Violence to staff in social work and social care settings is a comparatively recent area of concern and study. This chapter will examine the factors we need to take into account in managing risk of violence to staff, drawing on our knowledge of risk factors, and the problems there are in assessing and utilizing approaches to risk management. In particular, the incidence, types, settings, and locations of violence will receive attention. The client groups who pose most risks will be set out, and why they might pose such risks.

The deaths of several workers during the course of their duties focused professional and public concern on the issue in recent years. Several deaths of social workers have occurred, including those of Peter Gray, a social worker in Hampshire; Norma Morris and Isabel Schwarz in London; and Francis Bettridge in Birmingham.

Approximately 90 per cent of assaults on staff are by people who are known, and the assailants often have a previous pattern of violence. Incidents of violence, especially where the assailant is known, frequently engender feelings of guilt, self-blame, anger, and fear concerning further repercussions. Rowett (1986) found that 42 per cent of victims of physical assault said it had adversely affected their practice. In addition, workers often feel that they will be judged harshly by managers and colleagues. They often have concerns about their future safety, which can affect their work performance, and confidence in confronting situations; and suffer a severe denting of professional self-image (Littlechild 1993a).

Incidents can affect not only individuals, but also the morale, and the commitment, of groups of staff. To convince staff that the agency does take violence seriously, there need to be policies in place which ensure that consistent monitoring of the situation takes place. Such monitoring needs to take into account the experience of victimization, and allow identification of the specific nature of the types of risk, venues, and the effectiveness of responses.

To address fully the issues which we need to take into account when assessing and managing the risk of violence to staff in social care and social work settings, we need to look at three separate, but inter linked levels. These are the personal, the team, and the agency. The inter-relationship between these areas is a dynamic one, and in this chapter, each area will be covered and the inter-relationship made clear.

THE RAP/REVIEW MODEL

The RAP/Review model for risk assessment and management is one way of approaching this area systematically, by processes of Recognition, Awareness, Planning, and Review.

Recognition

This has to take place at all three levels, personal, team and agency. In most agencies, there is now some level of recognition that their staff are at risk. In many, though not all, this has not been transferred into effective policies which are based on staff's experiences and difficulties, as is demonstrated in the research of Johnson (1988), and of Norris (1990). At the team level, recognition of the real issues needs to be aided by an enabling central agency policy. At the personal level, staff need to recognize when, and in what situations they are at risk; how to ensure effective support; how to reduce risk in face to face situations; and how to gain support if they have to face the effects of incidents. It is important for those at all levels to recognize that no matter how well individuals employ violence reduction tactics, they cannot guarantee it will not happen. This reflects a culture of support, as opposed to a culture of blame. The latter has often been the experience of many workers (Heining 1990; Johnson 1988; Littlechild 1993b; Norris 1990).

Awareness

It is important that the potential for violence, and strategies to deal with it, are kept constantly in mind. Such awareness, which can be helped by proper induction of new staff into policies and practice of violence avoidance; a constant personal awareness; and proper planning and review systems in the agency/team. This in turn provides the key to better recognition of areas and types of risk, which should lead to greater awareness and better planning, as part of a feedback loop.

Planning

At an individual level, workers need to recognize when they might be at risk, and then plan support and protection. Independent workers need to determine how to deal with the wider issues with their contracting agency. Where someone is an independent practitioner, s/he may need to take these issues to a support group of similar workers, and make representations to their employer/contractor to get such processes into place. The contractor can still be seen as having a responsibility for the safety of those contracted.

At team level, there needs to be agreement on when, and how, the issues set out in the Recognition and Awareness sections above are dealt with. Different teams examine what violence occurs in their settings, and what they intend to do about it, for example in a residential unit there might be statements laid out in an admission agreement, which state the acceptability (or not) of certain types of behaviour, and what will happen if this is breached. This might include training and policy development work with the staff group.

For the agency, there needs to be one senior manager who has responsibility for collecting and collating information, and developing policies in conjunction with front line staff.

Review

Any planning must include an element of review. This is necessary at all three levels – for each individual workers, for the team, and the agency. Such review is the key to learning and effectiveness in planning to deal with violence. This could include regular reports – six monthly, possibly; based on the individual definitions and policies drawn up; numbers of incidents, of what type, to

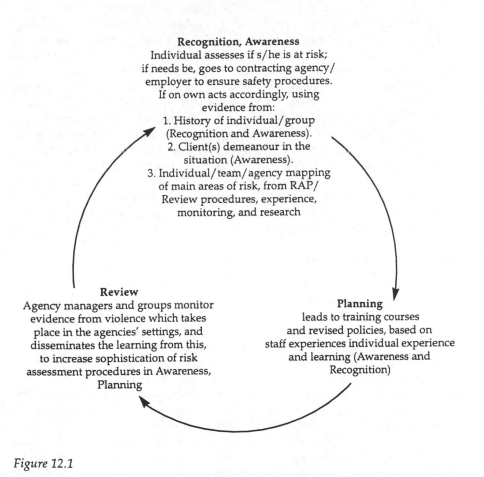

Figure 12.1

whom, for example. Suggestions drawn from this process are collated and analyzed by a senior manager with this area of responsibility, and an agency group, comprising front line staff representatives then suggests ways forward to develop agency and team policy and practice. Such review in turn provides the key to developing better recognition and awareness at all three levels, and feed into better planning – completing the all important feedback loop.

The whole system – personal, team and agency – is a dynamic one which can be represented in Figure 12.1.

A Definition of Violence

As we all have different, individual definitions of what might constitute violence, there needs to be agreement in agencies and teams on what we mean by violence. This then becomes an essential feature of the RAP /Review model, and the means by which individuals are empowered to recognize when they are at risk, and demand appropriate support.

There are various 'official' definitions we can draw on, and they provide a perhaps surprising unanimity. The Association of Directors of Social Services (1987) adopted the following: 'Violence is behaviour which has a damaging effect either physically or emotionally on other people'. The British Association of Social Workers (1988) definition is virtually the same. This can include threats, verbal abuse, racist abuse, and sexual harassment.

The importance of taking a baseline definition which takes into account the victim's feelings of whether, and to what degree, they feel violated, and how this is taken into account in agreed policies, and procedures within agencies, is difficult to overstate. Frequently, staff believe incidents are not serious enough to report, or they believe they are expected to soak up such behaviour as part of their work (Norris 1990). Workers often fear how others, especially managers, will judge them (Rowett 1986, p.122). This then leads to under reporting, due to concerns from the worker that they will be seen as weak, provocative and poor workers if they do report. Such attitudes were frequently reported in Rowett's study.

The Importance of Recording and Reporting

Under reporting is wide spread in social work. For example, Rowett found that only five per cent of all incidents of physical violence were properly reported and recorded in written form in the Social Services Departments that he studied. Poyner and Warne (1986) state in their Health and Safety Executive report that the essential feature of any strategy to reduce the risk of violence at work is the effectiveness of reporting procedures. If procedures, policies – and most important of all, a culture of support to report – are not in place, it will not be possible for colleagues, teams, or the agency to map out areas of risk, be they from individual clients, work settings, particular types of work, times of greatest risk, and so on. If there is no such mapping, or review of learning from such incidents, it is not possible to plan for safe environments. A vital aspect of ensuring proper reporting, and therefore proper risk assessment, is the need for staff to feel safe to report, and meet supportive response from managers. All the research within this field conclude that there is a major problem of under reporting. Ways of improving reporting are pursued in Bibby 1994, Littlechild 1993a and 1993b, and Norris 1990.

Individual Awareness

The individual needs to make use of the opportunities afforded from the learning emanating from RAP/Review procedures, and link this to his/her own knowledge of themselves; how do they respond to threats, and the various forms of violence and aggression (recognition), i.e. in what situations is s/he most at risk? What happens in their behaviour, which might aid the upwards spiral of aggression (awareness), and what do they do/could they do to minimize this? (planning). Every individual has learnt to deal with aggression and violence through different experiences, for example in their home environment; at school; in youth clubs; discos; clubs; on the street.

Table 12.1. shows a brief checklist, offered as a means for individuals to make an initial assessment of the types of situations in which their previous learning might affect their assessment of, and ability to deal with a potentially difficult situation. Rate your responses to the situation; 1 means you are not threatened; 2 means you are threatened to some extent; and 3 means you are very fearful.

Table 12.1. Checklist		
I am least able to think clearly, and be appropriately assertive, when dealing with:		
	Not threatened	*Threatened to some extent*	*Very threatened*
	1	*2*	*3*
Males			
Females			
Older people			
Younger People adolescents; defiance, threats, challenges,			
Young children tantrums, etc.			
People exhibiting paranoid schizophrenia			
One-to-One situations			
Group Settings			

Table 12.1. Checklist (continued)		
I am least able to think clearly, and be appropriately assertive, when dealing with:		
	Not threatened	*Threatened to some extent*	*Very threatened*
	1	*2*	*3*

When Working Alone

When working with a co-worker

When exerting authority
e.g. setting/enforcing limits/
boundaries, rules, in field residential
or day care setting

When on client's territory

When on your territory

Other areas of concern for yourself:
(List and indicate level of concern)

Look at the overall results of your deliberations, and think through in what sorts of situations, in what type of settings, and with which clients you might be most at risk. You may think of other situations or settings relevant to your own experiences. Relate this to the evidence of risk set out in this chapter. This should then give you a good idea of your own individual needs and risk within the overall picture. Use this as a basis for discussion with your line manager as part of planning how you best use your strengths, and develop the areas you find most threatening.

GROUP CARE AND FIELDWORK SETTINGS

This section examines what we know of risk in different settings, and the risk from each client group within that setting.

Group Living and Group Care Situations

The main issues in residential care relate to the close relationships formed between care workers and residents. The dynamics are very different from fieldwork; in residential work, the working relationship is based on seven to eight hour (or longer) shifts, where meals, group living, and domestic living arrangements provide the framework for staff/resident relationships. Unlike fieldwork, staff cannot just walk away from a difficult situation. The build up to and aftermath of an incident or incidents, can take place over days, sometimes weeks. In addition, residential workers, and to a somewhat lesser extent day care workers, are working with residents on an everyday basis to achieve social work values and aims in the development of a resident's skills and attitudes, by way of individual care plans, for example. They try to maintain a balance between the rights of an individual, and the resident group as a whole. For example, if one person is exhibiting anti social and/or dangerous, violent behaviour towards other residents, or staff, this needs to be dealt with. Such controlling is a necessary part of caring; it should not be our task to allow such behaviour to continue unchecked, not only for the safety and well being of others in that situation, but also in helping residents learn how to manage their behaviour in such situations; a vital element for someone learning to exist in any community. If residents learn that such behaviour is not dealt with, it is likely they will continue with such behaviour; and if it means they do get their own way over other interests which should be legitimately defended, they are liable to do it more. This is a clear and real lesson we can learn from behavioural psychology (Sheldon 1982). Tutt (1976) quotes a study which looked at the background of young people in Community Homes with Education, where a correlation was found between violent male figures in their previous home life, and current attitudes and use of violence, to others.

The implications are clear; a major element of care plans, and overall aims of establishments, will need to take into account the need to help clients to overcome such previous learning. However, such work leads to confrontation; and when and how we use our power, authority and control, is a key feature in when violence will be offered to staff, as Brown, Bute and Ford found in their study in the Wessex area (1986). Other pressures are also brought into the situation from outside influences, for example on a Friday evening when a young person in residential care may be let down by her/his family with whom they may have an ambivalent and difficult relationship, when told at the last moment the family cannot, after all, have them home that weekend. It then becomes essential that the rules of the establishment are seen as being implemented fairly. The group care situation can become a cauldron of difficult feelings; rejection, poor self-image, learnt aggressive behaviour, competitiveness within the group, immediate external pressures on individuals; all can fire a violent incident, and need to be taken into account in risk assessments.

We do have some knowledge of particular settings, and difficulties within them. Rowett (1986) found the same as Smith (1988) in respect of violence in residential establishments. Whereas a high proportion of incidents occur in residential establishments, 89 per cent in Rowett's study, and 78 per cent in Smith's, in each case many of the incidents were attributable to a small number of individuals who were the perpetrators on a number of occasions. Leavey (1978) found that 5 per cent of residents accounted for 37 per cent of the violence in his study, and Smith comments that his figures for residential incidents were skewed by a high number of incidents from two individuals; one adolescent, and one adult with learning disabilities. Rowett found that in terms of violence suffered in the previous five years, residential workers in one shire county had been victims at roughly twice the rate of fieldworkers; for example, 17 per cent of basic grade fieldworkers reported being victims, whereas 38 per cent of basic grade residential workers reported being victims. Of all who reported, 18 per cent reported moderate to serious effects – moderate was extreme tissue damage, or broken limbs, for example (and 19 of these 20 were residential workers); and 6 per cent reported permanent physical harm. The group most at risk were males who were deputy officers in charge; perhaps because they intervene on behalf of other staff in difficult situations, and then become the focus for aggression themselves.

In Brown *et al.*'s study, they found that residential and day care settings accounted for over half of all incidents, though there may have been more staff employed in these settings; or they may just have returned their questionnaires more regularly. They found that 9 per cent of all incidents to all staff were due to advice giving or disciplining residents. They also found a high level of violence within day care settings; 22 per cent of staff reported they had been victims of such violence which differs from Smith's and Rowett's findings, although Brown *et al.* used a wider definition of violence. They concluded that residential staff were at greater risk than field social workers; 45 per cent of the former reporting having been victims, and only 22 per cent of the latter. These findings accord with a Surrey Social Services Department study in 1986 which showed that most staff in residential establishment had been assaulted on two or more occasions during the previous five years (Bibby 1994, p.22).

Fieldwork

Fieldworkers tend to work on their own, carrying out home visits, transporting clients in their cars, interviewing in the office. Avoiding isolation is a key feature of risk assessment and management, and in RAP/Review procedures; fieldwork staff in many settings have ensured that some planning and policies are in place, at some level, to reduce such isolation.

The situations in which staff are most likely to be at risk are when dealing with situations where clients see them as exercising 'unfair' power and control, and in particular, where their, or a relative's, liberty is at risk. This is so for mental health clients, where someone is being assessed for compulsory admission, or where s/he is in a very paranoid and psychotic state, and to a large degree, out of touch with reality. It is also true for child protection and child care work, which has been recognized as having particular risks for workers.

The House of Commons Health Committee's report on Child Protection services (1991) expressed concern at the number of people leaving the social work profession, due partly, they believed, to the level of violence and abuse which such staff suffered. The Department of Health's review of findings of child abuse death inquiries (1991) found that the threat of violence to staff had been identified as having had significant negative effects on social workers practice in a number of such situations.

Rowett also noted that 11 per cent of assailants were relatives of clients; and this was a particular feature of child protection situations in fieldwork. One in four assailants in fieldwork were clients' relatives. If we consider how much face-to-face contact there is in such situations, and therefore opportunity for this to happen, compared to other social work settings, this would seem to be a very high risk area; and unlike the profile of assailants overall – most were men – such violence was usually from women, probably as it was often single parent families where the intervention took place. Brown *et al.* found that 26 per cent of incidents in fieldwork in their study were in relation to taking children into care, as they termed it. In Probation Service work, one study shows that the group of workers most at risk are Court Welfare Officers; again, this is because such workers are seen to be making judgements about people's parenting skills, and whether the child(ren) should be with that parent, or someone else (Littlechild 1993b).

A survey by the London Boroughs Training Committee (1983) found that 67 per cent of assaults occurred in the social work office; 10 per cent were in the street; and 21 per cent were in client's homes. Brown *et al.*'s figures were 42 per cent in the client's home; 19 per cent were in the social worker's office, and 11 per cent took place in cars or ambulances. Rowett found that 50 per cent of assaults on fieldworkers occurred in the client's home; 7 per cent in psychiatric hospitals; 3 per cent in community homes; and 2 per cent in each of the following: cars; the social worker's office; police cells; reception areas; and the client's bedroom in residential child care units. In Probation Services, the only research into setting indicates that the reception area is much the most frequent area for incidents to occur (Littlechild 1993b).

OTHER FACTORS

The Relationship Between Social Worker and Client

There is a clear correlation of risk, to the relationship with the social worker. Rowett found that 85 per cent of assailants were established clients; and 84 per cent of incidents were repeats of incidents from the same assailant, in similar circumstances. Many of these were attributable to older people in residential care. Smith found that in 98 per cent of incidents in his study, the victim knew the perpetrator; and in 90 per cent staff knew of previous violent behaviour from the perpetrator; again, many were in residential care.

In his scanning survey of a number of Social Services Department, Rowett found only 3 of 112 assaults on fieldworkers took place on first meeting. He also found that more than one in four assailants had previous convictions for violence. He considered that 92 per cent of the clients were under some form of stress at the time of the assault. This emphasizes the need to record what factors may have led to violence in that particular situation.

Issues of Ethnic Origin and Racism

There is no clear evidence on whether there is any significant differences in victimization in terms of ethnic or racial background.

Norris (1990) quotes from an internal study into abuse and assaults on residential staff carried out by a Metropolitan Borough Social Services Department (original source not given) which found that racial assault had been suffered by 11 per cent of staff. We do not know if this is an accurate figure, or if there might be under-reporting in the survey. It is a much greater figure than other studies have produced, however. From the results of this research, he concludes that: 'Issues of race and gender, especially the former, are poorly served at the present time'; and 'Matters of race are not mentioned at all in the vast majority of responses' (Norris 1990, p.82). He recommends that '...Such complete failure to address the problem is clearly unhelpful and needs to be speedily put right'. Smith (1988) suggests that black staff in particular may be wary of reporting incidents, because of a concern at being judged even more harshly by management than their white counterparts.

Issues of Gender and Sexism

It may be the case that women do not feel safe to report such matters as there is a concern that predominantly male managers will not look sympathetically either at the woman's experience of the incident, or at attempting to stop the sexist harassment. Women have had to struggle for years in work-places (amongst other settings), to have it accepted that sexual harassment is not acceptable from colleagues and higher managers, or from clients in social work agencies. Norris (1990) noted that sexual harassment '...needs to be logged as a discrete area of inquiry (in report forms and agency monitoring) and properly researched, not least because its sensitive nature may make it especially prone to under reporting'. (p.82). Littlechild (1993b) found that 1 in 17 of female probation staff reported such harassment.

Smith found that 'women outnumbered men 2:1 in the reports of violence suffered and male perpetrators outnumbered female by the same ratio', and 'male victims appeared to be at particular risk from male perpetrators' (as in Rowett's study). In fact, where males were victims, 83 per cent of the perpetrators were males, and only 17 per cent females. He also found that where females were the victims, they were almost as likely to be assaulted by a male as a female – 56 per cent and 44 per cent respectively. This last finding may be of importance at looking at who might be potential victims in certain settings, as it would seem there are significant gender issues here.

MANAGING RISK: WHEN VIOLENCE IS ASSESSED AS BEING A POSSIBILITY

Some Do's and Don'ts

Use the checklist in Figure 12.2 having first considered how you react to violent situations – see relevant section in this chapter.

Figure 12.2

- Do, if possible, discuss and think through the situation with your supervisor or colleagues.
- Do organize back-up. If you are to be alone with a potentially violent client take a colleague with you, have one wait outside the door (which will perhaps be left open), or arrange for a colleague to call after a certain period if you have not returned, if you are on a home visit. Prepare what action will be taken on your behalf by colleagues in a given situation.
- Do think through, and plan, how you will approach and deal with clients in advance, if possible, if you are to be the bearer of distressing or explosive news. Invite them to the office; or your territory, if day/residential setting. Do not attempt to do this in front of their peer group.
- Do remove or hide in advance any potential weapons, e.g. knives, bottles, tools, plant pots, furniture, ashtrays, which may be nearby.
- Take off ties, earrings, etc. which could be used to cause injury.
- Don't put yourself or the client, either physically or psychologically, in a corner. Make sure that you each have exits and that either of you can back down without losing face. Arrange to meet a further time, agree to discuss matters with your boss. Perhaps suggest that the client complains to your managers, as another route through which they can direct their anger.
- Don't get into a verbal battle or feel or act as if you always have to win a point if it seems something is intractable between you and an aggressive client.
- Don't show that you are afraid or get into an aggressive mode in trying to conceal your fear. Hear your own voice; modulate it and try to keep it firm but calm. Use eye contact, but don't stare. Too forceful eye contact can appear threatening and increase your client's hostility. In particular, be very careful of use of eye contact with psychotic people.
- Do sit down if possible, at the same level as the client. You are then in a less aggressive stance. Try to maintain a relaxed posture. Squaring up to the client is rarely helpful. Sitting at a 45 angle is much better than sitting face to face.
- Do stay aware of your own feelings and reactions to those of your client. You are then more able to adjust your own responses to reduce the risk of violence.
- Do recognize the client's thoughts and feelings and communicate that recognition – but do not be patronising.

Figure 12.2 (continued)

- Do remove yourself and your client from a group if the group presence is exacerbating things. It is harder to back down in front of peers, for the worker, as well as the client.
- Do be aware of any drugs or alcohol which the client may have taken or be taking. The more taken, the less a reasoning approach will be effective.
- Don't point at the client, gesticulate or offer threats (as opposed to realistic limits).
- Do remove yourself immediately if it becomes obvious the client is rapidly becoming more aggressive or is about to attack you.
- Don't go to touch a potentially violent person to try to eject them or to prevent damage to property. Again, this issue needs to be discussed by the staff group, and perhaps more widely, as an agency.
- Do lock doors and windows if necessary until it is safe, to prevent an aggressor's access to you. Once someone has been successfully led out of the premises, there is a risk they may return very quickly, having decided they still have a score to settle.
- Do obtain support afterwards.

For further guidance on such individual techniques, see Bibby (1994) and Breakwell (1989).

MICRO-SIGNALS

These are the elements of body language which can alert us to a client's emotional state, and their propensity for violence or aggression in a situation.

Body Language
- Pacing jerky movements
- Use of space – theirs and ours
- Way of sitting/standing – towering above someone, sitting below them
- Threatening gestures
- The use of a lighted cigarette as a jabbing, threatening object
- Stiff posture
- Violence to inanimate objects

- Wagging, tense feet
- Pointing finger
- Drumming fingers
- Clenched fists
- 'Tight' facial muscles.

Eyes
- Fixed eye contact
- Averted Eyes
- Narrow eyes
- Dark glasses – someone wearing these is hiding an enormous amount of information about their attitude and emotional state from you
- Closed eyes, as part of a tense face and attitude.

Voice
- Silence
- Raised
- Ranting
- Menacing
- Shouting.

The important elements of the situation to note are how the above factors may be changing. Changes in attitude to you, or the situation, will be signalled by how these factors are changing in the interview. The worker should remain vigilant to these and adjust their approach and strategies accordingly, as their awareness of micro signals they are giving to the client(s) is of just as much importance as observing theirs. Are you in control of the signals you are giving, to reduce your messages of threat or submission?

History of Violence by an Individual

This is the most important warning factor; if there is such a history, we need to get as much information as we can on previous behaviour, and on the client's present circumstances.

Questions to ask of those who have known the client or from previously written records, will be:

- What was his/her mental state at the time?
- What was his/her domestic/social situation at the time, and what stresses were they perceiving?
- What were the stresses/trigger(s) for the violence?
- What clues do we get from these deliberations?

Questions to ask about present circumstances, will depend on answers to the above. Are the circumstances similar? If so, we need to take the precautions; if not, are we satisfied violence will not occur? If not, then set up the precautions.

Do record the incident fully, and in context, in a way which could be shared with the client. Include any possible triggers for the violence or aggression you can identify in a de-briefing session after the event, and any other ways the same sort of situation could be dealt with again in the future. Place this prominently on the front of the client's file, in a way which is in line with agency policies for recording, and open records. This is to give colleagues and future workers clues as to how to approach the client, to reduce the risk to these workers, and to reduce stress and potential further difficulties for the client if s/he is violent again. Such recording can also be useful as a tool in debriefing for the victim, and use in work with clients on their behaviour, if appropriate (Littlechild 1993a).

POTENTIAL CAUSES OF VIOLENCE FROM INDIVIDUALS

This section presents some of the theories on possible causes of violence

Mental Ill-Health

Some people suffering from certain forms of mental ill health may be more prone to aggressive and violent behaviour. This is by no means the norm for people suffering from the different forms of mental ill-health, but it can be the case that when someone has paranoid schizophrenic tendencies, normal interaction may be interpreted by the sufferer as a threat to which they could react violently. Three of the deaths of social workers in recent years have been at the hands of people with mental health problems. Rowett (1986) found that 38 per cent of assailants had been admitted to psychiatric units on at least one occasion, and of assailants to fieldworkers, this was the case for nearly 50 per cent. Brown et al. (1986) found that in fieldwork, 30 per cent of incidents were in relation to mental health admissions. Psychopathy, where the sufferer is only interested in their own ends, could lead that person to decide violence is a way to achieve them. The Approved Social Worker role under the Medical Health Act 1983 frequently puts the member of staff of risk.

Drug Use

Anyone using drugs illicitly – or legally, in the case of alcohol – may be subject to unpredictable behaviour. Rowett (1986) found that 15 per cent of incidents of physical violence in his study occurred when the client was under the influence of drugs.

Emotional

Stress and frustration are the two key elements to violence arising from a person's emotional state. We need to be aware of myriad of areas in a person's life which could lead to different levels of stress and frustration; from previous experience of abuse, through to structural reasons, such as poor service at DSS offices, housing offices, and so forth.; to his/her experience of 'us' as an agency, and our response; and, if we know the client, what gives them as individuals most stress and frustration, and what their reaction to different levels of these are; we all vary in these last respects.

Physical and Chemical Influences

Where physical or chemical causes may be present in someone we are working with, we should pursue these possible causes through medical channels; otherwise, we may be judging the person on behaviour they cannot control without medical help. Often those we work with have poor access to medical care. For example, Alzheimer's Disease can produce changes – sometimes rapid – towards aggressive behaviour, through the person's fear and confusion. Deafness or the inability to speak, can lead to great frustration in stressful situations, due to the constant failure of others to understand and appreciate what the person is trying to communicate. Constant pain in an individual which is unbearable can lead to aggression.

Defensible Space

When someone is in an emotionally and physically charged state, their need to have defensible space increases. We all have different distances within which we feel imposed upon by others; this is extended when we are in such an aroused state. When someone deliberately or inadvertently invades that space, this could easily be the trigger for violence. This will also vary depending upon whose territory the interaction takes place upon, and signals to the participants about threats and submissions can be a significant element in the outcome. Being aware of not invading an enlarged area of defensible space when someone is in an agitated state is one of the most important features of risk assessment and management.

Isolation

Research by the Labour Research Department (1987) demonstrated that the risk of violence is increased – and can lead to more severe violence – when the worker is isolated from what can be seen as supportive surveillance; this was a factor in 87 per cent of incidents in social services departments. This need not be in someone's home, this could be in a residential establishment, or in an office where interview rooms are away from easy view. Avoiding isolation is a key factor in risk assessment and prevention (Littlechild 1993a), particularly on home visits.

EFFECTIVE POLICIES

The aim of an effective policy for risk assessment and management is to:

(1) Enable effective recognition of areas of risk, in terms of work setting, types of situations, client groups and individual responses;

(2) Reduce risk of aggression and violence; by agency, team/peer group, and individual awareness of these;

(3) Reduce isolation of staff members, physically and emotionally, by proper planning, based on (1) and (2) above, and to increase collective support.

Who Owns the Policy of Risk Assessment and Management?

It is important that any policy relating to matters of managing violence and aggression is owned by the local staff group who operate and are subject to it. Whilst a policy on some of the areas to be covered is best formulated within central decision-making bodies in the organization, in consultation with front-line workers, such a policy needs to also encourage and enable staff groups to develop, operate, and regularly review their policy. The policy should enable staff groups to develop a culture within their setting which empowers and enables staff in their dealings with potential and actual aggression, and does not disempower them. Policies can be perceived by front-line staff as inhibiting good and creative practice, rather than promoting it, if a policy does not make clear it is in place to protect and support workers, and not just to protect the agency (Johnson 1988). Such policies need to reflect the fact that aggression and violence towards staff is an issue under the Health and Safety at Work Act, 1974 where agencies – and individual employees – have a duty to ensure employees safety, as far as possible.

Policies need to ensure that staff know what to expect from the members of their staff group and their agency in terms of support and protection. The more confident staff are in a situation, being aware of back-up procedures and knowing how they might work, the less likely violence is to occur, and if it does, to minimize risk to the worker, by ensuring they are readily accessible for support and protection. Staff need to know what measures they can count on, rather than be uncertain about this as well as being confronted with the aggressor(s).Whilst individuals need to examine what they may have been able to do differently in any particular situation, and therefore try to do differently in the future, they must feel confident that this is within a central and local policy which recognizes that aggression towards him/her is not their fault. Aggression and violence happens to staff at work because they are at work, and the work staff in caring agencies do is inherently risky. The purposes of the policy would be to move away from blaming the individual; to minimize risk to staff; minimize isolation of staff; and maximize supportive surveillance, and confidence, in back-up procedures; and to define areas for consideration for agencies, services, and state groups/peer groups to consider in defining risk.

REFERENCES

Association of Directors of Social Services (1987) *Guidelines and Recommendations to Employers on Violence against Employees.* Reading: ADSS.

Bibby, P. (1994) *Personal Safety for Social Workers.* Aldershot: Arena.

Breakwell, G. (1989) *Facing Physical Violence.* London: British Psychological Society and Routledge.

British Association of Social Workers (1988) *Violence to Social Workers.* Birmingham: BASW.

Brown, R., Bute, S. and Ford, P. (1986) *Social Workers at Risk: The Prevention and Management of Violence.* Basingstoke: MacMillan Education.

Department of Health (1991) *Child Abuse: A Study of Inquiry Reports 1980–1989.* London: HMSO.

Heining, D. (1990) 'Workers at risk.' *Social Work Today*, 19th July.

House of Commons Health Committee (1991) Public Expenditure on Personal Social Services: Child Protection Services. Second Report, session 1990–1991. House of Commons Papers 1990–1991, 570–1. London: HMSO.

Johnson, S. (1988) 'Guidelines for social workers in coping with violent clients.' *British Journal of Social Work 18.*

Labour Research Department (1987) Assaults on Staff. Bargaining Report, July 1987, London.

Leavey, R. (1978) Violence in Community Homes. Clearing House for Local Authority Social Services Research. London.

Littlechild, B. (1993a) *Managing Aggression and Violence towards Social Work Staff: Moving from Individual Blame to Agency Support.* Hatfield: Centre for Social Work Studies, University of Hertfordshire.

Littlechild, B. (1993b) *I needed to be told I hadn't failed: A research report into aggression and violence experienced by probation staff in Hertfordshire.* Hertford: University of Hertfordshire/Hertfordshire Probation Service.

London Boroughs Training Committee (Social Services) (1983) Analysis of Response to a Questionnaire to ascertain the level of violence/unreasonably aggressive behaviour experienced by fieldworkers and other staff in area teams. London: unpublished report.

Norris, D. (1990) *Violence Against Social Workers.* London: Jessica Kingsley Publishers.

Poyner, B. and Warne, C. (1986) *Violence to Staff – A Basis for Assessment and Prevention.* London: Health and Safety Executive.

Rowett, C. (1986) Violence in the context of local authority social work. Cambridge: Institute of Criminology Occasional Paper No. 14, Cambridge University.

Sheldon, B. (1982) *Behaviour Modification.* London: Tavistock.

Smith, F. (1988) *Analysis of violence towards staff in a Social Services Department.* Croydon: Croydon Social Services Department Monograph.

Tutt, N. (ed) (1976) *Violence.* London: HMSO.

CHAPTER 13

APPLYING RISK IN PRACTICE
CASE STUDIES AND TRAINING MATERIAL

This chapter consists of a series of case studies which can be used as training material. They have been complied in different ways, by different contributors to the book. They are presented in the order of the authorship of the chapters in the rest of the book.

CASE STUDY 1

Jacki Pritchard

Maria is 23 years old and has learning disabilities. She lives with her mother, father and two sisters. Her mother, who is the main carer, is a very domineering person and is physically disabled herself.

Maria is not physically disabled, but she has mild learning disabilities. For a long time she has had respite care in a local authority residential unit – two weeks in the unit followed by six weeks at home. She thinks that everyone is her 'friend'. Maria is described as being 'very capable' by people who work with her. She belongs to a user-led group who are very active in art-based activities, for example producing videos.

Recently, after she returned home from a respite stay Maria cried constantly and she told her mother that she never wanted to go to the unit again. She disclosed that a male member of staff had touched her breasts and put his hand down her pants. Maria's mother contacted the police who interviewed Maria and then the alleged perpetrator. The police concluded that there was no case with which to proceed. It was said that Maria could not be specific enough about what had happened to her and that staff in the unit thought highly of the alleged perpetrator, who had worked in the unit for years. The police had interviewed Maria in the presence of her mother; the social services department had not been contacted.

A student social worker was already involved with Maria when the incident occurred. Maria's mother refused to let the student talk to Maria by herself, because she did not believe that Maria should talk about sexual matters to anyone else except herself. After the police investigation, Maria refused to go for respite care because the care worker was still working there.

Risk Issues – Points for Discussion

- Discuss why Maria may think that everyone is her friend.
- What were the risks involved through Maria thinking that everyone is her friend?
- Is there a risk to others?
- Why had no-one talked to Maria about her sexuality/sexual matters?
- Who should take responsibility for discussing these matters if it is an issue?
- Was Maria able to give informed consent?
- Do you think a proper assessment had been carried out regarding Maria's level of understanding?
- What issues do you think should be given specific attention in this risk assessment?

CASE STUDY 2

Jacki Pritchard

Eric is 33 years old and has learning disabilities. He can hold a conversation and has good comprehension if simple, basic language is used. Eric is very much at risk of physical abuse in the local community where he lives.

Eric lives alone in a council flat. He says he loves his girlfriend, who also has learning disabilities. The couple have been engaged for years, but they do not have a sexual relationship, which Eric finds very frustrating. He has now got into the habit of exposing himself and saying rude things in public. The neighbours started bullying him and on occasions when they have physically attacked him the police have been called out.

Eric has been known to the local social services department for many years. He has had several social workers and his case has often been passed over to students. However, very little intensive work has been done with Eric over the years. A day centre place was arranged a long time ago and Eric still attends regularly. He enjoys crayoning and drawing flowers. He has never been considered a priority because he is not 'a high risk case' from the social services point of view.

However, other professionals assess his case differently. The police are concerned that Eric is at risk of further attacks in the community and believe that social services 'should do something'. The community psychiatric nurse has expressed concern, because of the harassment Eric suffers but she also believes that someone should be working with Eric regarding his sexual needs and behaviour.

```
┌─────────────────────────────────────────────────────────────┐
│                Risk Issues – Points for Discussion            │
├─────────────────────────────────────────────────────────────┤
```

- Discuss why you think Eric is at risk.
- What are Eric's needs?
- Are other people at risk?
- How could the risks be reduced?
- What work should be done with Eric?
- What strategies could be developed to manage this case?
- How can other professionals push for Eric's case to be made a priority in social services?

CASE STUDY 3

Jacki Pritchard

There are two good friends, Emma and Anne, who are both in their early twenties. They have known each other for many years, having met through a day centre for people with physical disabilities.

As a result of a head injury, Emma cannot walk at all and uses a wheelchair. Anne has cerebral palsy and also uses a wheelchair. The girls have decided that they now want to live together, but their parents are objecting to this idea saying that they would be too vulnerable in the community. Anne's parents also consider Emma to be 'too dominant and manipulative' regarding their own daughter.

The social worker considers that the girls could live together successfully. They have actually gone away together to a holiday camp for several years. They have never been accompanied on these holidays. They can help each other with practical basic care tasks and there have never been any problems whilst they have been away on holiday. Both girls acknowledge that there will be different problems to face, i.e. risks if they lived independently on a permanent basis, but they are sure that they will be able to manage.

The social worker believes that it is the two sets of parents who are presenting problems rather than Emma and Anne. The girls do have a sexual relationship, but they do not discuss this with anyone except the social worker. The social worker thinks that the parents are against the idea of the girls living independently because it would seem as if they were condoning the relationship.

A risk assessment has been undertaken by the social worker in conjunction with other professionals, who are involved with the girls. It is recognized and acknowledged that there will be certain risks for the girls living in the community, especially at night-time. But, as the social worker pointed out in a care planning meeting, both girls are capable of making their own decisions and have realistic views about the risks they will be taking.

Another suggestion has recently been put forward. Rather than move into a council tenancy, the girls should apply to live in a ten-bedded sheltered accommodation unit as a first step towards independence. The social worker also wants to work with both sets of parents to help them 'let go' of their daughters.

Risk Issues – Points for Discussion

- Are the girls being realistic about living together in the community?
- Discuss the principle of self-determination in regard to this case.
- Make a list of possible risks you think Emma and Anne may be taking.
- Discuss the possible positive outcomes of taking these risks.
- How would you reduce the risks?
- What work needs to be done with the girls?
- How would you achieve this?
- What are the needs of the parents?
- What work needs to be done with the parents of the girls?
- How would you achieve this?
- What are the conflicts of interest in this case?
- Do you think the girls should move into a semi independent unit before moving into their own tenancy?

CASE STUDY 4

Jacki Pritchard

Mr A is a Somalian man who is about 50 years old. He was wrongly placed in a sheltered housing complex for older people. He is physically disabled as a result of the injuries he sustained to his legs back in Somalia. He cannot walk and uses a wheelchair. Mr A cannot speak any English and refuses to admit the interpreters brought by the social worker. He insists that his friends translate.

Mr A is known to be a drug dealer in the locality. It is felt that he is putting the other people who live in the housing complex at risk, because of the activities which are carried out in his flat. Neighbours report that people are coming to the flat throughout the day and night. There is often a lot of noise and sometimes fighting. Other neighbours have said that they are very 'frightened' sometimes. They also object to 'the filthy state' of the corridor outside Mr A's flat, where there are piles of broken bottles, cans, cigarette ends and on occasions syringes have been found.

Mr A has a nine-year-old daughter living with him in the one bedroomed flat. His daughter does not attend school very often and an education welfare officer has just become involved. It was the education welfare officer who made contact with social services, who were unaware of the girl's existence.

Risk Issues – Points for Discussion

- Who is at risk in this case?
- Why are they at risk?
- How many assessments need to be undertaken and by whom?
- What issues would you be considering regarding:
  - (1) Mr A
  - (2) Mr A's daughter
- What concerns do you have for the welfare of Mr A's daughter?
- How would you go about getting a history of the family?
- Is the use of drugs in the household likely to influence people's assessment of risk?

CASE STUDY 5

Jacki Pritchard

Thirteen-year-old H is Somalian. He is physically disabled and also has learning disabilities. He can speak some English. He has just started to have respite care in a residential unit for disabled children.

On the first couple of stays in the unit, staff discovered that H had peculiar marks on his legs and old wounds on his body. The staff tried to find out how these wounds could have been inflicted and a risk assessment was instigated. The social workers who undertook the assessment were told that there is a ritual where children are burnt with twigs. It was necessary to conduct the assessment very sensitively by finding out about Somalian culture and rituals. The social workers spoke with elders within the Somalian community.

However, other concerns developed as the assessment proceeded. It became known that H was locked away in a cupboard by his mother when he was naughty. He had no toys or games in the house. Workers also noticed that H cowered everytime he saw his eldest brother.

Staff at the school H attends said that on occasions H had tried to strangle other children when engaged in playing games. He knew exactly where to find pressure points. He also seemed to enjoy other children hitting him when they became angry with him. Female staff were also concerned about his display of sexual behaviour towards them.

> ## Risk Issues – Points for Discussion
>
> - What do you see as the main concerns in this case?
> - What would you be assessing?
> - How would you carry out a risk assessment?
> - Were the social workers correct in only talking to the elders in the Somalian community about culture and rituals?
> - Who else could give them this information?
> - Where could they check whether this information is correct?

CASE STUDY 6

Jacki Pritchard

Sybil had lived in Dorchester Heights, a local authority run home for older people, for the past six years. When she had been admitted as a permanent resident, she was described as being 'educationally sub normal'. Her health deteriorated so much that she became wheelchair bound. Her behaviour then became very difficult. She suffered from mood swings and could be very nasty to staff. She then started to refuse to transfer from her wheelchair to an ordinary chair or to bed. The GP diagnosed that Sybil was starting to dement.

Some of the staff started complaining about Sybil saying 'she shouldn't be in here'; 'she's too much work for us'. The staff group became very split in their opinions about Sybil. This was very evident in handovers. Some staff were obviously very fond of Sybil and others really disliked her. The principal of the unit became very concerned about the situation, because she felt that Sybil could be at risk of possible neglect and physical abuse from some members of staff.

The principal asked the area social work team for a full needs assessment to be undertaken. Sybil had no family, but a volunteer visitor was involved and became an advocate. While the assessment was being carried out two incidents occurred. One morning the principal found Sybil sitting on the floor in her nightdress, propped up against her bed. Two care assistants had found Sybil on the floor after she had fallen out of bed, but said it had been impossible to lift her. They had heard an alarm from another resident, so *both* of them had responded to that, leaving Sybil propped against the bed on an uncarpeted floor for fifteen minutes until she was found by the principal. She had not been covered by a blanket nor had she been made comfortable with a pillow or cushion, which were available in the bedroom. Days later a temporary care assistant reported that a permanent member of staff had slapped Sybil across the face when she had refused to transfer from her wheelchair.

A social worker started a full needs assessment, but found herself being dragged into to listen to the gossip of the different staff factions in the unit. When she checked Sybil's file she was concerned that many records were missing and she also felt that Sybil may have been overmedicated. As she discussed Sybil's situation with all the people involved it became obvious that there were serious conflicts in opinion.

The GP thought Sybil now needed one-to-one attention because of the decline in her health. She diagnosed that Sybil did not have very long to live. She said she felt that Sybil's physical needs were not being met in the unit. Sybil was not mobilizing at all at this stage and she was not eating properly. The GP said it was also very obvious that she was not receiving any emotional stimulation. The GP wanted Sybil to be transferred to a nursing home.

The principal of the unit acknowledged what the GP was saying and was realistic about the problems she had with her staff group. However, she felt that Sybil should die in the home where she had lived for the past six years.

Sybil herself told the social worker that she did not want to move. The advocate supported Sybil in this.

Risk Issues – Points for Discussion

- Why was Sybil at possible risk of:
  (1) neglect
  (2) physical abuse?
- What were the other risks in this case?
- Was anyone else at risk in the unit?
- Discuss the conflicts of opinion/interests
- Discuss the principle of self-determination in relation to Sybil
- What role could the advocate play?
- How would you assess the use of medication if you suspected Sybil was being over-medicated?

CASE STUDY 7

Jane Lawson

Mary was 81 years old when she was admitted to a large teaching hospital where her leg was amputated below the knee. She had lived for 12 years with one artificial limb and was now a bilateral amputee. Despite a high degree of scepticism amongst professionals Mary mastered life in her own home with two artificial limbs.

Professionals and care staff had been sceptical because:

- Mary lived in large unadapted accommodation.
- They felt that mastering the second artificial limb would require strength and determination which might be beyond Mary's capacity.
- They were concerned at her high degree of isolation associated with the risk of falling.

Most felt that residential care would be more suitable. Mary on the other hand wanted to return to her own home because:

- it was her lifelong family home
- she would be able to pursue all of her interests (above all her interest in gardening) – she would retain her own choices and independence.

The benefits of continuing to live independently are significant. The importance and value of those benefits for Mary can be more fully appreciated against the background of the personal significance of the things surrounding Mary in her home:

- a library: a room full of fascinating literature of continuing interest to Mary
- furniture which had been carved and built as a wedding present for her parents
- a grand piano belonging to her sister
- a living room cluttered with all the things that made her life interesting (books, music, radio, evidence of letter writing, seed trays) and a view into her magnificent garden
- a garden which despite Mary's incapacity is outstanding.

Their importance is also evident in the lengths to which Mary is prepared to go to pursue her interests:

- To continue to enjoy the garden Mary has installed a ramp and rail and chairs of the correct height at intervals along the garden.
- She has at times endured immense discomfort from chafing caused by the artificial limb.

The potential harms for Mary are:

- pain, discomfort and sometimes exhaustion from coping with the second artificial limb
- danger that Mary might fall and the particularly hazardous transfer during the night (without the limbs) from bed to commode.

The potential harms were reduced by installing an intercom/door release system, a personal alarm, and other aids around the home. A stair lift had already been installed.

The risk assessment then clearly demonstrated that for Mary the benefits outweigh the practical harms. The likelihood of the harms occurring was monitored with a greater amount of home care/district nurse support initially.

Mary has succeeded now for five years in living independently and the likelihood of the harms occurring is now seen as far less likely. The pattern of home care support was altered once this became apparent.

The role of supervision of the staff involved was important in supporting them in their task of helping Mary to take the risks.

CASE STUDY 8: MENTAL HEALTH

Tony Ryan

FAMILY HISTORY AND DEVELOPMENT

John is the only son of white, working class parents who lived in an inner-city area all their lives. His father left the family house when John was ten years old after a volatile marriage. John had been the focus of attention from social workers until his father left because of his father's history of violence towards his mother, particularly when intoxicated from alcohol, and suspicions that John may have been at risk of violence from his father. John's mother died five years ago when he was 25 years old. His mother had brought John up by herself for the previous 15 years and died from chronic heart disease at the age of 56 years.

John's childhood development was uneventful and in his early school years he demonstrated an average intelligence. During his adolescence John became quite introverted and found friendships difficult to make with other adolescents. When he left school at 16 John commenced an employment training scheme but never gained full time work of any form and has remained unemployed.

ONSET OF SCHIZOPHRENIA

During John's late teenage years he began isolating himself in his bedroom and rarely communicated with anyone unless they initiated the interaction. During this period he began to keep a diary in which he recorded information on people in the media spotlight who he felt were responsible for everything that was wrong in the world. As time passed he became obsessed with the idea that a number of prominent people controlled his life. He also believed that several neighbours were being directed by these famous people to control him. These ideas became apparent to his mother when he threatened the paperboy, milkman and postman as they made their deliveries one day when he was 19 years old. Shortly afterwards his behaviour became increasingly bizarre and his general practitioner referred him to a psychiatrist. John refused to go into hospital and was eventually admitted for assessment under Section 2 of the 1983 Mental Health Act a week later when he assaulted the postman. During the admission John was diagnosed schizophrenic and accepted treatment with neuroleptic medications; he was discharged six weeks later. Aftercare was provided by community psychiatric nurses (CPN) who administered depot injections on a monthly basis. No social care assessment was arranged.

ACUTE PHASES OF SCHIZOPHRENIA

During the next three years John was compulsorily admitted to hospital on seven occasions and spent a total of 21 months in hospital. Each admission was precipitated by either minor acts of violence, often to his mother or callers to the family home, or bizarre behaviour in public places.

During this period he developed friendships with several other people who were frequently admitted into the hospital and began to drink and take cannabis. His cannabis use ceased after a short period but his alcohol intake increased dramatically. He soon began to drink daily and constantly pressurized his mother for money to subsidise his drinking.

CHRONIC PHASE OF SCHIZOPHRENIA

Over the next three years John was able to stay out of hospital due to a combination of his mother capitulating to his demands for money to finance his drinking and regular contact from his Community Psychiatric Nurse (CPN) who supervised his compliance with his medications.

John spent long periods drinking in isolation or with others who he met in hospital. He has refused all attempts to get him to attend structured day care or sheltered work of any form.

CURRENT SITUATION

Since his mother died five years ago John's life has become increasingly chaotic. He was found new accommodation by the social services department when he was asked to vacate his mother's council house. John did not maintain payments for his new flat and caused a lot of damage to the property and was ejected. He spent most of the time during the next few years moving between hostels for homeless men. His drinking increased and his mental health deteriorated. His mental state was masked by his drinking until he again came to the attention of the mental health services. He was referred by the police who removed him to a place of safety under Section 136 of the Mental Health Act. He had been found by the police begging aggressively and had threatened to assault a young female shopper who had ignored him in the city centre. Upon admission John smelt very strongly of alcohol and, although he was not drunk, he was very unkempt.

RISK ASSESSMENT AND MANAGEMENT ISSUES

It is important to realize that risk assessment and management are not two distinctly separate activities and that good risk management involves ongoing risk assessment whether formal or informal. The components of the assessment of risk relating to John should cover a range of areas which can be subdivided according to risks he poses to others and risks he poses to himself. The initial assessment should be undertaken by a multi-disciplinary team (MDT) which at the least includes medical, nursing and social work staff. It may also be useful as time progresses to include others in the assessment and management process such as staff involved in any residential scheme he moves into, CPNs and the police.

ASSESSMENT OF RISK

The assessment of risks is an ongoing process which provides a series of snapshots in the life of an individual. A combination of the approaches advocated by Carson (1990) and Ryan (1994) are useful when exploring both assessment and management of risk. Early assessment should focus upon John's mental health and whether he will remain in hospital for assessment and accept treatment. This will determine his legal status and direct the immediate management. If he remains in hospital on a voluntary basis this should make the task of developing a therapeutic relationship easier than if he is compulsorily detained. It will also encourage the MDT to focus on the issue of informed consent as John could not be treated against his wishes.

In addition to the initial assessment of risk in relation to mental state it will also be necessary to assess for signs and symptoms of alcohol withdrawal and medications may be required on an PRN or 'as needs' basis.

After the initial period where John is stabilised in relation to his mental state and alcohol withdrawal it will be necessary to undertake a full risk assessment of all areas of health and social circumstances. In doing this it is useful for all members of the MDT and John himself to list what they regard the risks to be. In this case they would be violence to others, accidental self injury due to intoxication or withdrawal from alcohol, homelessness and risk of offending behaviour. There may be other risks which people identify and these should be discussed in relation to their potential. Once all parties have agreed the range of risks each should be rated with regard to their likelihood by each person. Although such an exercise is not as scientific as some might wish it does provide a clear basis upon which to discuss the issues and combines clinical and actuarial approaches in a manner in which John can participate. It also ensures that clinicians can demonstrate that they took the issues seriously and made reasonable decisions based upon the information they had at the time.

A second issue which can also be assessed is the range of strategies which could be available at times of future crisis. By working through potential situations it may be possible for all parties to agree in advance what will happen if particular circumstances occur and thereby have a degree of advance consent from John when he is not otherwise able to give it.

Finally, a clear record should be made of the decision making process, how the decisions were reached and who has particular responsibilities. This can be useful for evaluation purposes and also an aid to improved practice where things have gone wrong.

MANAGEMENT OF RISK

There are two risk management strategies which need to occur in the case of John. The first relates to his stay in hospital where he may require close observation during the early phase as he may present risks to himself and others. Risks to himself can be through the physical aspects of withdrawal and also a desire to leave hospital in a vulnerable state if he is not a detained patient. The risks to others could come from aggression associated with his mental state, possible detention or alcohol withdrawal.

The management of risk after John has been discharged commences during the hospital stay. Hospitalization provides an opportunity for those who are going to be involved with him upon discharge to develop their professional relationships with him. The admission provides opportunities to agree a management plan with John for each of the areas highlighted in the risks assessment. Invariably his drinking, homelessness and mental state are interdependent to some degree and using the Care Programme Approach to draw together both health and social care would seem to be pivotal to the future success of John's resettlement. A suitable risk management strategy for each of these areas would include initial supervision and monitoring of medications, stable accommodation, regular contact with health and social services practitioners, a longer term programme of contact and integration within the local community and 24 hour access to crisis interventions of the type highlighted in the risk assessment. Whilst compliance with medication regimes and the desire to address his alcohol use may be longer term objectives for the MDT the issues can still be raised and discussed with John whilst in hospital.

Finally, once a plan has been agreed it should be flexible enough to adjust according to changing circumstances. Regular risk assessment of the progress or decline is part of the risk management process and ensures that only little mistakes can made. The frequency of assessment allows for incremental progression and learning each step of the way.

CASE STUDY 9: OFFENDER RISK: THE CASE OF DARREN AND PAROLE RELEASE

Hazel Kemshall

Darren is 22 years old. He is diagnosed as a person with learning difficulties, with poor self-esteem and difficulties in understanding the consequences of his behaviour. He is presently serving a five year sentence for arson with intent to endanger life and criminal damage of many thousands of pounds.

The offence occurred in the family home, shared by his mother and his step-father. Darren had been at home in the care of his sister (she lives nearby) whilst his parents went on holiday. He set the fire on the day they were due to return from holiday. He says he set the fire because they left him but does not seem to appreciate the possible harm he could have done them. A neighbouring house as well as his home was badly damaged, and neighbours were helped to safety by the fire brigade.

He expresses a wish to apply for parole, and to return to his parents' home if parole is granted. The Probation Officer, in preparing the parole report must consider the issues of risk. The framework proposed for assessing offender risk (see Chapter 10) may be useful for the officer.

GENERAL PREDICTIVE HAZARDS

(1) The known reconviction rate of young offenders upon release.

(2) Age of the offender.

(3) Gender of the offender.

(4) Type of offence.

SPECIFIC PREDICTIVE HAZARDS

(1) The specific circumstances of the offence and the likelihood of these being repeated. He proposes to return to a similar situation in which the offence occurred.

(2) His lack of remorse and lack of understanding about the consequences of his offending.

(3) His poor self-esteem and learning difficulties which exacerbate (1) and (2) above.

(4) The family situation itself which appears to have contributed to the 'offending event' and which remains unresolved.

DANGER

The same offence or something very similar will recur and people and/or property will be seriously harmed.

STRENGTHS IN THE SITUATION, EITHER OF THE PERSON, OF OTHERS, OR OF THE GENERAL ENVIRONMENT

These need to be investigated and identified. There may be extended family support, other networks which can be accessed, or the offender may need to be negotiated into an alternative environment, such as a hostel, which may provide a source of strength in this situation. Are there are any unidentified strengths in the offender, or in the relationship the offender has with his parents?

LEVEL OF RISK PRESENT

The hazards and the resulting danger clearly outweigh any identified strengths. The risk must be considered as high.

RISK OF WHAT?

That any tension in the relationship with his parents, or any perception by him that he is being rejected will result in fire setting to harm his parents or other harmful behaviour directed at them. There is also the possibility of unrelated others being harmed.

RISK TO WHOM?

To parents, other family members, public, offender, officer, and agency.

CONSEQUENCES OF THE RISK, TO WHOM?

There are consequences of serious physical harm to family members, public and offender. There are serious professional implications for the officer and the agency if 'things go wrong'.

COSTS OF ACTING/NOT ACTING. TO WHOM?

Not acting is the more costly option in terms of the potential risks and the resulting dangers. Whilst investigating this situation thoroughly and pursuing other options for release involve substantial use of throughcare resources, this must be balanced against the cost of not acting.

ACTION REQUIRED TO MINIMIZE THE HAZARDS

A recreation of the situation and factors which led up to the 'offending event' *must be avoided*. This will require attention to family relationships, the offender's perception of that relationship and his demands upon it, perhaps the creation of other networks of support (for example by using a hostel and/or extended family members), and a further assessment of the offender's situation with regard to his self-esteem and learning difficulties prior to commencing either offence focused work or victim empathy work. A number of these points need to be addressed prior to release.

ACTION REQUIRED TO ENHANCE THE STRENGTHS

Investigation and identification of the possible strengths, access to, or request for a full psychological assessment of the offender, investigation and if appropriate mediation of family dynamics, the pursuit of alternative support networks, offence focused and victim empathy work when appropriate, vigilant monitoring of the case if released.

CONSEQUENCES OF NO ACTION, FOR WHOM?

Lack of action will result in a number of the issues important in the commission of the offence remaining unresolved, presenting a high likelihood of the offence being repeated with danger of significant harm to others occurring.

RECOMMENDATION AND CASE PLAN, (REFLECTING WORK PROPOSED ON HAZARDS AND STRENGTHS, AND INCLUDING EVIDENCE FOR LEVEL OF RISK DETERMINED)

Readers are invited to insert their own case plan and /or to write a parole report.

DATE FOR REVIEW

This case will probably require ongoing review in the early stages, with monthly updating in formal supervision with the officer's supervisor, and a three monthly evaluation of progress.

CASE STUDY 10: MANAGING AND ASSESSING SEX OFFENDER RISK

Sue McEwan and Jo Sullivan

The aim of this case study is to illustrate the use of the 'Intergrated Model' for managing and assessing risk in cases of child sexual abuse. Although our experience is primarily based upon work with perpetrators and non-offending partners, we will be referring to issues appertaining to all parties and agencies represented in cases of this nature.

We acknowledge the variety of case types encountered by agencies and the various circumstances which apparently require differing responses in cases of sexual abuse:

- convicted perpetrator wishing to return to the family within which the abuse took place
- convicted perpetrator who offended outside of the home who wishes to remain with his family
- convicted perpetrator wishing to move into a new family setting
- alleged perpetrator within family, denying allegations
- alleged perpetrator, against children outside of family denying allegations
- convicted perpetrator of offences against adults
- alleged perpetrator of offences against adults.

We would argue for a consistent approach and the development of a standardized multi-agency response to all cases irrespective of apparent differences.

CASE HISTORY

NB has one previous conviction for offences of indecent assault and gross indecency against young boys, aged eight and nine years. He was sentenced to two years' imprisonment in 1981, when he was 22 years of age. At the church youth club where NB was working as a volunteer in 1994, an eight-year-old boy alleged an indecent assault. Although the matter was investigated, a prosecution was not brough due to NB's total denial and the Crown Prosecution Service's view that the boy would not make a good witness. The Child Protection Team notified the local area Social Services that NB was a Schedule 1 offender now living with a partner, her two daughters, aged seven and nine, and the couple's two-year-old son.

CASE DEVELOPMENT

In her report to the initial case conference, the social worker stated that NB continued to deny the allegation and dismissed as irrelevant his previous conviction; TB his partner, who had been unaware of his previous conviction, continued to support him and stated that she was certain he would never pose any risk to her children; the family appeared to function well and the children seemed happy and well-cared for. The case conference decision was made to place the names of the three children on the Child Protection Register and appoint the social worker as the keyworker, with responsibility for providing a comprehensive risk assessment for the next case conference.

An invitation to attend the initial case conference was sent to the local Probation Service; however, there were no current involvement with NB and records of his previous contact could be found, consequently, a representative did not attend.

In the intervening six months, the core group, comprising the social worker, family doctor, head teacher and school nurse for the girls, were due to meet on three occasions; however, only the school nurse and the social worker attended all the meetings.

Reporting back to the case conference, the social worker indicated that both NB and TB had been unco-operative by cancelling meetings at short notice and continually moving the focus away from child protection issues by highlighting practical difficulties within the family unit. She stated that this was preventing her from completing the risk assessment. The conference recommended that assistance be sought from the Probation Service regarding assessment of NB. Although reluctant, NB stated that he would co-operate with the risk assessment as it appeared this was the only way he could prove he was not at risk.

The case was referred and, in the first instance, the Probation Service agreed to undertake a Preliminary Assessment to ascertain NB's suitability for sex offender groupwork programme on a voluntary basis.

The Preliminary Assessment found NB unwilling to discuss the recent allegations, although he did admit his previous sexually abusive behaviour but felt that this was 'in the past' and no longer relevant. NB expressed anger at the inference that he could present any risk to his own son or stepdaughters.

The findings of the Preliminary Assessment were reported to the core group:

- NB admitted the use of fantasy, masturbation and planning in the previous offences but denied any ongoing sexual arousal to children. He stated that he had an excellent sexual relationship with his partner and would never re-offend
- He could offer no explanation as to how he controlled his behaviour since the previous offences; he stated that if he ever realized he was becoming aroused to children, he would block out his thoughts – although he could not explain how.
- He stated he had told his partner everything about his past and she had forgiven him knowing that he would never do it again.
- He acknowledged that agencies (Social Services and Probation) assessed him as presenting a risk and, for this reason, he accepted that he needed to join the sex offender assessment programme.
- It was felt that NB would be suitable for inclusion in an assessment programme, where work would focus initially on his previously admitted offending but would move towards helping NB to acknowledge the continuing risk he presented.

The social worker reported that work with the family was being obstructed as NB and TB considered the work unnecessarily intrusive and did not believe the children were at risk.

It was decided that the social worker and the probation officer would engage in co-work with NB and TB alongside NB's attendance on the sex offender assessment programme. The aim of this work would be to ensure that TB had full information regarding the pattern and cycle of sexual offending, relating particularly to NB's previous offending. It was hoped that TB would be encouraged to recognize the continuing risk presented to her children.

Unfortunately, anything achieved in the meetings appeared to be undermined in the intervening period and the overall feeling was that little progress was being made.

During his attendance at the sex offender group NB appeared to be making slow progress, admitting sexual arousal to young boys since his adolescence up to the present time. He blamed this on the fact that he was abused himself. However, he continued to deny any risk to his own children.

This information raised concerns at the next case conference and, for the first time, the issue of NB's continued presence within the household came into question. NB retracted the admissions he had made, stating that the felt he had been pressurized by the sex offender group.

This retraction and refusal of ongoing intervention by NB and TB were viewed by the case conference as confirming that the children were at risk and legal proceedings were initiated. Ultimately, the children were removed from the family home and placed in the care of the local authority by order of the Court. The parents were granted supervised contact on an interim basis whilst individual assessments were completed upon all family members.

Consequently, NB returned to the sex offender programme, having moved out of the family home, TB began attending a non-offending partner programme and work was undertaken with the children individually. It is important to not that the family reconstruction was not set as an aim: the aim of all the work was to assess if family reconstruction would be viable.

CASE ANALYSIS

AGENCY PROCEDURES

One of the main problems with the management of this case, as with many other cases of this nature, was that no agreed multi-agency procedure existed in the area where this case was reviewed. Consequently, the Probation Service, the agency which generally will have the most information about sex offenders, did not attend the initial case conference and decisions were made which, with the benefit of hind-sight, were not in the long term interest of the children in this case.

It is of considerable importance that all agencies engaged in the preparation of risk assessments have mutually agreed what the expectations and limitations of such assessment are. In our opinion it is also vital that assessment work is undertaken by specially trained staff who closely liaise with practitioners in other agencies completing work with the various members of the family. All too often inappropriate agency expectations of inexperienced staff, leaves workers feeling vulnerable and de-skilled and open to manipulation.

AGREED MULTI-AGENCY PHILOSOPHY

Simply assembling the appropriate agencies is, however, only the first step in effective management of risk in cases of child sexual abuse. Without agreeing a multi-agency philosophy with clearly stated principles upon which can be built a consistent approach to all cases of child sexual abuse, the response of case conferences will continue to be diverse and retain a tendency to completely change direction, depending upon the personalities attending the conference. This phenomenon is, understandably, perceived by the parents as a dubious and unsettling, 'changing the goalposts'. In addition, it focuses frustration on the changing processes employed in managing the case and draws attention away from the content or actual behaviour necessitating the case conference in the first place.

Whilst full consideration of the arguments for and issues relating to commonly agreed multi-agency philosophies and procedures will require more space than is available in this book, some of the key component elements of this debate are raised in this case study and earlier chapter.

CASE STUDY 11: A PRACTITIONER VIEW OF RISK: A CASE STUDY FOR LIFE LICENCE

Avril Aust

In considering risk assessment for Life Licences as an illustration of probation risk assessment, I thought of my most long-standing Life sentence Licencee as a case example. This would focus my mind on issues of risk assessment prior to discharge from prison and whilst on licence. However, when I came to consider the case, from the day it was allocated in 1985 to the present time when I am awaiting a response from the Home Office to my request that supervision requirements be lifted, I realized that my thinking about risk had been somewhat vague when I first took on the order and has been clarified by a number of influences. Given the length of time that I have held this case, I feel that this development in practice has not simply been a personal process, but has been a reflection of changes in the management of high risk cases in both the prison system and the Probation Service.

This case was initially allocated to me on the basis that I was an experienced officer and, therefore, could hold Life sentence cases. No guidelines were given to me in relation to through-care of Life sentence prisoners. I feel that I learned most about the process of being a Lifer and being a Lifer Supervisor from two sources, first, the Lifer himself and other Lifers with whom I worked and, second, from working in a Dispersal prison and seeing how the Lifer system operated or failed to operate, particularly in relation to the assessment of risk.

In the case of Jack (the name has been changed to ensure confidentiality), risk was generally assessed to be low. His offence was murder and the circumstances were that he and a co-defendant had been involved in a dispute with a man in a public house. The three of them went outside, a fight took place and the man subsequently died of his injuries. Alcohol was a major factor in the offence since Jack had been drinking for most of the day having left home earlier after a dispute with his partner. The Judge's comments were: 'In the circumstances, there is only one sentence I can pass and I make no recommendations'. Jack was sentenced to Life imprisonment in 1978. He had only two previous offences, both committed as a juvenile and neither for offences of violence.

At the time that the case was allocated to me in 1985, Jack was in open conditions in HMP Leyhill. Guidelines relating to management of Life sentence prisoners outlined in Prison Department Circular Instruction 1/1982 which recommended the setting of tariffs, career planning and regular reviews of prisoners had been implemented but carried out with varying degrees of efficiency depending on the institution which held the prisoner. Even in those institutions with a higher proportion of Lifers the implications of the review system had not been clearly thought through. A number of factors had been identified in the Circular Instruction referred to above, including the following:

(1) Analysis of information and recognition of change over protracted time scales.

(2) The concept of dangerousness, patterns of behaviour and assessment of risk.

Decisions about Jack seem to have been made on the basis that he was a hard-working, albeit anxious individual who related well to staff and had not been involved in any violent activity during his prison sentence.

Since he had been sentenced in 1978, prior to these guidelines being introduced, Jack had no official tariff. However, he was hoping that his 'unofficial' tariff would be about 10 years. With hindsight, the areas of concern which would probably have been identified in relation to his offending would have been:

(1) Dealing with conflict.

(2) Managing stress.

(3) Awareness of the effects of alcohol on behaviour and the ability to use alcohol in a responsible way.

None of these areas of concern had been identified for Jack. He felt that he had to guess about the judgements being made about him and frequently felt powerless to influence the decision making process. This, in turn, added to the stress he (and other Lifers and potential parolees) felt.An incident that occurred in 1986 highlights the inability Jack had to engage in the process of risk reduction and the lack of resources available to him. He was found to be involved in the smuggling of a bottle of spirits into the prison. He was returned to closed conditions and for some time was very anxious about his progress through the Lifer system. Given the significance of alcohol in his offence, this anxiety was understandable. However, the incident was investigated and it was concluded that he had acted under duress and that this behaviour was not typical. At that time prisoners were not allowed access to reports written about them and so Jack could not take part in the process of assessment of risk by acknowledging concerns about previous abuse of alcohol and by taking concrete steps to demonstrate that his attitudes and behaviour had changed since the time of his offence. At no time during his sentence was he offered any work in any prison on the management of stress, dealing with conflict or alcohol education.

An important way in which Lifers are expected to demonstrate fitness for release is by expressing remorse for their offence. Jack was fortunate that he had an extremely supportive partner and was able to maintain good relationships with her and his children. His valuing of these relationships and his wish to make reparation to them for the distress he had caused them by committing his offence was a major motivation to get through his sentence. He also expressed remorse for the loss of the victim's life and the pain he had caused the victim's family. However, I do find discussions about the sincerity of Lifers' expression of remorse problematical. In the course of a lengthy sentence, Lifers will have to discuss their offence on numerous occasions. If a review system is operating efficiently, they will be seen at least on a yearly basis and will be interviewed about their offence by a number of different people, for example Case Officer, Wing Manager, Probation Officer, Psychologist, Lifer Governor, Medical Officer. It would not be surprising if, after such repeated discussions of the same event, their views were not to sound 'rehearsed'. I feel that overt expressions of remorse need to be set beside judgements about the capacity of the individual to relate in a positive and empathic way in current relationships. This was demonstrated by Jack in his awareness of his partner's and children's feelings and, also, in his awareness that he could, occasionally, become so concerned about his own situation that he, temporarily, lost sight of theirs.

During the course of time that I was supervising Jack, I was seconded to HMP Long Lartin. Observing a large number of Lifers I became acutely aware of what needs to be in place to enable an offender to 'own' his own sentence, to recognize what it is about his attitudes and behaviour that are considered to cause concern and what he needs to work on to demonstrate change. Having reached this point he also needs to be provided with resources in terms of offence-focused programmes to do the necessary work. Whilst I was in Long Lartin the issue of open access to reports was beginning to be discussed. It has been the practice of the Probation Service to show reports to inmates for some time and I tended to see them as a useful working 'tool' to highlight areas of agreement about ongoing work and to note progress where it had been made. I would invite inmates to think about what the Parole Board had to consider when making decisions about risk of re-offending and what they had to do to demonstrate that they had changed since committing their offence and that they could be trusted with the responsibility of increased freedom. Often their answers would indicate a lack of change and a maintenance of risky attitudes and would serve as an indicator to the readers of the report that caution was needed in terms of management.

An anxiety which is frequently expressed about open access to reports is the fear that dangerous, possibly irrational, individuals may bear a grudge against a particular individual for a negative report and make that person a target for revenge. Clearly, this is a possibility and help needs to be given to staff to ensure that judgements are owned collectively rather than being left with individuals. However, I have also found that offenders can accept the reporting of opinions which are different from their own if their own views are at least registered. I tend, therefore, to outline the views of the client and then use formulae such as, 'The Parole Board may be concerned, however...' or 'The Court may feel that...' and then go on to discuss issues which are indicative of areas to which the offender may not have paid sufficient regard. This indicates clearly that it is not I as an individual who makes decisions about risk but the decision-making body taking into account all the information available.

With regard to demonstration of progress through a prison sentence, paradoxically the period of time leading up to release often seems more difficult to manage than the main bulk of the prison sentence. I maintained contact with Jack as he moved from closed conditions to another open prison and then to a pre-release hostel, finally being discharged in 1987. The gradually increasing levels of freedom can put great strain on the prisoner and the family. It is very hard to return to prison after a period of freedom and short periods of time at home can be overshadowed by the prospect of separation once again. Families have often adjusted to life without the prisoner and his presence for short periods can be seen as disruptive rather than an opportunity for real integration as a family. Children, particularly, can be confused about the fact that a parent seems to be home again but not really home. These strains can put at risk the support systems that prisoners need to help them to readjust to life in the community.

Fortunately, Jack and his family coped with these difficulties well. In assessing risk, I took into account their very realistic attitudes to their own relationship. They did not pretend that all was perfect but could acknowledge the stresses and strains that they each had to cope with and their different ways of dealing with them. Jack used work as a way of keeping occupied and maintaining self-esteem, as well, of course, as meeting the family's basic material needs. He was fortunate in finding work quite quickly. His use of alcohol had to be monitored and, since his job involved driving, he would not risk using alcohol whilst at work. He and his partner would occasionally go out for a meal and have a drink together then.

However, there was no evidence of a return to the pattern of heavy drinking with male friends which had preceded his offence. After release, the attitude of the offender to supervision can further clarify thinking about risk. Jack's attitude to supervision was positive and accepting of the need for close surveillance. Whilst regular reporting is not, in itself, an indicator of low risk, I do feel than an awareness on the part of the offender of the reasons why supervision has to take place and the areas on which it must focus gives some indication of the level of engagement with the supervisory process and, therefore, of a possible wish to avoid re-offending.

In the case of the Lifer to whom I have referred throughout this discussion, my views of risk have been consistent with those of members of staff in the institutions he has passed through, the Parole Board and, more recently, the Courts. After release, further offending reinforced issues of appropriate risk assessment and the need for realistic decision-making. A year after his discharge, Jack was found guilty of one minor offence.

There was no evidence of the concerns relating to his original offence recurring and he was dealt with by means of a fine, with no action being taken by the Home Office. However, he has also been through the process of being charged with a more serious offence to which he pleaded not guilty and was acquitted. This was an offence relating to property rather than against the person and, though he was at risk of imprisonment had he been found guilty, again there was no evidence in the allegations made against him of abuse of alcohol and failure to manage conflict. Indeed, the strength of character which he and his partner showed in the long months preceding his trial and acquittal seem to me to be further evidence of their capacity to deal with stress and to cope with problems.

In conclusion, I would say that I feel management of risk should include the following factors:

(1) Identification of the areas of concern.

(2) Engagement of the offender in the process of managing his or her own sentence or order so that he or she identifies what work must be done to demonstrate change.

(3) Clear contacts so that the offender knows what is required of him or her and what action will be taken in the event of failure to comply.

(4) Appropriate sharing of information with other informed people and sharing of responsibility for decisions.

(5) Awareness of the perspective of the victim and/or victim's family so that the offender is not allowed to retreat into an avoidance of responsibility by seeing himself or herself as a 'victim of the system' or of 'society'. (This is particularly important when the offender has experienced victimization, i.e. as a woman, a black person or as an abused child, in which case that victimization needs

to be acknowledged but the offender must address it in an appropriate way rather than by abusing others.

I would like to offer these thoughts, not as an indication that my practice is ideal, but to share a process of learning by experience and with an awareness that I need to continue to learn more. Jack's permission was obtained to use his case to illustrate this discussion of risk assessment. I would like to offer thanks to Jack and his family and to other Lifers from whom I have learned so much.

REFERENCES

Carson, D. (1990) 'Risk-taking in mental disorder.' In D. Carson (ed) *Risk-taking in Mental Disorder; Analyses, Policies and Practical Strategies*. Chichester: SLE Publications.

Ryan, T. (1994) 'The risk business.' *Nursing Management 1*, 1, 9–11.

The Contributors

Avril Aust is a Probation Officer with the Hereford and Worcester Probation Service. Her present role consists of half-time practice teaching and half-time sex offender specialist work.

John Blakeney is a senior social worker with the City of Birmingham Social Services Department. He is employed as a hospital social worker based at the Queen Elizabeth Psychiatric Hospital within the Mental Health Service for Older Adults South Birmingham.

David Carson is a Lecturer in Law at the University of Southampton. His principal interests lie in inter-disciplinary and inter-professional studies of a preventative nature. He is a founding editor of *Expert Evidence* and established the Behavioural Science and Law Network.

Brian Corby is a Senior Lecturer at the University of Liverpool. He has experience as a statutory social worker, and extensive research in the areas of child protection, social work practice, and policy. His published works include *Working With Child Abuse* (1987) and *Child Abuse – Towards a Knowledge Base* (1993).

Ann Davis is currently Director of Social Work Research at the University of Birmingham. Her principal interests are in poverty, welfare rights and mental health. She has extensive research, teaching and practice experience in these areas, in addition to a number of publications.

Ronno Griffiths is a qualified social worker who has worked in the area of sexual abuse since 1978. She is currently an independent trainer and management consultant specializing in working with adults who were sexually abused as children. In addition, she provides training in substance misuse in a wide range of organizations in the statutory and voluntary sectors. She has published on both alcohol and substance dependence.

Hazel Kemshall is a Lecturer in Probation Studies at the University of Birmingham. Her current research interests are in risk assessment work with offenders. She is presently a holder of an Economic and Social Research Council award to investigate 'Risk in Probation Practice' under the ESRC's 'Risk in Human Behaviour Programme'. She has ten years' experience as a probation practitioner and manager in a range of fieldwork and specialist settings.

Jane Lawson is Advisor, Services for Older People, Hampshire Social Services Department. She has over ten years' practice experience in a number of local authority departments.

Brian Littlechild is Director of Social Work Studies at the University of Hertfordshire. He has worked in residential care and Social Services area teams, specialized in child care, child protection, and youth justice as a practitioner and manager. He has over ten years' experience in the provision of training on the management of violence for staff in a variety of settings.

Rosemary Littlechild is currently a Lecturer in Social Work at the University of Birmingham. Her principal interests are in practice, research and teaching on work with older persons. She has recently completed a research study into hospital discharge of the elderly.

Sue McEwan is currently a Probation Officer working in the regional sex offender unit of the West Midlands Probation Service. She has extensive group work and individual case work experience with sex offenders.

Jacki Pritchard is a freelance trainer/consultant working as a practitioner, manager, and trainer in Social Services and Probation. She has a particular interest in the areas of child abuse and adult abuse.

Liz Ross is currently a Lecturer in the Department of Social Policy and Social Work and Research Facilitator in the Department of General Practice, both at the University of Birmingham. She is an experienced community worker, and has undertaken research in a number of areas with the primary focus on the experiences and perspectives of users of health and social services.

Philippa Russell is the Director of the Council for Disabled Children and Associate Director of the National Development Team for People with Learning Disabilities. She is Chair of a Mental Health Foundation Committee on children with learning disabilities, an honorary member of the Council of the NSPCC and the British Paediatric Association.

Tony Ryan has worked within the field of mental health since 1982 in a variety of practitioner and managerial positions, including both the public and 'not-for-profit' sectors. He is currently Area Manager for the mental health charity Turning Point. He is also Honorary Research Fellow at the University of Lancaster where he is researching risk in relation to people with mental health problems.

Joe Sullivan has experience as a Probation Officer specializing in work with sex offenders with the Staffordshire Probation Service. He was responsible for creating and co-ordinating regional services for sex offenders. In 1995 he became senior clinical therapist with the Faithful Foundation.

Jan Waterson is a Lecturer in the management of social care in the Social Services Management Unit at the University of Birmingham. After starting her career in generic social work, she specialized in working with client groups who are now described as 'community care' clients. Since she moved into teaching she has maintained close contact with practice through research projects.

Subject Index

References in italic indicate tables or figures.

Author Index

ACMD (Advisory
   Council on the
   Misuse of Drugs)
   126, 130
ACOP (Association of
   Chief Officers of
   Probation) 137
Adler, Z. 153
Advisory Council on
   the Misuse of Drugs
   (ACMD) 126, 130
Alaszewski, A. 80
Allan Roehr Institute 32
Allen, I. 70
Ammons, P. 16
Apsler, R. 127
Asen, K. 26
Association of Chief
   Officers of Probation
   (ACOP) 137
Association of Directors
   of Social Services 68,
   118, 162
Aston, D. 22, 23
Audit Commission 32,
   35, 48, 82, 111, 112,
   118, 133, 157

Baldwin, N. 68
Baldwin, S. 32, 121
Barham, P. 114, 115
Barker, I. 115, 118
Barnes, C. 84, 86
BASW (British
   Association of Social
   Workers) 121, 162
Beardshaw, V. 87
Becerra, R. 14
Beckett, R. 151, 152, 155

Beckford, J. (London
   Borough of Brent)
   22, 23, 136, 141
Beech, A. 151
Beitchman, J. 16
Bell, C. 14
Bentovim, A. 16, 25
Bibby, P. 163, 166, 170
Biehal, N. 87
Binder, R.L. 102
Blom-Cooper, L. 93, 110,
   111, 112, 113, 117,
   118
Bottoms, A. 134
Bowling, A. 102
Box, S. 133
Braye, S. 109, 114, 115,
   116
Breakwell, G. 170
Brearley, C.P. 1, 5, 81,
   86, 136, 139
Bridge, The 14, 23
Bristol University 33
British Association of
   Social Workers
   (BASW) 121, 162
British Medical
   Association 7, 97
Brown, P. 98
Brown, R. 165, 166, 167,
   172
Brown, R.A. 94
Browne, A. 155
Browne, K. 17, 18
Brun, W. 94
Burns, W.J. 82
Burti, L. 114, 116
Bute, S. 165
Bytheway, B. 70

Campbell, J.C. 102, 136,
   141
Campbell, M. 20
Campbell, T. 98
Carlile, K. 23
Carlisle, J. 32
Carnie, J. 21

Carson, D. 9, 11, 55,
   58–9, 93, 94, 102, 185
Carson, E.R. 82
Carter, P. 139
Carver, V. 85
CCETSW 89
Charlton, J. 98, 110
Chester, R. 121
Christie, N. 134
Clark, D.A. 133
Clark, R. 133
Cleveland Report 16,
   23, 24, 26
Clifford, P. 101
Cohen, N.L. 103
Coleman, J.L. 95
Collins, S. 121
Colwell, M. 14, 22
Combs, B. 94
Comstock, G.W. 99
Connolly, N. 80
Conroy, S. 14
Convit, A. 136
Corby, B. 18, 20, 21
Corker, M. 81
Cornish, B. 133
Crepaz-Keay, D. 115,
   117, 118
Crichton, J. 113

Dale, P. 25
Dartington Social
   Sciences Research
   Unit 33
Davies, M. 25
Department of Health
   see DoH
Department of Health
   and Social Security
   (DHSS) 23, 97
Dick, D. 110, 113, 117,
   118, 139
Dingwall, R. 18
DHSS (Department of
   Health and Social
   Security) 23, 97